LONG ISLAND

LONG ISLAND

People and Places · Past and Present

A NEWSDAY BOOK

Bernie Bookbinder

Photography by

HARVEY WEBER

HARRY N. ABRAMS, INC.

Publishers, New York

To Marilyn

HALF-TITLE:
Summer at Long Beach

TITLE PAGE:
Fire Island Lighthouse

PAGES 4–5:
*Parades in Northport and
Centerport*

COPYRIGHT PAGE:
*Old First Church in
Huntington*

PAGE 8:
*Canada geese; Home Sweet
Home and Pantigo Windmill,
East Hampton*

PROJECT DIRECTOR: *Hugh L. Levin*
EDITOR: *Nora Beeson*
DESIGNER: *Judith Michael*
PICTURE EDITOR: *Barbara Lyons*
RESEARCHER: *Gaynell Stone*

LIBRARY OF CONGRESS CATALOGING IN PUBLICATION DATA

Bookbinder, Bernie.
Long Island : people and places, past and
present.

"A Newsday book."
Bibliography: p.
Includes index.
1. Long Island (N.Y.)—Social life and customs.
2. Long Island (N.Y.)—History. 3. Long Island
(N.Y.)—Description and travel. I. Weber,
Harvey. II. Title
F127.L8B66 1983   974.7'21   83-2819
ISBN 0-8109-1259-7

Illustrations © 1983 Newsday

Printed and bound in Japan

Contents

Introduction   11

1. TAKING SHAPE   13

2. CHALLENGE AND CONFLICT   25

3. DEFEAT AND SURVIVAL   59

4. MOVING AHEAD   83

5. CITY AND SUBURB   117

6. FUN AND GAMES   141

7. OVER HERE   167

8. FAST TIMES   177

9. TURNING THE CORNER   201

10. TAKING STOCK   223

Some Places to Visit   247

Historical Societies   254

Selected Bibliography   257

Acknowledgments   259

Index   260

Photo Credits   264

Introduction

ABOVE
Irrigation hoses and wheels near Riverhead

BELOW
Racks for drying fishnets in Promised Land

Long Island's story has been determined largely by forces it could not control. It has been compelled to deal with the inescapable reality that it is surrounded by water. And, more than most, it has been a victim and beneficiary of natural phenomena, glacial and oceanic, that have shaped its profile, its surface, and its character.

Its story begins before recorded history, when Long Island's endowments—a temperate climate, rich soil, abundant game, and beneficent seas—enabled Indians to develop a culture that provided them with peace, progress, and purpose. Successive societies have seen in Long Island a similar opportunity for fulfillment and have bent it toward their own needs and ends. From the earliest English and Dutch colonists who braved uncertainty and deprivation to the most recent former New Yorkers looking for a good place to raise the kids, newcomers have altered Long Island's appearance and its direction.

Still, its location in the shadow of the greatest city in the world has made Long Island hard-pressed to assert itself. Politically, economically, culturally, it rarely has succeeded in diverting attention from New York City. Yet historically, it enjoys a background and a tradition rivaling that of any place in America, of America itself.

For many of us, Long Island's past is, at best, hazy, disjointed, incomplete: a montage of Indians, clamdiggers, and potato farmers. It was a past without a presence. The purpose of this book is to resurrect that past. To recreate, through words and pictures, the Long Island that *was*, that is responsible for the Long Island that *is*. This is not intended as a definitive history, but as an evocation of time and of place, of how people lived, and even of what they thought. Its goal is to make today's Long Islanders more aware of what preceded them. For if it succeeds, they will be more concerned about what follows them.

CHAPTER ONE

Taking Shape

Long Island is *new*, a recent addition to the Atlantic coastline, to the silhouette of America. Its familiar fish shape—mouth nibbling at Staten Island, flukes pointing eastward toward Europe—is only about 6,000 years young; just a tick or two of the geologic clock, a blink of God's eye.

Its origins lie in New England, where the stuff from which the Island is made once reposed. Think of Long Island as a three-tiered layer cake: its base, called bedrock, is really a 500-to-600-million-year-old extension of southern Connecticut that slid beneath Long Island Sound; its middle layer of sands, clays, and gravels is thought to be the deposits left by ancient rivers 60 to 70 million years ago, when dinosaurs roamed the earth.

But the top, or surface, layer concerns us most: it is where we live. And it is essentially the product of a vast continental glacier that visited the Island twice—first about 60,000 years ago and again about 21,000 years before the present. This glacier, called the Wisconsinan, is largely responsible for writing the history of Long Island. It determined where and how the Battle of Long Island would be fought, where the Long Island Rail Road would run, where ships would be built, potatoes would be grown, and housing developments would sprout. It gave the Island its contour, size, terrain, and soil. And each of these factors affected the kind and location of vegetation and wildlife, which, in turn, influenced where people lived and what they did.

Like the blade of a monstrous snowplow, the glacier moved imperceptibly but inexorably south across what is now Canada and the northern United States, filing the peaks off mountains, scraping the surfaces of plateaus and valleys, and carrying along with it the natural debris of boulders, rocks, gravel, and soil in a frozen, unending wall of ice hundreds of feet high. Nothing could stand in its way. But it was vulnerable to heat, and when it reached a point roughly between Long Island's North and South Shores, the glacier's leading edge began to melt. As it melted, it deposited the huge mounds of debris it had carried—the way dirt and stones scraped up by a modern snowplow line the roadside after the piled-up snow thaws. These mounds, actually a string of hills stretching from Brooklyn east to Montauk, comprise what geologists call the Ronkonkoma Terminal Moraine.

Besides the moraine, the melting of the Wisconsinan gave birth to great rivers which flowed from the glacier's face to the sea, creating a vast expanse of flatlands. These flatlands, extending from the moraine south to the Atlantic Ocean, are called the Hempstead Outwash Plain.

During this period of the earth's history, the northern hemisphere was undergoing radical temperature changes, fluctuating between warm and cold over intervals that lasted tens of thousands of years. After the first advance of the Wisconsinan Glacier as far south as Long Island, a global warming trend caused it to melt back, or recede. The change of climate also caused the sea level to rise, probably separating what is now Long Island from the mainland.

Some 40,000 years later, the climate began to cool once again, the glacier readvanced almost to the same position, stayed for a while along what is now the North Shore, began melting again, and deposited another terminal moraine. This ridge, which runs from Brooklyn Heights to Orient Point, including Harbor Hill in Roslyn, is named the Harbor Hill Moraine. It, too, has an outwash plain, called the Terryville Outwash Plain after the community south of Port Jefferson.

These four major features, going from north to south—the Harbor Hill Moraine, Terryville Outwash Plain, Ronkonkoma Terminal Moraine, and Hempstead Outwash Plain—make up Long Island's surface. Because of the glacier, the Island is not all hilly like the North Shore, nor pancake-flat like the mid-Island area; there is an elevation to Brooklyn Heights that enables its residents to look down on New York Harbor, while those in Coney Island stare the Atlantic Ocean in the eye.

The glacier left Long Island other mementos of its visits. Geologists believe that claws of ice projecting out of its main wall carved the deep indentations on the North Shore that now bear names such as Oyster Bay and Cold Spring Harbor; and that when these claws melted, their deposits created the bluffs on the peninsulas such as Great Neck and Manhasset Neck.

The Wisconsinan can also be credited with giving lakes, gullies, and boulders to Long Island. The depressions that dot the terrain are called kettle holes, and were created by huge chunks of glacial ice that had torn loose, had been buried, and later melted. Some became dry hollows while others, fed by underground streams, became lakes and ponds (Lake Ronkonkoma, Lake Success, Artist Lake). Except for some exposed bedrock near today's Hell Gate Bridge in Queens, no rocks or boulders are indigenous to the Island's surface. Those found here, such as Shelter Rock in Manhasset, the large graffiti-covered rock on the campus of the State University at Stony Brook, and many others were borne from New England and are called erratics to indicate that they came from elsewhere.

When another warming period sent the glacier on its final retreat, it also raised the worldwide sea level once more and gave Long Island's shoreline, as well as coastal areas around the globe, its present contour.

ABOVE
Originally a salt marsh, Sanctuary Pond was dammed and is now the largest freshwater pond on the Mashomack Preserve, Shelter Island.

LEFT
Stones, typical of North Shore beaches, were carried from New England by the Wisconsinan Glacier that helped shape Long Island; these line the beach at Caumsett State Park, Lloyd Neck.

RIGHT
Not only rocks and stones, but large boulders called "erratics," such as these at Caumsett State Park, were borne by the glacier during its two visits to Long Island. Long Island Sound, in background, probably was formed more than 30,000 years ago, separating Long Island from the mainland.

Scientists think that Long Island was free of ice about 18,000 years ago; that Long Island Sound was reflooded by sea water about 12,000 years ago; and that the Island's fishlike outline emerged some 8,000 to 6,000 years ago.

After the Wisconsinan Glacier disappeared, its influence lived on through a chain of causes and effects that began with the distribution of different types of soil. In and around the moraines, Long Island's generally sandy soil is mixed with a silty sediment that enables it to retain moisture and nutrients and thus sustain such moisture-loving hardwoods as white and red oaks, hickories, chestnut trees, and tulip trees.

By contrast, the sandier, drier soil of the outwash plains primarily supports softwood pitch pine forests. Because the dryness greatly increases the chances of fire, flames swept repeatedly across the outwash plains for thousands of years, shaping—and transforming— its vegetation. Some trees even have become dependent upon fires: in the Dwarf Pine Plains around Westhampton, the pigmy pine trees cannot reproduce unless flames singe their closed cones, melting the resins, and causing the cones to open and disperse their seeds.

These differences in vegetation between the moraines and outwash plains attracted different types of animal life to each. The cool shade and numerous springs and ponds of the morainal hardwood forests appealed to deer and turkey; these, in turn, drew predators such as wolves, bears, and cougars. One exception to the pattern of rich morainal soil and sandy outwash is found on the extreme eastern end of Long Island, where silt, carried by the winds, blanketed the sandy plains that characterized most of the North Fork and some of the South Fork. This windblown silt, called loess, enriched those areas, making them fertile and the eventual site of productive farmland.

The life and history of Long Island also have been influenced significantly by other distinctive landscape features: the Hempstead Plains, the barrier islands, and the tidal marshlands.

The Hempstead Plains, a 60,000-acre portion of the Hempstead Outwash Plain in the heart of what is now Nassau County, is the easternmost prairie in North America and something of an enigma because it cannot be explained from its geological foundation. Some scientists speculate that the vast expanse was burned every year or two, possibly by the Indians as an aid to hunting or farming. Such fires might have killed trees and shrubbery while stimulating the growth of grass which provided forage for generations of Long Island cattle and sheep.

Another important asset that developed after the glacial epoch are the barrier islands, particularly those off the South Shore, such as Fire Island, Jones Beach, and Long Beach, which were—and still are—built and shaped by the powerful Atlantic. Ocean waves acting on the shallow sea bottom have reworked the sandy glacial outwash into offshore islands, which then have been extended westward by the prevailing currents.

After their formation, these islands served as a buffer between the mainland and oceanic storms. They also created quieter bodies of salt water—lagoons that are named Shinnecock, Moriches, Great South, South Oyster, and Jamaica Bays. For thousands of years, the barrier islands and bays have participated in a process that has enriched the bay floors and shoreline. As the tides swept in and out of the bays through breaks in the islands called inlets, they brought nutrients into those sheltered waters to nurture marine life on the bottom. They also fostered the growth of salt marshes, which served as a breeding ground for both vegetation and sea creatures. These marshes proved extremely important during the colonial period, when they provided salt hay that was rich in nourishment and a valuable source of food for livestock.

The shallow waters surrounding both shores of Long Island produced bountiful quantities of shellfish that played a key role in the lives of the area's early human inhabitants. Evidence unearthed from the campsites of prehistoric Indians suggests that they, like the Island's contemporary residents, enjoyed clambakes, savored venison, and kept dogs as pets. (While dogs may have been man's best friend even then, the reverse was not always true: bones found at some sites indicate that dogs occasionally served as food for their masters.)

The presence of these people dates to about 5,000 years before the present time, during what is called the Archaic or Hunting and Gathering Stage. That stage is the second of four prehistoric periods designated by archaeologists to reflect the evolving development of Indians in this region. Based on the way people lived, these periods have been reconstructed from artifacts, such as weapons and tools, and from "garbage," such as shells and bones.

These early Indians also shared today's predilection for waterfront sites, making their camps along bays, streams, and the Island's four rivers: the Peconic, Carmans, Connetquot, and Nissequogue. Such locations provided abundant hard-shell and soft-shell clams, oysters, and scallops, which were gathered and cooked in pits of burning coals or hot stones. Waterfowl, turtles, and fish also were readily available, along with many deer.

The lifestyle of the Archaic people was eased by the use of stone tools, such as adzes, gouges, drills, and scrapers. These primitive versions of today's basic handtools enabled the Archaic Indians to engage in woodworking, hide processing, and food preparation. They also used spear points, blades, and knives, possibly inherited from those believed to be the area's first humans, the so-called Paleo-Indians. (While little is known about them, archaeologists speculate that the Paleo-Indians—or their ancestors—probably originated in Asia and followed the retreating glaciers more than 12,000 years ago in pursuit of huge elephantlike mammoths and mastodons. Consequently, the period of their presumed

ABOVE
Salt marshes, such as these at Bass Creek in the Mashomack Preserve on Shelter Island, provided farmers during colonial times with nutritious salt hay for their cattle. The shadbush is a white blaze from April to June.

BELOW
The innumerable bays, coves, and harbors that delight North Shore sailors, such as Northport Bay seen here at dusk, are, geologists believe, the result of fingers of ice that reached out of the glacial wall as it melted back during a worldwide warming trend.

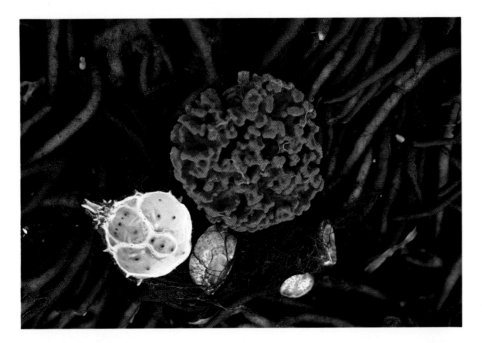

ABOVE
Marine life has thrived for thousands of years in the quiet waters and marshes that comprise much of Long Island's shoreline. This horseshoe crab, one of the earliest anthropods, lived in Flax Pond, Old Field.

LEFT
A sponge and the shell of a crab give evidence of the variety of creatures that inhabit the shallows of Peconic Bay.

BELOW
Shellfish always have appealed to Long Islanders. Some, like the scallops whose familiar ribbed shells are seen here with boat and yellow jingle shells, were a staple of Indian diets.

ABOVE

Pollution and other attacks on the natural environment by modern Long Islanders have affected deeply the area's vegetation and wildlife. Ospreys are beginning to reappear after being threatened with extinction.

RIGHT

Long Island was involved with ducks for centuries before farmers began raising them in the 1870s. Its location on the migratory routes accounted for the presence of many species of waterfowl, including these canvasback ducks.

BELOW

Prehistoric Long Island Indians started steaming shellfish in pits, similar to this one constructed for an exhibit at the Garvies Point Museum in Glen Cove.

ABOVE

The adze, a woodworking tool, was used by Long Island Indians during the Archaic or Hunting and Gathering Stage about 5,000 years ago and was useful in fashioning dugout canoes.

LEFT

These projectile points found in the Glen Cove area were used about 3,000 years ago by Indians during what archaeologists call the Transitional Stage, one of four prehistoric developmental periods.

RIGHT

This Indian clay pot, found at Crabmeadow Beach, Northport, is identified with the Woodland Stage.

existence on Long Island is called the Big Game Hunting Stage.)

A major advance during the Hunting and Gathering Stage of the Archaic people was the development of the dugout canoe. Paddling these sturdy craft out of the fine natural harbors of the North Shore, they were able to extend their mobility considerably and even trade with other groups in upstate New York and the Great Lakes. The canoes, made mostly from tulip trees felled and hollowed out with the aid of fire, enabled Long Island's Archaic Indians to exchange rare or strategic materials with nearby groups. These, in turn, were traded for desirable items only available in distant regions to the north and west. Such networks explain the discovery on Long Island of flint implements, when flint came from the region along the Hudson River; copper jewelry, when the nearest source of copper was in the Great Lakes; and jasper beads and pendants, when jasper was located in New England and Pennsylvania.

About 3,000 years ago the Archaic people were supplanted, during what has been labeled the Transitional Stage, by Indians who are thought to have come from New England and the Pennsylvania-New Jersey region. Their lifestyle is referred to as the Orient Culture because their campsites were discovered in the Orient area on the North Fork, where they left extensive evidence of their preoccupation with death and life beyond death. From their elaborate burial rituals, archaeologists have learned that virtually every item used by the living was buried with the dead: spear points for hunting, celts and adzes for woodworking, quartz and iron pyrite for firemaking, stone vessels for cooking, and graphite and hematite paintstones for body painting.

For their burial ceremonies, the Orient Indians selected hilltops in eastern Long Island from which they could simultaneously look out over several bodies of water: the Sound, Plum Gut, and Peconic Bay in one case, and Peconic Bay and the Atlantic Ocean in another. Fire played a significant role in Orient funerals and one can imagine the dramatic sight of a communal burial with its bonfire blazing on a windswept hill.

Sometime during the Transitional Stage, but before the Indians of Long Island came into contact with European explorers about 500 years ago, a new prehistoric lifestyle emerged. It is called the Woodland Stage, although its most significant development was farming. Trees were cleared and, using the prototypes of hoes, these Indians planted fields with corn and possibly beans and squash. Their mortars and pestles imply a more sophisticated diet, probably some type of meal cake, while the utilization of smaller projectile points suggests the evolution of spears into more effective arrows and bows.

Artifacts from the Woodland Stage include pottery pipes of a size and shape that indicate these Indians had acquired the nicotine habit—something, like Long Island itself, they would soon pass along to as yet unimaginable strangers.

Challenge and Conflict

From the beginning, Long Island enjoyed what colloquially might be called "a good press." Early explorers sent back glowing reports to Europe extolling the natural beauties and bountiful resources of this portion of the New World.

One of the first visitors, Florentine explorer Giovanni da Verrazzano, sailing in 1524 under the French flag, "found the country . . . well-peopled, the inhabitants . . . being dressed out with the feathers of birds of various colors" until "a violent, contrary wind forced us to return to our ships, greatly regretting to leave this region which seemed so commodious and delightful." Henry Hudson, an Englishman outfitted by the Dutch East India Company, sent some crew members ashore in Brooklyn in 1609 who reported that "the lands were as pleasant with grass, and flowers, and goodly trees as ever they had seen, and very sweet smells came from them." Sir Edmund Plowden, who sought a grant of Long Island from Charles I of England in 1632, found that "there is great variety, and also all deputies [kinds] of fruits that Italy or the gardens of Spain affordeth may be had out of those rich grounds, for it is as hot as Spain or Italy, and as full of pleasure and comfort."

While this was news to the Europeans, Indians had been enjoying the fruits of Long Island, figuratively and literally, for a long time. By the time America was being "discovered" during the so-called Contact Period of the 1500s, Indians were living in Long Island from one end (Brooklyn) to the other (Montauk Point). Loosely divided into between six and twenty groups (many historians have settled on thirteen), Long Island Indians were not, strictly speaking, organized into tribes: they did not wear different costumes, inhabit separate territories with fixed boundaries, and have different customs. Rather, they comprised extended family groups living in geographic areas—along a river, near a beach, beside a pond—from which each group took its name.

These early Long Islanders were among the first American Indians to come into contact with Europeans. For this, they paid heavily, becoming the first to be acculturated through intermarriage and to be decimated through violence, slavery, and diseases such as smallpox and alcoholism. By the early 1700s, their presence was barely felt on Long Island; before

long, their existence was reduced to life on the Poosepatuck and Shinnecock Reservations, and preserved largely through the names of places: Montauk, Shinnecock, Setauket, Massapequa, Matinecock, Rockaway, and Canarsie.

Anthropologists suggest that the Indians of Long Island were peaceful and industrious, far more interested in trading with the Europeans than in fighting with them. One researcher speculated that the Long Island Indians' lack of aggressiveness, compared with the Plains Indians of the West, stemmed from the relatively "soft" life afforded them by the availability of shellfish and other seafood.

Dealings between the Indians and the Europeans were aggravated by a host of misconceptions and deceptions on both sides. The Europeans assumed that Indian society was organized along the same lines as their own—a faulty perception that led them to seek out a chief, or sachem, with whom to negotiate. But the Indians frequently had two leaders, one for war, the other for ordinary affairs. And neither was reluctant to accept whatever designation—and resultant reward—the Europeans seemed so eager to extend in their zeal to make a deal. It is thought that some chiefs sold the same land several times to different Europeans, as well as selling land over which they had no jurisdiction. This somewhat tarnishes the legendary cleverness of Europeans for having obtained vast tracts for trinkets.

The confusion resulting from differences in political organization was compounded by dissimilar concepts of property. The Europeans assumed that the purchase of land gave them ownership and total control; the Indians assumed that they were merely allowing the Europeans to use their land, and that the Indians would be able to hunt and fish on it as always. Such misunderstandings often led to disputes, some of which found their way into the colonial courts. Generally, the Indians lost and were forced, one way or another, to move to successively smaller and less desirable areas, or off Long Island.

Perhaps the most cynical appraisal of the interaction of the Indians and Europeans on Long Island came from an Indian chief in 1788:

The avidity of the white people for land and the thirst of the Indians for spirituous liquors were equally insatiable. The white men had seen and fixed their eyes upon the Indians' good land, and the Indians had seen and fixed their eyes upon the white men's keg of rum; and nothing could divert either of them from their desired object, and therefore there was no remedy; but the white man must have the land and the Indians the keg of rum.

Alcohol addiction almost claimed one of Long Island's most extraordinary Indians, Samson Occom, a convert to Christianity, who was ordained by the Suffolk Presbytery in 1759, taught and preached among the Montauks and Shinnecocks, and even went on a British lecture tour raising funds for the establishment of a college for Indians that became Dartmouth College. Occom, hailed in England as "the first Indian gospel preacher that ever set foot on this island," confessed his alcoholism, from which he subsequently recovered, in a 1764 letter to the Presbytery.

The devastation of most of the Long Island Indians so soon after contact with the Europeans has severely limited our knowledge of their culture and lifestyle. Probably the most comprehensive—if biased— first-hand account of how those early Long Islanders appeared and behaved to seventeenth-century European eyes survives in a report by Daniel Denton, one of Jamaica's first settlers and a prominent representative of that community. Published in 1670 as *A Brief Description of New York*, it offers a fascinating look at those for whom the advance of one civilization meant the termination of another. The son of a minister, Denton wasted no time in finding religious justification for the mistreatment of these people:

To say something of the Indians, there is now but few upon the Island, and those few no ways hurtful, but rather serviceable to the English, and it is to be admired, how strangely they have decreast by the Hand of God, since the English first settling of those parts; for since my time, where there were six towns, they are reduced to two small Villages, and it hath been generally observed, that where the English come to settle, a Divine Hand makes way for them by removing or cutting off the Indians either by Wars, one with the other, or by some raging mortal Disease.

With an observant eye—and the racism and condescension of his European contemporaries—Denton examined many aspects of Indian lifestyle. Tasks were determined by gender, with the males hunting and fishing while females tilled the land and planted corn. "The meat they live most upon is Fish, Fowl and Venison; they eat likewise Polecats, Skunks, Racoon, Possum, Turtles, and the like."

The Indians of that period were mobile, moving seasonally from their cornfields to their hunting grounds and fishing waters by simply packing up their possessions and transporting them to the new site. For recreation, they played "Foot-ball and Cards, at which they will play away all they have, excepting a Flap to cover their nakedness."

Denton seemed particularly interested in the Indians' drinking habits and described them in some detail:

They are great lovers of strong drink, yet do not care for drinking, unless they have enough to make themselves drunk. And if there be so many in their Company, that there is not sufficient to make them all drunk, they usually select so many out of their Company, proportionate to the quantity of drink, and the rest must be spectators. And if any one chance to be drunk before he hath finisht his proportion (which is ordinarily a quart of Brandy, Rum, or Strongwater), the rest will pour the rest of his part down his throat.

He noted that drinking frequently got out of hand and violence resulted. "They often kill one another at these drunken Matches, which the friends of the murdered person do revenge upon the Murderer, unless he purchase his life with money, which they sometimes do. Their money is made of a Periwinkle shell, of which there is black and white, made much like unto beads, and put upon strings."

The fighting style of the Indians, which contrasted sharply with the open formations of the British troops, was the focus of many early European observers and did not escape Denton's observation. He wrote that when an enemy approached, the Indians would hide their wives and children, "and then with their guns and hatchets they waylay their enemies, some lying behind one, some another, and it is a great fight where seven or more is slain."

When Indians died, it was considered highly disrespectful ever to mention their names, since doing so would renew the grief of their loved ones. Similarly, all those named for the deceased would change their names to spare the feelings of the survivors. "Their names are not proper set names as amongst Christians," Denton explained, "but every one invents a name to himself, which he likes best, some calling themselves Rattlesnake, Skunk, Bucks-horn, or the like. And if a person die, that his name is some word which is used in speech, they likewise change that word, and invent some new one, which makes a great change and alteration in their language."

Denton was fascinated by the sexual and marital practices of the Indians and could not resist passing judgment on their moral code. "Their Marriages are performed without any Ceremony, the Match being first made by money. The sum being agreed upon and given to the woman, it makes a consummation of their Marriage, if I may so call it. After that, he keeps her during his pleasure, and upon the least dislike turns her away and takes another."

Adultery was permissible for wives if they informed their husbands or close relatives; if not, they could be put to death. "An Indian may have two wives or more if he please; but it is not so much in use as it was, since the English came amongst them; they being ready, in some measure, to imitate the English in things both good and bad. Any Maid before she is married doth lie with whom she please for money, without any scandal or the least aspersion to be cast upon her, it being so customary, and their laws tolerating of it."

Their criminal justice system, according to Denton, included capital punishment, although he pointed out that it was used sparingly. The death penalty was carried out by sending the condemned prisoner into the woods with the "King" (chief) and his executioners in hot pursuit. When found, he was shot to death (the "King" taking the first shot) and then scalped.

Finally, Denton described the cosmetology of Long Island's Indians:

While Indians still live on Long Island on two reservations, the Shinnecock near Southampton and the Poosepatuck near Mastic, intermarriage has altered the racial characteristics of many. A Shinnecock from an earlier generation, shown in the photograph taken by W. R. Harrington about 1900, was Mary Ann Cuffee, 81, with a wooden mortar and pestle then in use.

"They grease their bodies and hair very often, and paint their faces with several colours, as black, white, red, yellow, blue, &c., which they take great pride in, every one being painted in a several manner."

The relationship between the Europeans and the Indians on Long Island, as elsewhere in America, was essentially based on exploitation. Yet, for the most part, it was surprisingly peaceful. This pattern was ripped apart in 1643 by a merciless attack on a group of Indians in what is now New Jersey. It was launched from New York by Governor William Kieft of the Dutch West India Company, a harsh authoritarian who earlier had imposed stringent penalties for offenses by Indians against Europeans. David De Vries, who had been with Kieft when the assault was ordered, described the aftermath:

When it was day, the soldiers returned to the fort, having massacred or murdered eighty Indians, and considering they had done a deed of Roman valor, in murdering so many in their sleep, where infants were torn from their mothers' breasts, and hacked to pieces in the presence of the parents, and the pieces thrown into the fire and in the water, and other sucklings, being bound to small boards, were cut, stuck, and pierced, and miserably massacred in a manner to move a heart of stone. Some were thrown into the river, and when the mothers or fathers endeavoured to save them, the soldiers would not let them come on land but made both parents and children drown—children from five to six years of age, and also some old and decrepit persons.

Those who fled from this onslaught, and concealed themselves in neighboring sedge, and when it was morning came out to beg a piece of bread and to be permitted to warm themselves, were murdered in cold blood and tossed into the fire or the water. Some came to our people in the country with their hands, some with their legs, cut off, and some holding their entrails in the arms, and others had such horrible cuts and gashes that worse than they were could never happen. And these poor simple people, as also many of our own people, did not know any better than that they had been attacked by a party of other Indians. After this exploit, the soldiers were rewarded for their services and Director Kieft thanked them by taking them by the hand and congratulating them.

As might be expected, this atrocity provoked retaliation by the Indians against Europeans throughout the area, including Long Island. Yet, within a decade or so, relations had improved to the extent that a number of Indians were invited to what is now Brooklyn to attend their first religious meeting, which was being conducted by Domine Johannes Megapolensis of the Dutch Church of Long Island. Apparently the recent hostilities had not been forgotten entirely. When the Indians asked the minister why he was speaking at such length to the congregation and he replied, "I admonish the Christians that they must not steal, nor drink, nor commit lewdness and murder," they reportedly considered this for a moment and then inquired, "Why do so many Christians do these things?"

Dealings between the Dutch and Indians had been alternately friendly and strained from the outset. When Hudson, under Dutch sponsorship, first visited the Brooklyn area in 1609, one of his crew, John Colman, was shot to death with an arrow and buried at Sandy Hook at a spot the captain named Colman's Point. Hudson and his men admitted having killed three Indians during their exploration of the river that was to bear the adventurer's name.

The Dutch reinforced their early claim to New Netherland with a series of exploratory and trading voyages, including the extraordinary experience, in 1614, of Captain Adriaen Block. When his ship was destroyed by fire on Manhattan Island, Block and his crew, using only the tools they had brought from Holland or could obtain from the Indians, built a 44-foot vessel named *Onrust*, meaning restless (the first constructed by Europeans in North America), sailed it through Long Island Sound, discovered "Adriaen Block's Eylandt" (subsequently shortened to Block Island), determined that Long Island was, in fact, surrounded by water, and drew the first map to show "Lange Eylandt" as an island and to bear the term "Nieuw Nederlandt."

While the Dutch were interested largely in trading with the Indians for furs, particularly beaver pelts, and focused their activities in Manhattan

The monument in Mill Neck commemorates the military exploits of Captain John Underhill, who defeated the Massapequa Indians in the only battle between English colonists and Indians on Long Island. It took place at Fort Neck, near what is now Massapequa in 1653 or 1654. Underhill later fought for the Dutch, as Jan Van der Hyl, against the Canarsie Indians.

(which they called New Amsterdam), up the Hudson, and in western Long Island (Brooklyn, Jamaica, and Flushing), the English were busy colonizing Long Island's eastern end and its northern shore. Although the Dutch settlers came to the Island directly from Europe during the early 1600s, most of the English took a much shorter route, sailing across Long Island Sound from Connecticut and Massachusetts, where the religious fervor and intolerance of the Puritan leaders, or the harshness of the New England climate and soil, or the lack of a sufficient market for their goods and services, had made life in that part of the New World too demanding.

The first substantial English property holder on Long Island was Lion Gardiner, a prominent engineer who lived in Saybrook, Connecticut, where he directed the construction of a fort. Gardiner purchased an island, which he called the "Isle of Wite" (now Gardiner's Island), from his friend, Chief Wyandanch, sachem of the Montauk Indians, for "one large black dog, one gun, some powder and shot, some rum and a pair of blankets." Their long and valued relationship was derived in part, so the story goes, from Gardiner's successful negotiation for the release of

ABOVE
The elaborate granite tomb of Lion Gardiner, one of the earliest Long Island colonists and friend of the Indian sachem Wyandanch, from whom he purchased Gardiner's Island. The tomb is located at the South End Burying Ground in East Hampton.

BELOW
Travel by horse-drawn vehicles could range from the crude to the elegant. This example of the latter was constructed during the nineteenth century by Brewster and Company of New York for the affluent Gardiner family and is on display at The Museums at Stony Brook.

Wyandanch's only daughter after she had been kidnapped by the hostile Narragansetts on her wedding day.

In colonizing North America, the English paid strict attention to the legal niceties associated with British law and custom. Complying with this policy, Gardiner confirmed his title to the island by obtaining a patent from James Farrett, an agent of the Earl of Stirling, to whom Charles I had given Long Island. Gardiner occupied his island, which is still owned by his descendants, in 1639, and two years later his daughter, Elizabeth, became the first English child born in New York State and the first European born in Suffolk.

Shortly after the Gardiners moved in, English settlements were established in Southold and Southampton in 1640, and soon colonists began spreading into East Hampton (1648), Shelter Island (1652), Huntington (1653), Brookhaven (1655), and Smithtown (1665).

Despite a charming myth and a bronze statue on Jericho Turnpike celebrating it, there is no evidence that the boundaries of Smithtown were established by Richard Smith, through a daylong ride astride his bull, Whisper. It is generally believed that Smith, nicknamed Bull because supposedly he rode one, purchased much of what is now Smithtown in about 1665 from Lion Gardiner, who had obtained it from Wyandanch.

The colonists most often established their first settlements where Indians had already cleared the forests. For while they came from a society that was technologically more advanced than that of the Indians, they had arrived in the New World with few European implements and little opportunity to repair or replace those they had brought. In most important respects, the colonists were as affected and controlled by the vagaries of nature as were the Indians, and they sought to exploit the same natural resources: fresh water, trees, and shellfish.

Although the English focused their efforts in Suffolk, they also settled in among the Dutch villages on the western end of the Island, principally at Hempstead, Jamaica, and Oyster Bay. Most of the Dutch were concentrated in nearby Brooklyn and Flushing, and so a confrontation between these two great colonial powers seemed inevitable.

An attempt to resolve the tensions between English and Dutch colonists took place in 1650 at Hartford with the signing of a treaty that divided Long Island between them with an "international line," which corresponds to the present Nassau-Suffolk border. It specified that "a line Run from the westernmost part of Oyster Bay, and soe in a straite and direct line to the sea, shall be the bounds betwixt the English and Duch there, the Easterly parte to belonge to the English, and the Westerly parte to the Duch."

Despite the fact that it gave the British control of about three-quarters of Long Island, the treaty was never ratified in London, perhaps because the British had even bigger plans. When the monarchy was restored in England following the rule of Oliver Cromwell, and exiled King Charles

II was put on the throne in 1660, he decided to take over New Netherland, including Long Island, and turn it over to his brother, James, the Duke of York. To that end, in 1664 a British expeditionary force of 500 soldiers and four warships under the command of Colonel Richard Nicolls arrived at New Amsterdam and demanded the surrender of New Netherland from the Dutch governor, Peter Stuyvesant. Unable to gain assistance from Holland, Stuyvesant soon capitulated.

New Amsterdam promptly was renamed New York in honor of James, Duke of York, by Nicolls, who changed New Netherland to Yorkshire Province, after Yorkshire in England, and divided that territory, including Long Island, into three sections in the manner of the original Yorkshire: West Riding included Staten Island and the extreme western part of Long Island; North Riding included Westchester and mid-Long Island as far east as the 1650 "international line"; and East Riding included the remainder of Long Island, what is presently Suffolk County. (This arrangement lasted until November 29, 1683, when the General Assem-

bly divided the colony into twelve shires or counties, including Kings, Queens, and Suffolk.)

But Nicolls' most controversial act was the imposition of a rigid code, called The Duke's Laws, dealing with everything from the compulsory establishment of churches to penalties for fornication. In the case of the former, it stated that "in each parish within this Government a church be built in the most Convenient part thereof, Capable to receive and accommodate two Hundred Persons." While in the case of the latter, it established that "if any Person commit Fornication with any Single woman they shall both be punished by enjoyning Marriage, fine or Corporal Punishment, or any of those According to the discretion of the Court."

Long Islanders bridled under the code's restrictive rules, which they were given an opportunity only to ratify, not to formulate. In fact, representatives of Southold and Southampton refused to sign them. This dissatisfaction surfaced significantly in 1673 when the Dutch threatened New York City with a small fleet. The colonists showed little enthusiasm for sacrificing their lives in defense of a government they regarded as harsh and authoritarian and so the English were compelled to surrender. The Dutch immediately changed New York's name to New Orange, but a year later it was New York once again as Holland exchanged New Netherland with England for the South American territory of Surinam. This trade marked the peak of Dutch influence on Long Island—and America—and indelibly stamped English on our nation's culture, laws, and, of course, language. One Dutch custom we may be thankful never prevailed was their system of giving names, which were systematically changed with each generation, so that no son ever bore the family name of his father.

In what the Dutch did pass along, their legacy is mixed: an architectural style (Dutch Colonial), a religion (Dutch Reformed Church), a myth (Santa Claus), and an abomination (slavery). For two hundred years, slaves, brought in chains from Africa or impressed from the local Indian population, greased the wheels of Long Island's economy. And it was the Dutch, in 1626, who were responsible for introducing that institution, although the English proved readily receptive.

It did not take the early settlers long to realize that the rigors of life in the New World would require additional manpower. The most available source to perform the boring and laborious tasks necessary for survival was the Indians. But by nature and experience they resented and resisted domesticity. The Dutch then asked the East India Company in Holland for indentured servants, but the request was rejected as too costly. Instead, the company directors suggested that the Long Island colonists imitate those in Virginia and import slaves from Africa. The idea gained ready acceptance, and soon slave ships, slave auctions, slave quarters, and all the paraphernalia and trappings associated with the antebellum South were in evidence throughout the Island.

The Dutch introduced slavery to Long Island in 1626 as an alternative to providing indentured servants for their colonists. The English soon took up the practice and scenes such as this became commonplace.

By 1700, there was a greater proportion of slaves in New York—15 percent of the population—than in Virginia. By 1732, the census showed 7,232 black slaves on Long Island among a white population of 40,048. Male slaves, being stronger and more versatile, were in greater demand than females, although both, and even children, were highly valued. For example, an estate inventory in 1719 appraised a black woman and child at sixty pounds, while five milk cows, five calves, three young bulls, and two heifers were collectively priced at twenty pounds.

Although slavery was more common in western Long Island, where the Dutch and a farming economy predominated, it was widespread both geographically and demographically; that is, it was practiced by virtually all economic and social classes. Merchants, farmers, even ministers and Quakers, owned slaves. Slaveholding was to colonial status on Long Island what car-owning is to contemporary status: prosperous families owned fourteen or more slaves, while poorer residents could afford only one or two.

The Quakers, however, began to agitate against slavery and soon were in the forefront of those calling for its abolition. It was not a quick battle. Slavery reached its peak on Long Island between 1750 and 1790; much of the impetus for its abolition came immediately after the Revolutionary War when, ideologically, freedom was in the air, and, economically, there was a labor surplus. Consequently, it was not unusual for owners whose slaves were no longer productive, being aged or infirm, to welcome the opportunity to get rid of them—to the accompaniment of moral platitudes.

As late as 1779, according to local records, slavery was still very much in style: "$5 reward. Ran away from John Lefferts, Hempstead, Charles, a very black negro. He speaks good English, had an old homespun bearskin short-coat, tow shirt and trowsers, and small old felt hat."

Slavery finally was ended legally in New York State in 1827, although it was carried on surreptitiously by seamen in the Fire Island area until the Civil War.

Besides having slaves to perform drudgery, the colonists used indentured servants, generally English, who contracted their labor for many years or hundreds of dollars in return for passage to America and maintenance. For them, living and working conditions were at least as bad as those experienced by slaves, for in the case of the latter, slaveholders had a lifetime investment in maintaining their health and well-being. Few indentured servants outlived the terms of their contracts; many died from illness or, in despair, took their own lives.

The resort to slavery and the tenacity to maintain it stemmed, among other reasons, from the difficulty of living in Long Island in those harsh times. Even the most well-to-do endured living standards far below those they had enjoyed in Europe. Since there was no industry during the early days of colonization, and because the cost of obtaining manufactured articles from England or Holland was prohibitive, the settlers were compelled to live without many of the tools, utensils, and other amenities they had taken for granted before emigrating. If it became necessary to replace worn clothing or bedding, they had first to weave cloth. To weave cloth, they had to spin woolen yarn or flaxen thread. And to get the yarn or thread, they had to raise sheep or cultivate flax.

This salt swamp at Caumsett State Park, Lloyd Neck, is typical of Long Island marshes.

Life was consumed with providing food, clothing, and shelter, and everyone, from children to grandparents, participated. Everything was scarce, nothing was wasted. When, for example, a cow was slaughtered, some use was found for every bit. Anything that could be eaten was consumed including the head, which was boiled until the meat fell off and was mixed with spices to make a pickled dish called souse. Organs, too, were boiled and eaten with spices, while intestines were stuffed with chopped meat to make sausages. The fleshy parts were either smoked or cured with salt and spices. The fat was melted for candles and soap; the hide was scraped, dried, and tanned for leather breeches, jackets, and shoes, or book covers, or drumheads. Even the horns and bones were utilized: after being heated, the horns were shaped into cups, combs, and powder horns, while bones were converted into buttons and knife handles.

But for the early colonists, domestic animal meat was a treat. Aside from shellfish, which were eagerly gathered and devoured by those living close to the bays and beaches, and the finfish they were able to catch by line or seine, their diet essentially was unchanged from medieval times: its mainstay was grain and corn, the latter being ground Indian-style into a meal called samp and eaten as samp porridge. Even so prosaic a dish as this required monumental effort to prepare, particularly by today's frozen-food standards.

The corn first was parboiled for at least twelve hours and then placed

in a hollowed-out tree stump. A short log, tied at one end to the top of a nearby sapling, was used to pound the kernels into cornmeal. The process was so noisy and so commonplace that seamen would joke that even in a fog they knew they were off the Long Island shore by the pounding of the samp mortars. It was a slow, tedious job, taking an entire day to convert a half-bushel of corn into meal, and so the work generally was assigned to slaves.

Farming was carried on with the most primitive implements made almost entirely from wood. In addition to corn, the colonists raised wheat, oats, rye, and barley, and, when they could obtain seed, peas, beans, parsnips, turnips, carrots, and pumpkins. Wild fruit was abundant: strawberries, raspberries, huckleberries, mulberries, cranberries, persimmons, plums, and grapes. The strawberries grew in such profusion that eating them became a form of recreation, as this account by Denton suggests:

Such abundance of strawberries is in June that the fields and woods are dyed red; which the country people perceiving, instantly arm themselves with bottles of wine, cream, and sugar, and instead of a coat of Mail, every one takes a Female upon his Horse behind him, and so rushing violently into the fields, never leave till they have disrobed them of their red colors and turned them into the old habit.

In the early years, the colonists were more concerned with building their herds of cattle, sheep, and hogs, than consuming them. But in time, cattle became plentiful: by the Revolutionary War, there were an estimated 100,000 head of cattle on Long Island and each was identified by a special ear notch that designated its owner. Cattle were so common that they became a unit of exchange in Hempstead: taxes were paid "in fatt cattle delivered alive."

The grassy Hempstead Plains comprised a vast communal pasture of 60,000 acres, and thousands of acres of South Shore salt marshes provided an almost unlimited source of nutritious salt hay. The salt hay grew in the high marsh, closest to solid land. Cattle were grazed there as recently as 1956 in what is now Caumsett State Park in Lloyd Neck. The marshlands were cut each year, and it was a community event that lasted into the twentieth century in parts of the South Shore. The adjacent low marshes, which yielded thatch for colonial roofs, were flooded twice daily by the tides and consequently were treacherous since cattle could become mired in them. The marshes' value was such that they generally were held in common trust, like the village greens.

Clothing was designed, using the term loosely, for wear not style. The farmer's everyday suit was made from homespun. Later in the seventeenth century, it is likely that he also owned a suit of broadcloth, which he wore on Sundays and holidays throughout his life. On his death, it

*These men settling their affairs show
the clothes worn during the period.*

*Colonial gentlemen had no
reluctance to dress up, as this silk
and satin waistcoat, embroidered
with metallic thread, clearly
indicates.*

was inherited by a son. Laborers wore buckskin, leather breeches, checked shirts, flannel jackets, felt hats, heavy shoes with huge brass buckles, and leather aprons.

In the latter stages of the colonial period, as people of wealth and substance began to emerge, they dressed in a manner that clearly set them apart from others. A gentleman powdered his hair, braided it in a queue, and placed a three-cornered hat over it. He wore knee breeches, striped stockings, and pointed shoes with large buckles. A vest was put on under a light-colored coat, which was decorated with silver buttons and worn beneath a small cape. And he carried a cane. His lady was likely to wear a gown of brocade or taffeta over hoops, which extended about two feet in every direction. A high hat or bonnet covered her hair.

For Long Island's earliest colonists, shelter was little more than a glorified cellar. They dug square pits six or seven feet deep, lined them with timber and bark, used rough planking for floors and ceilings, and raised a roof of spars, covered with bark or sod. Nevertheless, these underground homes enabled the settlers to survive the first few years until they could erect more substantial structures.

ABOVE
The earliest Long Island housing development was composed of glorified cellars similar to these in Salem, Massachusetts. Most of the living space was below ground.

OPPOSITE ABOVE
What has been described as one of the oldest houses in New York State and "finest example of English domestic architecture to be found in this country" is called, appropriately, Old House. Built in 1649 in Southold by John Budd, it was moved in 1660 to Cutchogue.

OPPOSITE BELOW
Although it was built by Captain Josiah Hobart sometime after 1676, this venerable structure on James Lane, East Hampton, is called the Mulford House after the family that lived here from 1712 until World War II.

The second generation of housing utilized stone foundations, timbers, and beams that were attached by a mortise and tenon joint using wooden pegs (nails did not come into general use until the eighteenth century), chimneys, and thatched or shingled roofs. Many of these houses were two rooms wide, one room deep, and one-and-a-half stories high. Bedrooms were located on the upper floor loft, although with family members invariably outnumbering bedrooms, beds were placed in virtually every room. The ground floor was dominated by the chimney-fireplace, which provided the only source of heat both for warmth and cooking.

The kitchen was the main room. Heavy three-legged pots hung from iron hooks and chains in the fireplace. An alcove off the kitchen contained a pantry for storing food and utensils, and often doubled as a bedroom at night. Because the lumber was roughly hewn with broadaxes, drafts swept through the walls and, in the dead of winter, would freeze any water left standing. The floors were bare, except in the Dutch communities where they were sprinkled with sand.

This desk of cherry, pine, and poplar at the Mulford House in East Hampton dates from 1749 and is an example of colonial workmanship.

Featherbeds, filled with duck and goose down, were comfortable but bone-chilling until a covered metal pan filled with hot coals was rustled between the sheets. The only light other than that provided by the fire came from candles, which were made by dipping flaxen wicks repeatedly into melted fat. Whenever possible, the colonists saved labor by adapting natural objects to their own uses. Turkey wings became brooms and brushes, clam shells became spoons, and gourds became cups and ladles.

If material life was hard, so was the life of the spirit. Perhaps total religious commitment was essential to the colonists' survival; surely, it was present in all aspects of colonial existence. Paradoxically, since they had fled Europe to seek freedom from religious oppression, both English and Dutch settlers were unremitting in their efforts to impose puritanism upon all who lived within their communities. Religion and government were inseparable and implacably hostile toward nonconformity.

Because the ecclesiastical and political leaders were the same people, settlers who disobeyed or questioned the prevailing narrow beliefs and practices of church and state were without recourse. Religious officials made the laws and the laws supported religious orthodoxy. For example, in many communities only church members in good standing were permitted to vote. The construction of churches and parsonages, and the salaries of ministers, were paid through taxes levied by the towns against all residents. Further, attendance at services was compulsory. In Hempstead, failure to go to church twice (morning and afternoon) on Sundays and holidays was punishable by fines initially, and by corporal punishment and even banishment for repeated occurrences. It was also against the law to travel on Sundays, except, of course, to attend church.

Among those most severely affected by this church-state collaboration were newcomers, Quakers, and "witches." To maintain the moral standards of their communities, townspeople throughout Long Island were very cautious about accepting new residents. Town committees were established to probe the character of those seeking admission and a three- to six-month probationary period was required so that their behavior could be observed. Those who failed to pass scrutiny were forced to move on; it was illegal to sell property or rent quarters to them.

Few groups in America have suffered such persecution as that felt by the Quakers under the Dutch and English during the colonial period. In New England, they were fined, imprisoned, whipped, shorn of their ears, had their tongues bored with hot irons, and were put to death. On Long Island, under Peter Stuyvesant, it was against the law to shelter them even for a single night, to "hold converse" with them, or to bring them to New Netherland by ship.

Yet dramatic support for freedom of conscience emerged when thirty freeholders reacted to this discrimination in 1657 by issuing the *Flushing Remonstrance*:

Ye have been pleased to send up unto us a certain prohibition, or command, that we should not retaine or entertaine any of those people called Quakers. . . .

We cannot condemn them, . . . neither can we stretch out our hands against them, to punish, banish or persecute them. . . . Wee desire . . . not to judge lest we be judged, neither to condemn lest we be condemned, but rather let every man stand and fall to his own Master.

Therefore if any of these said persons come in love unto us, we cannot in conscience lay violent hands upon them, but give them free egresse or regresse into our town and houses.

Stuyvesant promptly jailed the principals, forced apologies from them, and outlawed town meetings for Flushing in favor of a seven-member "advisory" board. A few years later, when Stuyvesant banished Quaker John Bowne to Holland, he got his comeuppance from the directors of the West India Company, who voided the banishment with the rebuke: "The conscience of men ought to remain free and unshackled. Let every one remain free, as long as he is modest, moderate, his political conduct irreproachable, and as long as he does not offend others or oppose the government."

When the English took control of Long Island during the following decade, the Quakers received somewhat better treatment, and in 1672 their founder, Englishman George Fox, visited America and conducted meetings at Oyster Bay, Flushing, Gravesend, and Shelter Island. His stay at Shelter Island was particularly noteworthy because that area had served as a haven for persecuted Quakers.

What made the Quakers the targets of such hatred and abuse? For one thing, their principles, such as the refusal to take oaths, were regarded as a defiance of civil authority, contempt of court, and subversive. Further, their conduct was not always gentle and orderly. For example, they sometimes would "bear testimony" by running naked through the streets, cursing all who differed with them.

Even if justification could be found occasionally for the treatment of nonconformists, there is little doubt that Puritanical paranoia hit a peak of frenzy in 1692 in Salem, Massachusetts, when twenty people were executed within six months for allegedly being in league with Satan and practicing witchcraft. On Long Island, however, there was no corresponding panic, although belief in witchcraft and laws forbidding it existed.

Two cases did take place: one in 1657 against Elizabeth Garlick of East Hampton for causing the death of Elizabeth Howell, the daughter of Lion Gardiner; and the second in 1665 against Ralph and Mary Hall of Setauket for killing both George Wood and an infant child of widow Ann Rogers. When Elizabeth Garlick's husband, Joshua, retaliated by suing one of his wife's accusers for defamation, the town, uncertain of how to deal with the situation, put itself under the jurisdiction of Connecticut, thus passing the case to that colony. As a result, Goody (for Goodwife; only wives of distinguished men were called Mrs.) Garlick was tried in Hartford, where a jury found insufficient grounds to convict her but enough for suspicion. Both Garlicks were placed on a loose form of probation and eventually returned to East Hampton with a letter urging the town to "carry on neighborly and peaceably without just offense to Joshua Garlick and his wife and they should do like to you."

The principal basis of the charge against Goody Garlick was the ailing Elizabeth Howell's fevered cry, "Oh, Mother! I am bewitched!" and her vision of two figures at the foot of her bed, "Goody Garlick in the far corner and a black thing in the near corner. . . ."

The case against the Halls was tried in New York City, where they pleaded not guilty and "threw themselves to bee Tryed by God and the Country." In fact, they were tried by a jury which found that "there are some suspitions by the Evidence, of what the woman is Charged with, but nothing considerable of value to take away her life. But in reference to the man wee finde nothing considerable to charge him with." Considering that the charge carried the death penalty, Mary Hall may well have considered her sentence a triumph. The Halls were required to check in with the court periodically for about three years before being "released & acquitted from any & all Recognizances, bonds of appearance or othr obligations. . . ."

A third case involving a Long Islander, Mary Wright of Oyster Bay, illustrates both the unreasoning zeal of the witch-hunters and the dangers of unorthodoxy in those times. One of twenty-eight Quakers jailed in Boston in 1661 for telling the court to lay aside "carnal weapons" and stop slaughtering the Indians, she was tried for witchcraft but convicted of Quakerism. Her penalty was banishment.

By the eighteenth century the clamor over witches had begun to ebb throughout the colonies, to some extent through the excesses of Salem

ABOVE
Sheltering Quaker refugees, the Sylvester Manor on Shelter Island, rebuilt in 1733 since its original construction in the mid-seventeenth century, is said to have housed George Fox during the founding Quaker's 1672 trip to America.

LEFT
Clinton Academy, New York's first secondary school, was opened in 1784 in East Hampton and soon became recognized as a preparatory school for Yale. One of the academy's early teachers was William Payne, father of songwriter, actor, and playwright John Howard Payne, author of "Home Sweet Home."

RIGHT
A robust and enthusiastic man despite his forbidding demeanor, the Reverend Samuel Buell, a founder of Clinton Academy, had three wives and rode fourteen miles on horseback to preach on his eightieth birthday.

which resulted in greater demands for evidence; demands that of course could not be met. Time brought increasing skepticism about the supernatural, a possible consequence of the spread of public education.

The Dutch had been very educationally oriented in Europe and were quick to institute schools in their communities on the western end of the Island. This was true, too, of the English towns. In fact, the English community of East Hampton was the site of the first secondary school in New York State. Named Clinton Academy, after then-Governor George Clinton, it opened in 1784 largely through the efforts of the Reverend Samuel Buell, a dynamic Presbyterian preacher; installed by the famed evangelist Jonathan Edwards, Buell played an important role himself in the early eighteenth-century revivalist movement known as the Great Awakening.

Before Clinton Academy, public education was limited to the elementary level, although it was given a high priority in many settlements. In Huntington, for example, a schoolmaster, Jonas Houldsworth, was hired in 1657, just four years after the town's founding. He was appointed for four years, given a house, his "diet," firewood for the schoolhouse (to be supplied by the parents of attending children), and an initial salary of twenty-five pounds to be paid in butter, corn, wheat, cattle, cloth, and wampum.

The earliest reading materials in schools were hornbooks, so called because a transparent piece of animal horn was placed protectingly over the precious paper on which the lesson (usually the alphabet, phonic sounds, and the Lord's Prayer) had been written. The bone and paper were attached to a thin board, which, with a handle at its bottom, resembled a rectangular hand mirror. Sometimes the hornbook was hung around a pupil's neck on a string.

While there is no record of what transpired in Houldsworth's classroom, descriptions of early schools probably convey the general atmosphere. Discipline was very strict: a hickory stick was displayed prominently and used without hesitation across the back or shoulders of any disobedient boy. Some schoolmasters also wielded a long, broad ruler, called a "ferule," across the palm, pulled hair, or pinched ears. It would be some years before more "civilized" punishments came into vogue, such as standing on one leg, holding out a stick of firewood at arm's length, wearing a fool's cap, committing some lines to memory, or detention after school.

Learning was confined almost exclusively to reading, writing, and arithmetic. There were no steel pens, no ruled paper, no readymade writing books. The schoolmaster kept a sharp knife to make, mend, and nib the pens made from goose quills, as well as a leaden plummet and ruler to line the writing books. Each writer contributed a penny to buy a packet of Walkden's famous ink powder, which, when mixed with a gill of vinegar and three gills of rain or river water, made a pint of ink.

There is no doubt that education was less than universal in colonial

Elias Pelletreau, Sr., was born in 1726 and spent a seven-year indenture before perfecting his craftsmanship and becoming Long Island's most notable eighteenth-century silversmith, as this initialed porringer attests. A resident of Southampton and Patriot sympathizer, Pelletreau fled to Connecticut to escape the British occupation of Long Island during the American Revolution.

This gateleg table of maple and pine is one of the earliest (1700–30) examples of colonial woodworking on Long Island. It is said to have been used at the Sammis Tavern in Hempstead.

Long Island. Attendance was not compulsory; older boys (some of them nineteen or twenty years old) attended during the winter, while older girls often went during the summer with the younger boys. For the most part, education still was regarded as a luxury compared with the compelling necessity around the farm for helping hands.

This need began to ease somewhat toward the end of the seventeenth century, as farmers, while hardly prospering, at least found they could produce more than enough food to satisfy their own requirements and thus trade surplus crops for items they desired but lacked. This, combined with the growth of communities and the resulting availability of more diverse skills, led to the specialization of labor taken for granted today.

While farmers continued to predominate, many communities were able to boast a blacksmith, mason, carpenter, wheelwright, cooper, shoemaker, butcher, tanner, potter, weaver, ropemaker, glazier, sailmaker, chandler, and miller. There were also itinerant workers, frequently shoemakers and weavers, who visited those hamlets too small to support their own craftsmen. And there was, as well, a thriving wampum industry.

Long before the arrival of the Europeans, Long Island had been the Indian equivalent of a gold mine because of the abundance of shells from which wampum was made. So plentiful were quahogs (hard-shell clams) and whelks that the Island was called Seawanhacky, meaning Land of Shells. And the Indians were so adept at turning this raw material into wampum that Long Island became known as a colonial mint.

Black wampum was made from the purple part of the quahog shell and was worth twice as much as the white wampum of the whelk. The shells were worked into polished cylinders about one-quarter inch in diameter and one-eighth inch long, and strung on hempen or skin cords. Wampum was computed in terms of a "fathom," a string measured from the end of the little finger to the elbow, and was worth five English shillings or four Dutch guilders. The Dutch reportedly complained that the Indian agents either had very long or very short forearms, depending on whether they were buying or selling.

With colonization, parts of Long Island were transformed from a mint to a sweatshop, and some European traders, notably John Jacob Astor, hired Indians to grind out wampum day and night to trade for beaver and other valuable pelts. By 1641, the colonial economy had become so dependent on wampum that counterfeit had to be controlled. The Dutch passed an ordinance contending that "bad wampum is at present circulated here, and payment is made in nothing but rough, unpolished stuff . . . and the good, polished wampum is wholly put out of sight or exported." Consequently, the ordinance said, inferior wampum would have only three-fourths the value of good wampum.

Along with wampum, barter was the colonial medium of exchange, as farmers and craftsmen traded their produce and skills. The first industries that developed were mills, run by wind, water, and tides, to grind grain,

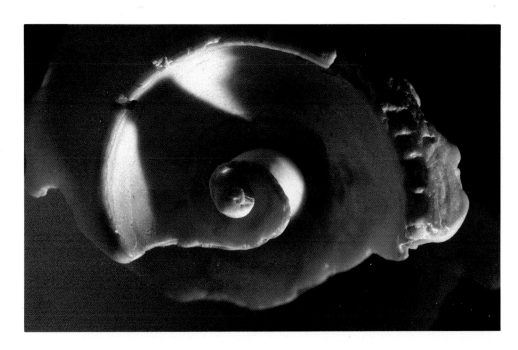

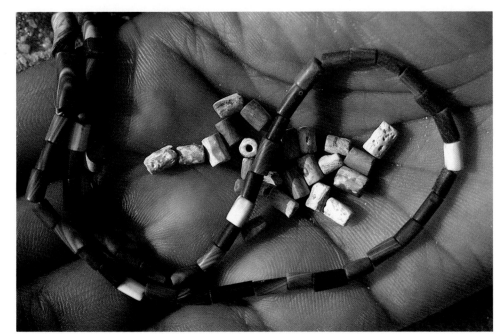

OPPOSITE ABOVE

The Thompson House on North Country Road, Setauket, was an unusually large timber-frame building for its time of construction, which was about 1700. It contains high ceilings and decorative detail on its exposed beams. There is a colonial herb garden on its grounds.

OPPOSITE BELOW

Sagtikos Manor in West Bay Shore was one of Long Island's earliest manorial estates when it was built in 1692. Used as a British headquarter during the Revolutionary War occupation, it later became one place where George Washington did sleep when he toured Long Island in 1790.

ABOVE

Wampum-making was one of the mainstays of the Indian economy during the colonial period since wampum was used by European settlers as a medium of exchange. White wampum was made from the columella—the central spiral—of whelk shells.

BELOW

Samples of black and white wampum are on display at the Garvies Point Museum in Glen Cove. Black wampum had double the value of the white.

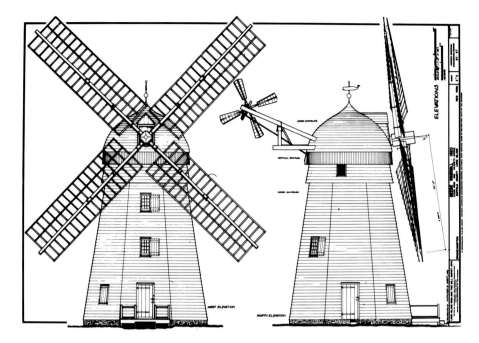

saw logs, and make woolen cloth and paper. The importance of grain was reflected in the controls exercised over grist mill operators, who could be made to forfeit their businesses if they cheated, performed unsatisfactorily, or unreasonably refused service. The usual method of payment was for the miller to retain a portion of the wheat or other grain he ground, trading this for other items or services.

As the colonists developed systems of journeymen and apprentices, improved the quality of their skills and products, and increased their output through mechanization, England became aware that it was not gaining its anticipated benefits from the exploitation of its New World holdings. The Crown had seen the American colonies as a market for British goods, which often were marked up from 100 to 300 percent, but the colonists were not buying.

Recognition of the incipient economic failure of the colonial system was expressed by New York Governor Lord Cornbury, when he noted: "I myself have seen serge made on Long Island that any man may wear. Now if they make serge, they will in time make coarse cloth and then fine. I hope I may be pardoned if I declare my opinion to be that all these colonies, which are but twigs belonging to the main tree, ought to be kept entirely dependent upon and subservient to England."

Attempts by subsequent colonial administrators to bring about such policies would not be accepted unquestioningly. The colonists, with their self-confidence fed by the knowledge that they had not only survived the wilderness but had tamed it and had begun to shape it to their own tastes, resented British attempts to impose British merchandise—at British prices—upon them. In time, that resentment would combine with others to become an ideology and to force a confrontation that would alter the future of the world.

CHAPTER THREE

Defeat and Survival

When Patriots, such as William Floyd, fled to Connecticut following the British occupation of Long Island during the Revolutionary War, their homes were often turned into barracks and stables. Floyd Mansion in Mastic suffered such a fate and was severely damaged.

For Long Island, the American Revolution meant seven disastrous days of battle and seven devastating years of occupation.

The battle was the least of it, although the losses were heavy and the implications dire. The brief Battle of Long Island, a clear defeat, came early in the war, in 1776, threatening the strength and spirit of the American cause. But the occupation was grindingly long, cruel, and destructive. It left deeper scars, claimed a heavier toll, produced more heroes and villains than the battle that preceded it.

"The history of that seven years' suffering will never be told," an East Hampton orator later said of the British military occupation of Long Island. "Left to the tender mercies of the foe; plundered by countryman and stranger of their property and ripened harvest; robbed of the stores which they reaped and garnered; slandered by suspicious brethren; taunted and scoffed at by the mercenary victors, they never wavered." Even discounting oratorical hyperbole, those were the harshest of times for Long Islanders. Surely, the war and occupation would have been painful enough under any circumstances. But their impact was heightened, coming, as they did, after the colonists finally had wrested a secure and decent life from the wilderness.

In the decades before the Revolution, the relationship between the Crown and the colonies was ambivalent. In part, there was a feeling of mutual interest and cooperation. Colonial militiamen had joined British troops to win the French and Indian War (1754–63), adding Canada to England's possessions and ejecting France from North America. Throughout the colonies, mere subsistence had given way to stability, even comfort. Many of the villages on Long Island had been in existence for a century by then and boasted attractive homes embellished with the works of American craftsmen. A tradition of higher education had been sown with the establishment of most of today's Ivy League institutions. Government and its foundation, law, were in place and functioning; there were doctors and ministers, artisans and artists, shopkeepers and innkeepers. In short, a society modeled closely on that of England and Holland had taken shape and was seeking to meet material and spiritual needs in much the same way that they were being fulfilled in Europe.

It was precisely this growth, this relative prosperity, that triggered the crisis with England. After all, the purpose of colonization was exploitation: a colony was supposed to be a source of raw materials and a market for imported products; its function was to serve the mother country, not rival it. But the Americans refused to accept such a definition, and while they were willing, in fact, eager to have the British represent them in foreign affairs, at home they wanted to run their own business.

And so tensions grew between England and its colonies as the British tried to make the Americans dependent, and the Americans sought to assert their newfound identity. An act by the colonists imposing a duty on European goods was repealed by the Crown (1724); the colonies were prohibited from exporting hats to the West Indies (1732); Parliament banned the establishment in America of slitting mills (1750); Parliament imposed a duty on molasses and sugar (1764) and passed the Stamp Act, compelling the use of stamps on all documents (1765); the Mutiny Act required the colonies to quarter and supply British troops stationed in America (1765); the Townshend Acts levied new duties on paper, glass, painters' colors, and, significantly, tea (1767); the Restraining Act threatened to suspend the New York Assembly if the colonists failed to comply with these impositions (1767).

Lacking any representation in Parliament, the colonists could rely only upon persuasion and recalcitrance. This they did with some effect. The Sons of Liberty was formed to oppose the odious Stamp Act, and succeeded in rallying the public against compliance, led demonstrations, and won support for a boycott of British goods. As a result, the Stamp Act was repealed in 1766 and the Townshend Acts, with the exception of the duty on tea, were rescinded in 1770. But these concessions by the British did not resolve the problem, which, while economic in origin, had escalated into a political and philosophic deadlock because Parliament and the Crown miscalculated the American will.

Still, there was far from unanimity among the colonists. Loyalists or Tories, those who supported King George III, comprised a substantial portion of the Long Island population, compared with the Patriots or Whigs, those who opposed the British position. These divisions were based on socioeconomic and geographic, as well as political alignments. Wealthier, higher-status Long Islanders, particularly merchants, tended to identify with the Crown, and since they were more likely to be concentrated in western Long Island, Queens was a stronghold of Loyalist sympathizers. Farmers, fishermen, and Suffolk residents, who tended generally to identify more with New England, the core of anti-British feeling, lent their backing to the Patriot cause. Differences were so intense within Hempstead between the Patriots in the northern portion and the Loyalists in the southern, that in 1775 the Patriots seceded, and in 1784 the area was split officially into the Towns of South Hempstead and North Hempstead, with the former becoming simply Hempstead later on.

Thus, it is not surprising that in 1774, fully two years before the

ABOVE
William Floyd, a fervent Patriot, soldier, politician, and one of the Long Island signers of the Declaration of Independence, made notable contributions to the founding of the nation.

LEFT
This portrait of Anna Floyd, William's sister, was painted by Ralph Earl, a prominent colonial artist, who also portrayed Floyd's son-in-law, Ezra L'Hommedieu.

RIGHT
Francis Lewis, who lived in Whitestone and achieved prominence as a signer of the Declaration of Independence, has been characterized by some as a shady businessman and war profiteer.

BELOW
Long Island craftsmen of the colonial period made furniture such as this writing table owned by William Floyd.

writing of the Declaration of Independence, a resolution foreshadowing that historic document was adopted at a town meeting in Huntington. Later called Huntington's Declaration of Rights, it stated in part:

That every freeman's property is absolutely his own, and no man has a right to take it from him without his consent, expressed either by himself or his representatives.

That therefore all taxes and duties imposed on His Majesty's subjects in the American colonies by the authority of Parliament are wholly unconstitutional and a plain violation of the most essential rights of British subjects.

The resolution went on to call for a boycott of British goods to pressure Parliament into repealing taxes imposed on the colonists, and to reopen the Port of Boston, which had been punitively shut down. It concluded by appointing a committee to work with other towns and New York City to achieve those goals.

As the Patriots organized, the Loyalists consolidated too, and it became increasingly difficult for colonists to remain neutral. Feelings intensified and positions hardened. There were conflicts within families rivaling those that would afflict the nation a century later during the Civil War. In Queens the following year, after Loyalists had soundly defeated a slate of Patriot delegates to the Provincial Congress, the Congress held the Loyalist voters in contempt, published their names in the newspapers (there was no secret ballot in those days), sent soldiers to disarm them, and arrested their leaders.

Colonel Nathaniel Heard of New Jersey, who headed the Patriot troops sent into Queens, won some measure of prominence when protesting Loyalists composed the following lyrics to the melody of "Yankee Doodle":

> Colonel Heard has come to town,
> In all his pride and glory;
> And when he dies he'll go to Hell
> For robbing of the Tory.
>
> Colonel Heard has come to town
> A'thinking for to plunder;
> Before he'd done, he had to run—
> He heard the cannon thunder.
>
> And when he came to Hempstead Town
> He heard the cannon rattle—
> Poor Colonel Heard he ran away
> And dared not face the battle.
>
> And now he's gone to Oyster Bay
> Quick for to cross the water;
> He dare no more in Hempstead stay
> For fear of meeting with a slaughter.

By the spring of 1775, the battles of Lexington and Concord already had been fought between the British and the colonists in Massachusetts, and while some leaders on both sides still hoped for an accommodation, it was becoming increasingly evident that this was unlikely. On July 4, 1776, Congress passed the Declaration of Independence, asserting the "right of the people to alter or to abolish it [any government that deprives them of the right to 'life, liberty and the pursuit of happiness'], and to institute new government," thus sealing the inevitability of all-out war.

Three of the signers of the Declaration—William Floyd, Francis Lewis, and Philip Livingston—had ties to Long Island, although Livingston's was somewhat tenuous, consisting of a summer house in Brooklyn Heights. Floyd, born in 1734 on the Mastic Beach estate now maintained by the National Park Service as an historic site open to the public, was one of the Island's most prominent native sons. A wealthy landowner and politician, he fought as a colonel in the First Suffolk Regiment during the Revolution and was commissioned a major general at its conclusion. More distinguished in his political than military career, he represented New York at the First and Second Continental Congresses, and served in the State Senate and first U.S. House of Representatives.

Despite his affluence, social position, and the fact that his first cousin, Richard Floyd, was a leading Loyalist, William Floyd steadfastly espoused the Patriot cause, a decision that compelled his family to flee to Connecticut during the war and, no doubt, encouraged the looting and damaging of his estate by the British or Loyalists. After the war, he rebuilt and expanded the manor house before moving to upstate New York to what is now Westernville, where he died at the age of eighty-six. Floyd is remembered both through the preservation of his home and the parkway bearing his name that traverses Brookhaven from Route 25A, near Wading River, to Smith Point on Fire Island.

Like Floyd, Francis Lewis has achieved immortality through Long Island's transportation network: Francis Lewis Boulevard runs through Queens from Whitestone to Elmont. Unlike Floyd, Lewis' reputation is somewhat questionable.

Born in Wales in 1713, Lewis emigrated to New York when he was twenty-five and formed a partnership with a former Englishman named Richard Annesley, whose sister he later married. During the French and Indian War, Lewis had a contract to clothe the British Army and, while handling this business at upstate Oswego, he was captured by the French. Upon his release, according to one version, the British rewarded him with a tract of land and he built a farm in what is now Whitestone.

In 1775, he was chosen to represent New York in the Continental Congress, where his business experience and executive talent were highly regarded. The following year, Lewis and fifty-five colleagues signed the Declaration of Independence; shortly thereafter, while he was in Philadelphia, British troops retaliated by ransacking his house and taking his elderly wife prisoner. Mrs. Lewis was held for months in a filthy room until finally freed in a prisoner exchange arranged by George Washington, the American commander-in-chief. But her health had been severely impaired and she soon died. Lewis moved to New York City in 1796, died in relative obscurity on December 31, 1802, and was buried in an unmarked grave in Trinity churchyard.

The controversy surrounding Lewis concerns his business activities. One account lauds him for spending "the bulk of his large fortune, for which he was never repaid," to obtain military stores for the colonial cause. However, a legal document in the New-York Historical Society's library accuses Lewis of having defrauded the estate of his late partner, Richard Annesley, a charge denied by Lewis, who portrayed himself as the victim.

A more scathing indictment came from Judge Thomas Jones, who, in a book entitled *History of New York During the Revolutionary War*, contended that before being captured at Oswego, Lewis, "by selling his tobacco, his pipes, his sugar, and his salt, at a most exorbitant price, extorted a great deal of money from the poor soldiery." Jones further charged that Lewis later made considerable money from privateering in collaboration with a corrupt judge of the Admiralty, and, during the Revolution, had speculated with his sons in soldiers' certificates, with which they bought confiscated lands. If, in fact, Jones' accusations were true, they were not extraordinary. Profiteering was widespread throughout the Revolutionary War and was imputed to many in high places.

Whatever the credentials of those who signed the Declaration, the effect of their efforts was galvanizing. In the days and weeks following July 4, 1776, the stirring document was read to gatherings of excited listeners throughout the thirteen colonies. In Huntington, for example,

An artist's recreation of a crucial phase of the Battle of Long Island, when Americans under General William Stirling retreated across Gowanus Creek. Stirling was one of two American generals captured during that disastrous encounter.

on July 22, the reading was accompanied by a flourish of drumbeats and an enthusiastic response. The British Union Jack, which had hung on the Liberty Pole, was replaced with one bearing the word Liberty in white on a red field. This became known as the Long Island Flag and was carried by Patriot troops in the Battle of Long Island.

Powder horns, such as this one made and ornamented by Gilbert Vail in 1762, were used in times of war and peace.

An effigy of King George III was made, wrapped in the discarded British flag, labeled King George III, filled with powder, hung from a gallows, and exploded. There was a parade of some three hundred members of the Huntington militia and volleys of musket fire. Later, thirteen toasts were drunk, one for each of the self-proclaimed independent colonies. Then Dr. Gilbert Potter, a lieutenant colonel in the militia, with Major Jesse Brush, one of Huntington's most noted Patriots, concluded the celebration by reading the following poem from the *Constitutional Gazette*:

> Rudely forced to drink Tea, Massachusetts in anger,
> Spills the Tea on John Bull; John falls on to bang her.
> Massachusetts, enraged, calls her neighbors to aid,
> And gives Master John a severe bastinade.
> Now good men of the law! Pray, who is in fault,
> The one who began, or resents the assault?

OVERLEAF

*Taking their history seriously, Long Islanders frequently don replicas of Revolutionary War uniforms to relive skirmishes by troops of both sides. During the 1976 Bicentennial celebration, military buffs reenacted activities of Continental Army regulars (*ABOVE LEFT*), Huntington Minutemen (*BELOW LEFT*), and British troops opposing the Americans (*ABOVE RIGHT*).*

OVERLEAF BELOW RIGHT

Built in 1740, this arsenal was used by the Huntington Militia to store arms and gunpowder until 1776, when the British took it over. It is located on Park Avenue, just south of Route 25A, in Huntington Village.

With their spirits high, Huntington Patriots, and thousands of like-thinking Long Island neighbors, made ready to take on John Bull. They did not have long to wait. A month later, in August 1776, the British fleet landed troops between Old Man's (now Mt. Sinai) and Wading River, where they shot cattle and carried off the beef. Potter, on learning of the foray, wrote to General Nathaniel Woodhull that, although he felt under-manned, he was preparing his militiamen for a possible attack in Huntington Bay, needed help, and thought that "General Washington should be acquainted."

Potter did not know it, but the Battle of Long Island already was under way, not in Huntington Bay, but in Brooklyn, and not with a few hundred or thousand British soldiers, but with one of the largest expeditionary forces ever launched against an enemy in the history of Great Britain: 32,000 troops. The immensity of that military effort was a tribute both to

the fighting skills of the Americans and the grand strategy of the British high command. A few months earlier, 7,000 British troops had been besieged in Boston by the Continental Army and compelled to evacuate. Clearly, the British generals learned, it would require far greater strength than had been assumed to put down the colonial rebellion.

The British also had determined from that experience the necessity of crushing the rebels throughout the thirteen colonies not merely by capturing a few key cities and towns. To this end, they decided to divide the colonies into three segments, isolating New England, the middle colonies, and those in the south. The first step was to cut off New England by sending one column down from Canada to meet another coming up from New York. That required the capture of New York City, which consequently made Long Island of vital strategic importance. The expeditionary force was being built up on Staten Island. There, British regulars, augmented by Hessian mercenaries, were under the command of General Sir William Howe, whose brother, Admiral Lord Richard Howe, had recently brought the bulk of the troops fresh from England aboard a fleet of 150 ships.

George Washington, anticipating an attack on New York, moved his 19,000 raw and poorly equipped soldiers into the area, noting that "it is the Place that we must use every Endeavor to keep from them. For should they get that Town, and the Command of the North River, they can stop the Intercourse between the northern and southern Colonies, upon which depends the Safety of America." He set his soldiers to work building fortifications on the southern tip of Manhattan and in Brooklyn Heights.

On the morning of August 22, 1776, Americans stationed at Gravesend (near the present Bensonhurst section of Brooklyn) awoke to see an armada approaching from Staten Island, ships loaded to the gunwales with British troops. The invasion was on. The Americans fled and soon joined the bulk of Patriot soldiers who were aligned either behind the Brooklyn Heights fortifications or along a ridge that ran from near Gowanus Bay eastward toward Jamaica. The ridge, called the Heights of Guan, was thickly wooded and formed a natural barrier, penetrable only through four openings, the easternmost of which was called Jamaica Pass.

After several days of skirmishing, the British took up positions in front of the three other passages, engaging the attention of about 2,500 American militiamen defending the ridge. While Washington waited for the attack, General Howe led his main force of 10,000 on an all-night march to Jamaica Pass, where only five Patriot officers had been posted. Capturing the five before they could warn their cohorts, the British learned that the pass had been left undefended and quickly poured through. Howe's strategy worked to perfection. He had positioned overwhelming forces both in front of and behind the American lines; the final blow was to be coordinated with a naval bombardment of Brooklyn Heights from the East River.

Had nature not intervened, it is possible that the Revolution would have ended then, with the capture or destruction of the entire American army, including Washington and three generals under his command. But a stiff north wind and an ebbing tide prevented Admiral Howe from moving his fleet northward, and so only the battle, not the war, was lost.

Yet, the situation was still desperate. Patriot troops, caught in the British pincers, suffered severely and were barely able to retreat behind the fortified Brooklyn Heights positions. There, they faced a force, superior in every regard, that was prepared to win victory by siege or assault. Confronted by this terrible dilemma, the American commander conceived and executed a brilliant stratagem, of which the noted English historian George O. Trevelyan said: "It may be doubted whether any great national deliverance since the passage of the Red Sea has ever been more loudly acclaimed or more adequately celebrated than the masterstroke of energy, dexterity, and caution, by which Washington saved his army and his country."

A witness to the operation, Major Benjamin Tallmadge of Setauket, who entered Yale at the age of twelve, served in the Connecticut militia, and later performed heroically during the British occupation, gave the following description:

General Washington was so fully aware of the perilous situation of this division of his army, that he immediately convened a council of war, at which the propriety of retiring to New York was decided on. After sustaining incessant fatigue and constant watchfulness for two days and nights, attended by heavy rain, exposed every moment to an attack by a vastly superior force in front, and to be cut off from the possibility of retreat to New York by the fleet which might enter the East River, on the night of the twenty-ninth [of August] . . . Washington commenced recrossing his troops from Brooklyn to New York.

To move so large a body of troops with all their necessary appendages across a river full a mile wide, with a rapid current, in face of a victorious, well-disciplined army nearly three times as numerous as his own and a fleet capable of stopping the navigation so that not one boat could have passed over, seemed to present most formidable obstacles.

But in face of these difficulties, the Commander in Chief so arranged his business that on the evening of the twenty-ninth by ten o'clock, the troops began to retire from the lines in such a manner that no chasm was made in the lines, but as one regiment left their station on guard, the remaining troops moved to the right and left and filled up the vacancies, while General Washington took his station at the ferry and superintended the embarkation of the troops.

The evacuation resulted in the extrication of some 9,500 American soldiers, with their equipment and supplies, from positions only 600 yards from the British lines to safety in Manhattan. Moments before its completion, with Washington still on the Long Island side, British scouts, suspicious of the silence, infiltrated the Patriot lines and discovered what was happening. But before they could act, a fog rolled in and concealed the departure of the remaining boats, one of which bore Washington. Of the 10,000 Americans actively engaged in the Battle of Long Island, an estimated 300 were killed and at least 1,100 were wounded, captured, or missing. These losses, which were appreciably worse than those suffered by the British, included two generals, Stirling and Sullivan, who were taken prisoner.

One of the most poignant (although possibly embroidered) incidents to emerge from the battle involved General Woodhull, the officer to whom Potter had addressed his belated warning about a British invasion. Woodhull had been given the vital, but hardly glamorous, task of rounding

Ranking high among the cruel and harrowing episodes of the Revolution were the rotting ships used by the British to hold American prisoners of war. The most notorious ship was the Jersey, *pictured above in Wallabout Bay, New York Harbor, which accounted for a significant share of the estimated 11,500 deaths attributed to these vessels.*

up the Patriots' cattle in Queens and driving them east of the vast Hempstead Plains to keep them out of enemy hands. Despite wholesale desertions, he accomplished his assignment and sought permission to join the fight in Brooklyn. He waited anxiously in Jamaica, within the sound of cannon fire, for orders that never came. Instead, a detachment of British dragoons arrived and took him prisoner. The general surrendered his sword, but when his captors demanded that he say "God save the King!" he replied instead, "God save us all!" This infuriated the dragoon leader, who slashed at Woodhull with his saber and would have killed him had not other officers intervened.

General Woodhull was treated by a doctor and then placed aboard one of the notorious prison ships that the British kept at Wallabout Bay in

Brooklyn. The wounds he had suffered required the amputation of an arm, and he died less than a month after his capture. From his deathbed, Woodhull wrote his wife, urging her to bring a wagon filled with provisions for his fellow prisoners.

The prison ships were among the most atrocious aspects of the Revolution and resulted in the death of an estimated 11,500 American seamen and soldiers from starvation, disease, and neglect. The following account by the Reverend Thomas Andros of Berkeley, Massachusetts, a prisoner who survived confinement on the former battleship *Jersey*, depicts the horrors of imprisonment.

When I first became an inmate of this abode of suffering, despair and death, there were about four hundred prisoners on board; but in a short time they amounted to twelve hundred, and in proportion to our numbers, the mortality increased.

All the most deadly diseases were pressed into the service of the king of terrors, but his prime ministers were dysentery, smallpox and yellow fever. There were two hospital ships near to the old "Jersey," but these were soon so crowded with the sick that they could receive no more. The consequence was that the diseased and the healthy were mingled together in the main ship. In a short time we had two hundred or more sick and dying lodged in the fore part of the lower gun deck, where all the prisoners were confined at night.

Utter derangement was a common symptom of yellow fever; and, to increase the horror of the darkness that shrouded us (for we were allowed no light betwixt decks), the voice of warning would be heard, "Take heed to yourselves! There is a madman stalking through the ship with a knife in his hand!" I sometimes found the man a corpse in the morning by whose side I laid myself down at night. . .

Washington's evacuation to Manhattan left Long Island to the British, and they wasted no time in taking control. Fearing the worst, Patriots and their families and slaves fled across the Long Island Sound to Connecticut. Refugees jammed the docks of North Shore communities, as about one in six Long Islanders—5,000 out of a population of less than 30,000—left their homes, farms, businesses, and most of their possessions for the next seven years.

Painful as it may have been to leave, the ordeal of those who remained made the decision to flee appear sound. Loyalists, particularly those who had suffered under Patriot rule, now emerged to welcome their conquering British heroes. To symbolize their support for the Crown, they wore red cockades or ribbons, a practice quickly adopted by boys, slaves, the elderly, and all who wished to avoid British persecution. The use of red rags for this purpose became so widespread that women had to tear up their red petticoats to meet the demand. The more ardent Patriots sneeringly derided these wearers of red as members of the Petticoat Brigade.

Not only the Loyalists regained stature and power. New York Governor

William Tryon, the Crown's appointee who had been forced out by the Patriots, now returned with the Howe brothers to reinstitute the Crown's authority. Martial law was declared and, with the assistance of Loyalists, Patriot leaders were identified, rounded up, and either imprisoned or kept under surveillance. The British also were interested in raising an army of Long Islanders to take part in their continuing effort to suppress the Revolution. But despite inducements and threats, recruitment of both Loyalists and former Patriots proved disappointing.

Aside from providing some manpower, Long Island served the British cause in two principal respects following the Battle of Long Island: it helped protect the British occupation of vital New York City, which Washington had been forced to abandon a few months later, and it supplied the British troops with food and shelter until the end of the war.

In exploiting the land and people to fulfill this latter function, the British exhibited the callousness, greed, and cruelty that bred hatred for them among generations of Long Islanders. Compelling the losers to sustain a victorious army was hardly a new concept; while the official British policy was to pay for goods and services, practice was something else. Long Islanders soon found themselves giving provisions, labor, and quarters to about 8,500 occupying soldiers, often with only the promise of eventual compensation.

When it came to the property and possessions of self-exiled Patriots, the British simply took what they wanted "for the King's use." Oliver De Lancey, whose family was prominent in New York affairs, commanded the Loyalists recruited into the regular British army and played an active role in subjugating Long Islanders throughout the seven years of occupation. His subordinates ordered their troops to "take into your custody all the grain, forage, and creatures you can find on L.I., being the property of persons actually in rebellion, or who have deserted their habitations."

Cattle, grain, and wood were given top priority by the army of occupation—the first two for food, the third for fuel and construction. Since one of four people living on Long Island at that time was a British soldier, the demand for meat, bread, cereal, and fresh fruit and vegetables was tremendous and immediate. In addition, Long Island was seen as a key source of food for the entire British expeditionary force, roughly equivalent in number to the Island's civilian population.

Keeping their cattle out of British hands (and bellies) required considerable ingenuity on the part of Patriot farmers who were continually on the lookout for places where herds could graze undetected. Among the best hideaways were the kettle holes, broad, deep cavities created by huge chunks of glacial ice. On one occasion, when British soldiers demanded to know the location of some Patriots' cattle in the Smithtown area, the Americans replied: "Oh, we sent them to Yorke"—the name of a nearby kettle hole. The British, assuming that New York City was

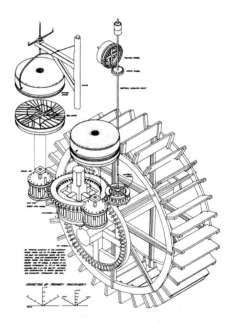

The mechanism of the Lefferts Mill is illustrated in this drawing; most of the fine gear is still intact.

meant, ended their search.

One devastating consequence of the war, although unintentional, involved the destruction of substantial wheat fields by an insect brought to America from Germany together with German wheat and Hessian troops. It soon ravaged the native wheat, beginning in western Queens where Tory farmers planted some of the infected imported grain, and became known as the Hessian Fly.

The effect would have been much worse had it not been for a farmer and miller from Flushing who, having heard of a type of wheat that resisted the Hessian Fly, acquired some and planted it. According to a 1786 newspaper account:

> The insect that has destroyed the wheat many years past continues to spread, but it has no effect on the white-bearded wheat raised on Long Island. This wheat was brought here from the southwest during the war, and a few bushels sown by a Flushing farmer grew well, and afforded a fine crop. He kept on, and has supplied his neighbors. It grew twenty bushels to the acre, and weighs over sixty pounds. It is of a bright yellow color, and makes fine flour. The straw is harder, and resists the poison of the fly, and supports the grain, while bearded and bald wheat were cut off.

Another indirect result of the war was the wasting of Long Island's vast hardwood forests, particularly on the North Shore. These woodlands held a special attraction for the occupation forces, but the appeal was hardly aesthetic. The British needed wood to construct fortifications and to burn as fuel, and they chopped down those forests indiscriminately, altering the look and the ecology of large portions of that area. After the war, logging operations continued for more than a century on Long Island and played an important role in the economy.

Generally, both during the occupation and later, the trees were cut and carted or dragged by horse to villages on Long Island Sound for shipment to New York. The method of loading the cordwood on the ships involved what was called "laying on." The sailboats would come as close to the beach as possible during high tide and stand by. As the tide receded and exposed more beach, the logs would be hauled across the sand and loaded aboard. When the tide rose again, the boats were ready to sail. This meant that men had to be available for loading whenever the tide made it possible, whatever the hour of day or night, and the British troops made certain Long Islanders responded.

But by far the most odious experience suffered during the occupation was the billeting, or quartering, of British and Hessian troops during the winter. This was done in an arbitrary manner, with concern only for the accommodations, not for the family's circumstances. British officers would tour the Long Island countryside, frequently with a Loyalist as guide, and inspect farmhouses to determine their capacities. Houses with only one fireplace were rejected, since soldiers were not supposed to become

ABOVE
Target Rock, off Lloyd Neck, got its name because it was used to sharpen the aim of British Navy cannoneers.

BELOW
A Revolutionary-era landmark still standing in Lloyd Neck is Lloyd Manor, which was built in 1766 and occupied by the British when its owner, Joseph Lloyd, joined other Patriots in Connecticut.

OPPOSITE ABOVE

Among the forts used by British troops during their seven-year occupation of Long Island was Fort Franklin in Lloyd Neck, overlooking Cold Spring Harbor. Its earthworks are still visible.

OPPOISTE BELOW

Raynham Hall in Oyster Bay, the home of Samuel Townsend, played a critical role during the Revolution when it served as British headquarters for a regiment of the Queen's Rangers. Townsend's son, Robert, was a member of George Washington's spy ring.

RIGHT

Although most of the British forts on Long Island were built on the North Shore to defend against assaults by Patriot troops stationed across the Sound in Connecticut, Fort St. George was located on the South Shore at Mastic Beach. As the plaque indicates, American Major Benjamin Tallmadge led a successful amphibious attack on the fort in 1780.

Woolen pocketbook belonging to Samuel Townsend of Oyster Bay, the master of Raynham Hall and bearing his name, was made in 1755, possibly by his wife or one of his daughters.

closely involved with the families, and fireplaces provided the only heat for warmth and cooking.

After some rooms were set aside for the family, and at least one fireplace was allotted for heating and cooking, the remaining rooms with fireplaces were assigned to soldiers. The touring officer decided how many soldiers a home could contain and marked the number on the front door with chalk. The owner was then informed: "Madam, we have come to take a billet on your house." And that was it. A door was nailed shut to keep the soldiers and family apart, but the number of intermarriages suggests that the separation was less than total.

To maintain their occupation of Long Island and to defend against anticipated Patriot forays from Connecticut, the British built a series of forts, principally on the North Shore: the Oyster Bay Encampment, Fort Franklin on Lloyd Neck, Forts Slongo and Golgotha in Huntington, and Fort St. George in Mastic.

The Oyster Bay Encampment served as headquarters for the Queen's Rangers, Americans who had volunteered to fight for the Crown, and its fortress was located at what presently is the intersection of Orchard and Prospect Streets in the village. Always ready to meet an attack, the fortification never was called upon to do so.

Fort Franklin, named for the Loyalist son of Benjamin Franklin, was designed by Colonel Benjamin Thompson, a figure of prominence and controversy who achieved a reputation in the military, scientific, and philanthropic fields, both in America and England. Thompson, later named Count Rumford, was born in Massachusetts and would have become a leader in the Continental Army but for internal wrangling and jealousy. Frustrated, he went to England, returning near the end of the Revolutionary War in 1781 to command the King's American Dragoons, a Loyalist regiment, and supervise construction of Fort Franklin and Fort Golgotha.

The earthworks of Fort Franklin, which dominated a bluff overlooking the entrance to Cold Spring Harbor, are still visible on the former estate of Mrs. Willis Delano Wood. It was Fort Golgotha, which ominously was given the Hebrew name for Calvary, the site of Christ's crucifixion, that earned Thompson notoriety as one of the most reprehensible figures of the occupation. Built in late 1782, when hostilities had ended and a peace treaty was being concluded, the fort—located at the present intersection of Nassau Road and Main Street in Huntington Village—was constructed by tearing down the Old First Presbyterian Church for lumber and uprooting a burial ground for tombstones.

The desecration was unbelievable: the tombstones were used for ovens, so that bread bore the reverse imprint of the epitaphs it was baked upon. Thompson reportedly pitched his tent over the grave of the Presbyterian minister, the Reverend Ebenezer Prime, so that when he entered or left he could "step on the damned old rebel's head." The Reverend Prime, before his death a few years earlier, had seen British officers take over his house, wreck his furniture, and destroy the most valuable books in his library. Thompson rounded out his unusual career in France, acquiring considerable wealth through various inventions, and bequeathed a portion of his estate to Harvard College.

Fort Slongo, named for its builder, Philadelphia contractor George Slongo, was located at Treadwell's Neck and commanded a magnificent view of Long Island Sound. The outline of its blockhouse still is visible on the ground behind the house at what is now 46 Brookfield Road, Fort Salonga. ("Salonga" is a corruption of "Slongo.")

Fort Slongo, along with Forts Franklin and St. George, became the target of raids by Major Benjamin Tallmadge, an heroic Patriot officer who launched hit-and-run guerrilla attacks against the British throughout the occupation. From the safety of Connecticut, which was held by Washington's forces, Tallmadge and other American soldiers waged "whaleboat warfare" across the Sound.

ABOVE
Major Benjamin Tallmadge, born in Setauket, escaped to Connecticut after the Battle of Long Island and launched whaleboat forays against British occupation forces.

LEFT
Portraitist Ralph Earl's painting of Major Benjamin Tallmadge's wife and child.

OPPOSITE ABOVE
Robert Feke's Self-Portrait *dates from about 1750. Born in Oyster Bay some forty years earlier, he became a prominent portrait painter.*

OPPOSITE BELOW
Feke's portrait of Josiah Martin, from 1746, shows the wealthy, successful merchant and landowner wearing a powdered wig and an elegant white brocade waistcoat. Martin is typical of the eighteenth-century aristocracy. His fine house, Rock Hall in Lawrence, was probably built in the early 1770s and included numerous outbuildings such as the kitchen building, smoke house, carriage house, and ice house.

In the assault on Fort Slongo, 150 Continental troops crossed to Long Island in the whaleboats, which were about thirty feet long, pointed at both ends, swift, light enough to be easily portable, and superbly maneuverable. After a brief engagement, the 140-man garrison was subdued, the fort destroyed, the blockhouse burned, and twenty-one prisoners, one field piece, and seventy muskets captured. Not a single Patriot was lost in the encounter, a tribute in large measure to the espionage activities of Henry Scudder, a refugee from Great Cow Harbor (now Northport), who visited the fort and made detailed sketches of it. Scudder, a lieutenant captured during the Battle of Long Island and released, took part in many of the raids against the British.

On one occasion, while Scudder hid in the chimney of his home in Crab Meadow, a British cavalry officer named Captain Coffin pointed a pistol at his wife's head and said, "If I don't find your rebel husband in a week, I'll be in my coffin." Less than a week later, Scudder and a Patriot raiding party surrounded a house where British soldiers were relaxing, took sixteen prisoners, and shot Coffin dead as he played cards.

While the Patriots used the whaleboats to great advantage in Long Island Sound, they by no means dominated that body of water. The British struck across the Sound on several occasions, destroying Danbury, Connecticut, and damaging New Haven, Fairfield, Green's Farms, and Norwalk for aiding the whaleboaters. However, the Patriots were not cowed by these assaults. In retaliation for the Danbury raid, Lieutenant Colonel Return Jonathan Meigs took 170 men across the Sound and, without a single casualty, returned to Connecticut within twenty-four hours of his departure after having attacked a British outpost at Sag Harbor with devastating effectiveness.

But perhaps the most spectacular of the amphibious assaults in and around Long Island was commanded by Major Tallmadge in November, 1780. The objective was Fort St. George, from which 200 Loyalists reportedly were plundering the countryside. It was located near Smith's Point on the South Shore, which meant the Patriots had to cross not only the Sound but the Island as well. Further, the base, consisting of three strongholds (the Manor of St. George, another fortified house, and a small fort), was protected by a triangular, twelve-foot-high stockade.

Tallmadge first visited the fort in disguise to familiarize himself with its defenses and plan his attack. Later, accompanied by eighty soldiers in eight whaleboats, he sailed across Long Island Sound to Mt. Sinai, was delayed a full day by a storm, and made an all-night march to strike at dawn with three columns. Shouting, "Washington and Glory!" his dragoons crashed through one stockade wall and scaled the other two to capture the fortification and fifty-four prisoners without loss.

The effectiveness of the whaleboaters tempted some to allow personal greed to overcome patriotic zeal. They eagerly sought "letters of marque," entitling private vessels to prey on enemy vessels—and retain part of the spoils. These "privateers" sometimes found it difficult to distinguish foe from friend and were accused of plundering their fellow Patriots as well. On Long Island, the line between privateering and piracy was anyhow a thin one historically. Captain William Kidd, a Scotch minister's son, was sent out in 1695 under the aegis of British King William III to curb piracy and, incidentally, capture enemy ships. Six years later, he was hanged in London for committing piracy, after part of his loot was unearthed on Gardiner's Island at a spot now marked by a bronze plaque.

At the time of the Revolution, the phenomenal success of the whaleboat expeditions stemmed to a large degree from the first-hand information gathered by Patriot soldiers and agents. During the course of the war, the Patriots developed an excellent espionage system—with the glaring exception of perhaps the most famous American spy, Nathan Hale.

Hale's career as a Patriot secret agent, which ended almost as it began, proved calamitous for him and useless for his sponsors. That he is remembered at all, much less in laudatory terms, seems less a tribute to anything he did or said than to the determination of many historians to perpetuate questionable anecdotes. Handsome, graceful, and refined, Hale, a native of Connecticut, graduated from Yale with honors, became a schoolmaster, enlisted in the Continental Army in 1775, and, at the age of twenty-one, bored with inactivity and fervent with patriotism, responded to a desperate request from General Washington and volunteered to spy. For about two weeks in the fall of 1776, Hale visited enemy forts on Long Island under the guise of being a job-seeking Dutch teacher. When captured, probably in Huntington Bay, possibly on a tip from a Tory cousin, Hale was carrying his own Yale diploma, and diagrams and descriptions of British fortifications. He readily admitted who and what he was.

Hale was hanged the next day in New York City. It was not until seventy-two years later, in a book published by the daughter of a friend and classmate, William Hull, that the famous phrase "I only regret that I have but one life to lose for my country" emerged. Those words were attributed to Hale by a British captain who witnessed the execution and described it to Hull.

Although Hale's information never reached Washington, his death inspired Tallmadge, also a friend and classmate, to accept an appointment from Washington in 1778 as head of the Secret Service, and thus chief of intelligence. Tallmadge recruited three Setauket neighbors—Austin Roe, a tavernkeeper, Abraham Woodhull, a farmer, and Caleb Brewster, a whaler—and an Oyster Bay merchant, Robert Townsend, to form what became known as the Setauket or Culper Spy Ring. (Samuel Culper Sr. was Woodhull's code name and Samuel Culper Jr. was Townsend's.)

Woodhull and, later, Townsend gathered information in New York City about British troop movements and transmitted it either on paper using invisible ink or orally to Roe, the courier. Roe took it to Setauket, where it was passed to Brewster, who carried it by whaleboat across the Sound to Tallmadge, who usually was stationed in Fairfield, Connecticut. Tallmadge would then send the intelligence to Washington, wherever he happened to be at the time.

The espionage ring also included two women: one, known only by her code number "355," became Townsend's sweetheart and bore his illegitimate child; the other was Anna Smith Strong, who lived alone on Strong's Neck since her husband, Selah, a judge, had been imprisoned by the British for aiding the Patriot cause.

Agent "355" circulated among the New York elite, where she was able to overhear the conversations of ranking British officers. She died aboard the *Jersey*, after being arrested in the wake of the execution of Major John André, the British soldier to whom Patriot traitor Benedict Arnold turned over plans for the capture of West Point.

Mrs. Strong's role was to designate in which of six hidden coves Brewster had moored his whaleboat so that Roe could deliver secret messages to him. She would signal Brewster's arrival on Long Island by hanging a black petticoat on her laundry line, and indicate the appropriate cove by adding from one to six handkerchiefs. The ring played a vital as well as romantic part in the Revolution and won the praise of Washington, who said succinctly of Townsend: "I rely upon his intelligence."

Although the war did not end formally until the Treaty of Paris was signed in 1783, its outcome had been evident since the surrender of Lord Cornwallis at Yorktown in 1781. For Long Islanders, more than most Americans, war's end was a momentous event. For Patriots, it meant freedom at last from the oppressive British occupation. For Loyalists, it meant the removal of British protection and the fear of Patriot retribution. And so, for many supporters of the Crown, it was a time to consider fleeing, as the Patriots had done after the Battle of Long Island. But their destination was not Connecticut but far-off Nova Scotia and New Brunswick, where the British provided land.

By the end of 1783, British troops had gone and Long Islanders were either celebrating or leaving. In Jamaica, according to a newspaper report, music, parades, and the display of the Stars and Stripes marked the afternoon festivities. At night, "every house in the village, and several miles around, was most brilliantly illuminated, and a ball given to the ladies concluded the whole. It was pleasing to view the different expressions of joy and gratitude apparent in every countenance upon the occasion. In short, the whole was conducted with the greatest harmony, and gave universal satisfaction."

But for Long Island, the satisfaction was short-lived. And this time humiliation came at the hands of their countrymen. In 1784, despite the degradation, deprivation, and suffering Long Islanders had experienced during the Revolution, the New York Legislature levied a tax against them to compensate the rest of the state for Long Island's failure to take an active part in the war against England.

Moving Ahead

One of innumerable paintings of George Washington by Charles Willson Peale. This relatively obscure portrait was done in 1772.

A bootmaker's sign used to advertise such trades to passersby and travelers.

The end of the Revolutionary War freed Long Islanders to wrest their farms and fields and forests from the ruin wrought by the enemy and the deterioration brought by abandonment. The ruin had come at the hands of British occupation troops; the deterioration had come while absent Patriots fled to Connecticut or fought under General George Washington.

Although some Americans may have been heady over the prospects of their newly gained political freedom, most were overwhelmed by the task of rebuilding their lives. It is not surprising that Washington, on a journey through Long Island just a year after his election as the struggling nation's first President, seemed more concerned with crop-yields-per-acre than with the spirits of his constituents. But, like many another prospective visitor, Washington had to contend with the weather. His diary entry for April 19, 1790, states: "Prevented from beginning my tour upon Long Island today from the wet of yesterday and the unfavourableness of the morning."

Once on his way, however, the President recorded daily comments and gave his overall impressions about the five-day coach visit that took him from New York City as far east as Patchogue, Coram, and Setauket. A wealthy Virginia landowner who has been described as "the first farmer of his day," he expressed interest in all the aspects of farming that he encountered, including the "living fences" that Long Islanders made by splitting live saplings and forcing their trunks to grow horizontally.

"Their fences, where there is no stone, are very indifferent," he wrote. "Frequently of plashed (entwined) trees of any and every kind which have grown by chance; but it exhibits an evidence that very good fences may be made in this manner either of White Oak or Dogwood, which from this mode of treatment grows thickest, and most stubborn. This, however, would be no defense against Hogs."

The President also took note of where he ate and slept, often commenting baldly on the quality of his hosts and their offerings. Thus, in Jamaica, a "Tavern kept by one Warne" was "a pretty good and decent house," while a meal taken with a Mr. Barre of New Utrecht, he dismissed as, "the Man was obliging but little else to recommend it."

Washington's focus, however, was upon agriculture. And he pursued it by questioning the farmers he met and analyzing their responses. "From

a comparative view of their crops," he concluded, "they may be averaged as follows: Indian Corn 25 bushels—Wheat 15—Rye 12—Oats 15 bushels to the acre. According to their accts. from Lands highly manured they sometimes get 50 of the first, 25 of the 2d and 3d, and more of the latter . . ."

Such concern reflected the times: Long Island and most of America were deeply involved in farming by the end of the Revolution; even as late as 1820, two-thirds of Long Islanders—and four-fifths of those outside Brooklyn—were engaged in it. Mostly they raised cattle, sheep, and the staples Washington had noted. But their methods were primitive, virtually unchanged from the Middle Ages, and the Long Island soil had become thin and unproductive from more than a century of exploitation.

Although, as Washington had noted, the value of manure was known, it was not in general use, nor was such a simple technique of soil enrichment as crop rotation. However, there were stirrings: Ezra L'Hommedieu, a Southold resident of broad interests ranging from public affairs and education to law and farming, pioneered in fertilizing with the inedible, herringlike fish called menhaden or "mossbunkers."

The fish were so plentiful in local waters, and the results proved so remarkable that a new profitable industry arose to revive and stimulate one that was languishing. The menhaden were readily netted in vast numbers and spread over the fields to decay at the rate of eight thousand to the acre. Caught by the hundreds of thousands in the early years of the nineteenth century, the once-useless fish were in such demand by 1850 that they were being harvested by the hundreds of millions, providing jobs and profits to Long Island fishermen and farmers alike.

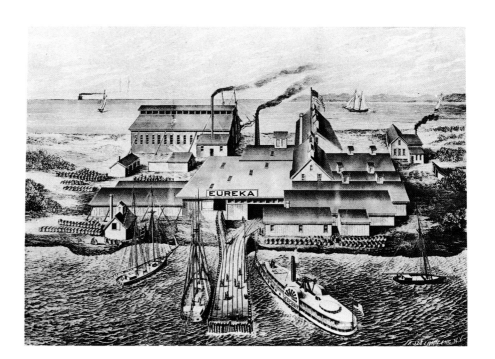

Menhaden were not the only bounty the sea provided. Long before the arrival of Europeans, Indians on Long Island had found a use for the whales that frequently ran aground on South Shore sandbars during migratory journeys. They boiled the blubber and mixed the resultant oil with their corn and peas, rubbed blubber into their leather moccasins and leggings to waterproof and preserve them, and offered the huge tails and fins as sacrifices to their gods. In time, they learned to pursue stragglers by canoe and drive them into shallow water where the enormous mammals became helplessly beached. The Indians then let the whales die naturally or shot them to death with arrows.

The early colonists found the blubber useful for lubricating and protecting their metal tools, and its oil effective for illumination. Further, they discovered that the waxy spermaceti in the sperm whale's head cavity could be used to make candles, and, when mixed with bayberry oil, provided a pleasant scent. Initially, the colonists depended largely on the whales that were washed ashore during storms, although this random harvest led to many disputes. To resolve them, Southampton in 1644 divided its beachfront into wards, with the residents of each entitled to whatever whales were washed up within its boundaries. This, apparently, was the first involvement of government in whaling, but hardly the last.

Before long, the colonists were going out, Indian-fashion, to force whales onto the beach or to kill them just offshore. They augmented this with the construction of watchtowers along the South Shore beaches from the Rockaways east, where, from fall until spring, observers would scan the seas and signal or shout at the sight of a "spout."

With that, the boats would push off through the breakers and pull for the whale. When they reached their target, wrote Charles Wooley in his 1678 diary, "About the Fin is the surest part for the Harpiner to strike . . . as soon as the whale is wounded he makes all foam with his rapid violent course, so that if they be not very quick in clearing their main ways to let him run upon the tow, which is a line fastened to the Harping-iron (harpoon), about fifty fathoms long, it is a hundred to one he oversets the boat."

Once the dead whale had been floated ashore, the men would begin the week-long task of converting it to their purposes. Most common were the right whales, large mammals with huge but harmless mouths lined with a sievelike substance rather than teeth like a sperm whale. Using long, razor-sharp cutting tools, the whalers would strip off the lips to extract the valuable baleen, or whalebone, from the jaws and remove the oil-rich tongue. Baleen was the bonus offered by right whales; from the sperm whales, there were ivory teeth and valuable spermaceti, which was dipped out of the cranial "case." The resilient baleen was used to make corset stays and umbrellas, while the bone and teeth were con-

Whaling was a major Long Island industry for decades and the inspiration for stories, poems, songs, and paintings. Three whaling scenes captured by artists include Captain Selah Young Striking a Sperm Whale on a Voyage Aboard the "Odd Fellow" Out of Sag Harbor (ABOVE); Whale Fishery "Laying On," *a print by Nathaniel Currier of Currier & Ives fame* (MIDDLE); *and* Sperm Whale "In a Flurry," *another Currier print* (BELOW).

OVERLEAF
The majesty of a ship under full sail was captured by Nathaniel Currier in a print entitled Homeward Bound.

verted into piano keys, fans, buttons, or scrimshawed into delicately carved cane handles, chessmen, and other art objects.

Then the whale would be decapitated, and the foot-thick blubber, actually a layer of fat separating the skin and flesh, peeled from the entire body. Finally, the blubber would be cut into smaller strips and rendered into "oyle" by being boiled in big iron try-pots. After cooling, the whale oil would be ladled into barrels for shipment.

Since the whales weighed considerably more than the try-pots, the pots would be hauled to the point where the whale was beached and the tryworks, consisting of the pots, a brick fireplace, and plenty of driftwood, was assembled on the spot. The stench of the boiling oil was so offensive, however, that in 1669 Southampton banned the operation of a tryworks within a certain distance of the community because "the trying of oyle so near the street and houses is soe extreme noysome to all passers by, especially to those not accustomed to the sent thereof, and is considered hurtful to the health of the people."

The cost of producing whale oil was relatively expensive, and soon whaling companies were formed as partnerships: one partner would contribute the boat, another the harpoons, and a third the try-pots. The boats were manned, as Wooley explained, by "four oarsmen or rowers; a Harpiner and a Steersman."

But it did not take long for the colonial governors, British appointees, to recognize the taxation potential of this shore-whaling trade. By the early seventeenth century, they were seeking to license the whalers, levy tariffs as high as 20 percent on their profits, and even claim for the Crown as "Royal Fishes" all "drifft" whales stranded on shore or found floating in coastal waters.

The profits from shore whaling were often considerable but usually uncertain. In 1708, Lord Cornbury, one of the governors, pointed out that Long Island's production of whale oil varied greatly from year to year and from whale to whale. "Last year," he wrote, "they made 4,000 Barrils of Oil, and this season only about 600. A yearling will make about forty barrils of Oyl, a Stunt or Whale two years old will make 50 or 60 barrils, and the largest I ever heard of yielded 110 barrils and 1,200 weight of bone."

Long Islanders resisted this governmental interference, frequently evading the tax collectors by illegally shipping their oil directly to New England instead of going through New York City. But the governors retaliated and the dispute raged for years. The tax finally was reduced in 1720 after Samuel Mulford, a leading citizen of East Hampton, took the whalers' case to London, where he petitioned King George I. Mulford not only endeared himself to Long Islanders because of his success, but to the British public as well when it became known that he had sewn fishhooks into his coat and trouser pockets to forestall London thieves.

ABOVE
One of the nation's first two ports of entry designated by President George Washington was Sag Harbor; the other, New York City. To carry out those responsibilities, this Custom House was built in Sag Harbor.

BELOW LEFT
Sag Harbor's importance as a port was represented by its authority over trading, fishing, and whaling. This coasting license was issued in 1790 to Captain Nathan Fordham of the sloop Polly.

BELOW RIGHT
Henry Packer Dering, member of a prominent Suffolk family, was appointed the first inspector of revenue for the Sag Harbor Port of Entry by President George Washington in 1791.

COASTING LICENCE.

DISTRICT OF SAGG-HARBOUR.

Nathan Fordham, Master of the Sloop Polly

of the burthen of *Twenty Seven* Tons, having entered into Bond with sufficient
Security for the Payment of one Thoufand Dollars to the United States, with Condition
that the faid Veffel fhall not be employed in any illicit Trade during the Continuance of
this Licence, and having paid the Tonnage Duty thereon, the faid *Sloop*
Polly _____ is hereby licenced to trade between the
different Diftricts of the United States, or to carry on the Bank or Whale Fifhery for
one Year from the Date hereof. —

Henry P. Dering
Collector

GIVEN under my Hand and Seal of Office, at the Cuftom-Houfe in Sagg-
Harbour, this *Twentieth* Day of *October* _____
one Thoufand feven Hundred and *ninety*

GEORGE WASHINGTON, Prefident of the United States of America,

TO ALL WHO SHALL SEE THESE PRESENTS, *GREETING.*

KNOW YE, That repofing fpecial Truft and Confidence in the Integrity, Diligence and *Difcretion of Henry P. Dering, of New York*
I DO APPOINT him *Inſpector of the Revenue for the Port of Sagg-Harbour in New York* and do authorize
and empower him to execute and fulfil the Duties of that Office according to Law ; AND TO HAVE AND TO HOLD the faid Office, with all the Rights and
Emoluments thereunto legally appertaining, unto him the faid *Henry P. Dering* during the Pleafure of the
Prefident of the United States for the Time being, and until the End of the next Seffion of the Senate of the United States, and no longer.

IN TESTIMONY whereof I have caufed thefe Letters to be made patent, and the Seal of the United States to be hereunto affixed.
GIVEN under my Hand, at the City of Philadelphia, the *Twenty firſt* Day of *March* in
the Year of our Lord one thoufand feven hundred and ninety *One,* and of the Independence of the United States of America the *fifteenth.*

G. Washington

By the Prefident

Th. Jefferson

Even before the Revolutionary War, the pods of whales that appeared close to shore in earlier days had all but disappeared, forcing whaling to enter a new phase: those seeking whale oil would have to pursue it on the open seas. To do so meant building or outfitting ships especially to track, kill, and process whales. Some whalers did go out, principally from Nantucket rather than Long Island, but the timing was poor. War brought the British Navy to the Island's coastal waters and prevented any attempts to take up the new business called "offshore whaling."

Nor did the American victory improve the situation. The defeated British, who had moved into whaling during the Revolution, remained highly competitive, placing duties on American oil to discourage its purchase in England. Disputes with Great Britain continued to forestall the growth of the whaling industry on Long Island at the turn of the century. In 1807, President Thomas Jefferson imposed his embargo on trade with both the warring French and British, thus virtually limiting the market for American whale oil to the United States.

Whalers suffered a further setback when a divided Congress declared war on Great Britain in 1812 over the harassment of American seamen and confiscation of goods. For the most part, the war was characterized far more by preparations for and fear of conflict than by conflict itself. On Long Island, the preparations primarily involved the construction of fortifications at Sag Harbor and in Brooklyn. But the anticipated invasion never came, possibly for the very reason that Long Island was prepared. A British fleet under the command of Commodore T. M. Hardy spent a good deal of the war in Gardiner's Bay, while its single attempt to land troops, a brief foray at Sag Harbor, was repulsed.

The War of 1812 ended in 1815, enabling Sag Harbor to resume its profitable activities as a port of entry, a designation it had received, together with New York City, from President Washington in 1789. In those pre-income tax days, the revenue from duties, which were collected through Sag Harbor's Custom House, was a principal source of governmental funds. More significantly, the end of the war brought a tremendous demand, both foreign and domestic, for whale products. The long-delayed advent of offshore whaling established Sag Harbor as one of the world's preeminent whaling ports and, with Cold Spring Harbor, earned Long Island whalers a global reputation.

Fired by dreams of romance and riches, young Long Islanders left their farms by the thousands during the ensuing decades to remain at sea for as long as five years on a single voyage and brave injury, illness, and death from winds, waves, whales, disease, and authoritarian masters. The crews, recruited and occasionally "shanghaied," represented virtually every racial and ethnic strain, with Long Island blacks and Indians playing important roles that until recently remained buried in time. Contemporary researchers have discovered black shipbuilders, owners, and

ABOVE

The Whalers' Church in Sag Harbor was designed and constructed in 1844 by Minard Lafever of New York under a commission from the port's whaling men. Its unusual Chinese-style steeple was blown down by the 1938 hurricane, leaving the remainder of the church as it appears today.

BELOW

Long Island boasts not one but two museums dedicated to the lore of whaling: one in Cold Spring Harbor and this one in Sag Harbor, in a building that originally was the home of whaling ship owner Benjamin Huntting and later became a Masonic Lodge. Both museums house memorabilia from the glorious days of whaling in the mid-nineteenth century.

captains, as well as crews, who, despite the restrictions imposed by racial prejudice, contributed significantly to the whaling and maritime history of Long Island.

The material rewards of whaling, especially for owners and captains, could be considerable. A successful voyage could yield as much as $100,000, with a captain receiving perhaps $5,000. Whaling captains were generally well-to-do, comparable to today's lawyers, enjoyed high social status, and often lived in substantial homes whose roofs were crowned with "widow's walks," permitting a view of the ship's return to the harbor.

Whaling exploits, while perhaps exaggerated (a contemporary writer contended that "no whaleman author has ever told the exact truth since Herman Melville set the standard of whaling mendacity"), lent an aura of mystery and danger to Eastern American life in the nineteenth century that paralleled the deeds of Western cowboys and cavalrymen. And, with the likes of Sag Harbor Captain Mercator Cooper, who sailed to Japan in 1845 and aided the State Department in opening the Orient to Western overtures, contributed considerably to the extension of American trade and influence abroad.

"I remember when black, bull-bowed whale ships lay three abreast along yonder dock, and eight hundred coopers, riggers, sailmakers, and stevedores went to and from the wharves to their work morning and evening," recalled blacksmith John Fordham about Sag Harbor's nineteenth-century days of glory.

In cellars along shore thousands of barrels of oil lay piled tier on tier and covered with sea weed. Yonder were great warehouses, three stories high, their upper stories filled with spermaceti and whalebone, the lower used as sail lofts and rigging lofts, and cheek by jowl with them were long cooper shops and here and there a candle factory.

The bosom of the bay was covered with lighters, piled high with products of the whale coming from ships at anchor and returning with provisions and outfits. An army of carts were moving oil and bone from the docks, the cooper's adse and the blacksmith's hammer made merry music all day long, and the streets were filled with crews of incoming and outgoing vessels, attended by their wives, daughters, sisters or sweethearts, making a strange jumble of welcome and farewell, smiles and tears, weeping and laughter.

Most of the sixty-four whalers that sailed out of Sag Harbor in 1845, Fordham said, were converted packet ships.

Sometimes it was an old craft that had become unsafe for passenger service. The vessels were of course overhauled, put in ship shape, refitted, and sent out on voyages of from one to four years' duration. At first the whalers cruised near home, in the North and South Atlantic mostly, but as the whales, hunted so remorselessly, foresook their favorite cruising grounds and withdrew to South

Black seamen were a common sight on nineteenth-century ships sailing out of Sag Harbor, but it was only recently that their contributions to whaling and maritime history gained recognition.

Pacific and the icebound fastnesses of the Arctic, their voyages were extended until they embraced the circle of the globe.

It was no light job to fit out a whale ship in the forties. First the sails, rigging, and boats were inspected with the greatest care, for on those depended the safety of the vessel and crew, and of course her success. This done, the captain picked out his crew of twenty-two men, aiming to get the most expert at this command, and ranging the country from Montauk to Shinnecock for them. The crew was a motley lot when gathered—whites, Indians, half-breeds, negroes—but they were picked men. To complete the outfit there was to be provided three boats, with tubs, harpoons, lances, lines, hatchets, spades, etc., with from two to three thousand barrels well-seasoned and a great variety of provisions and miscellaneous stores.

As Fordham indicated, whaling had a sizable economic impact on Long Island, particularly during its most prosperous era between 1820 and 1850. It triggered an expansion of the shipbuilding industry in North Shore villages such as Port Jefferson, Northport, Stony Brook, and Setauket, prompted the growth of subsidiary businesses such as sailmaking, ropemaking, and barrelmaking, and gave an important boost to the production and sale of the food and provisions required for long voyages.

The decline of whaling usually has been attributed to the discovery of gold in California in 1848, which, with its similar appeals of excitement and quick riches, supposedly siphoned off the whalers, and to the discovery of petroleum in Pennsylvania in 1859, which undercut the price of whale oil. However, recent research suggests that whaling had reached its peak in 1847 and that its end was brought about by overkill. Whales still could be found, but the time and distance consumed in finding them priced whaling out of the market. Further, a devastating fire ravaged the Sag Harbor waterfront in 1845, destroying almost one hundred structures.

At any rate, except for sporadic demands such as during the Civil War, the whaling industry on Long Island entered a depression in the mid-nineteenth century from which it never recovered. The last whaler to sail from once-proud Sag Harbor left port in 1871 and was condemned as unfit three years later at Barbados.

While the industry of whaling had a considerable effect on many aspects of local life, it did little to improve transportation, which always had constituted a challenge for Long Islanders. The surrounding seas were restricting, and the Island's long, thin shape limited the direction of road networks.

From Long Island's earliest days, its inhabitants showed a preference for traveling by water. The Indians used dugouts whenever possible to transport themselves and their goods in and across Long Island Sound, a practice followed by the colonists and their descendants using, progressively, oars, sails, steam, and gasoline. Trade between eastern

Suffolk and New York City was carried on almost totally by water. Packet sloops, carrying passengers, mail, and cargo, plied the Sound in a steadily increasing number. To New York, they brought wood and farm produce; to the Island, merchandise, ashes, and manure.

By 1824, one hundred vessels of all types were running between New York and the town of Brookhaven alone. Excursions were a popular form of diversion, although they occasionally proved disastrous. The most

ABOVE
Shipbuilding became a substantial industry on Long Island during the nineteenth century, particularly on the North Shore. This drawing by Edward Lange pictures the shipyards and residence of Jesse Carll in Northport Harbor.

BELOW
The silent splendor of two three-masted schooners off Orient has been preserved in this 1915 photograph.

The influence of the sea on Long Island life during the eighteenth and nineteenth centuries appeared in many unlikely places. Old First Church on Main Street, Huntington, was constructed by ships' carpenters in 1784.

terrible marine tragedy during this era occurred on January 13, 1840, when the steamboat *Lexington*, owned by Cornelius Vanderbilt among others, burst into flames on Long Island Sound off Eaton's Neck during a trip from New York to Stonington, Connecticut. Of eighty-seven passengers and forty crew members, all but four either were burned to death or drowned. The voyage was the ship's first after having been equipped to use coal, rather than wood, as fuel.

But the accident did not dim the demand for ships. They were needed and Long Island shipbuilders responded. In 1840, shipyards could be found in almost every coastal community. And by 1860, at shipbuilding's height, there were at least twenty-five yards in Suffolk, turning out catboats, fishing smacks, sloops, schooners, brigs, and barks. The Island's configuration and the accessibility of navigable waters made travel by land a reluctant choice even centuries before completion of the Long Island Expressway.

The earliest roads followed Indian trails, invariably accepting rather than challenging nature's design—skirting hills, forests, ponds, and other obstacles without regard to distance or time. These "cow paths," deeply rutted and often filled with sand or mud, were neither designed, repaired, nor maintained. The first real attempt at roadbuilding came in 1704 when the Legislature mandated a route from Brooklyn Ferry to East Hampton that still exists in part as King's Highway. In time, other east-west roads were constructed, however primitively, and served mainly to move produce and farming supplies.

The turnpike system—the introduction of toll roads—made its appearance in the country in 1801, and Long Islanders soon were driving their wagons and coaches from Brooklyn to Jamaica, Hempstead, Jericho, and Smithtown, for a price. With Jamaica as a hub, toll payers were able within a few years to travel to Oyster Bay on the North Shore and Babylon on the South Shore, while on the East End, a turnpike was operated between Sag Harbor and Bridgehampton. The roads were built by private enterprise and the tolls retained by the builders. There was a brief but frantic demand for wood-surfaced highways, called plank roads, to overcome mud, but the high costs of maintenance outweighed their relative comfort and they were abandoned after a short time.

Most developments arise out of need, and the need for good roads on Long Island during the colonial and Revolutionary periods was limited because of the self-sufficiency of most of the communities. Not even an interest in mail was sufficient to create the necessary demand for a decent highway network in those days. In fact, about the time of the Revolutionary War, mail was delivered not by the government but by "a respectable old Scotchman named Dunbar," according to a contemporary report, who made a weekly circuit from New York City to Babylon and Brookhaven.

Before the end of the eighteenth century, stagecoaches were running on a weekly schedule between Brooklyn and Sag Harbor, "but the service was miserable, the patronage poor, and . . . promptness in starting and arriving were neglected, while none of the schemes to promote the comfort of passengers . . . were ever dreamed of."

However, by 1835, a coach trip through Long Island could be a positive delight, as Gabriel Furman, author of *Antiquities of Long Island*, makes evident in the following first-hand account:

The practice was to leave Brooklyn about nine o'clock in the morning—they were not, however, particular to half an hour—travel on to Hempstead, where

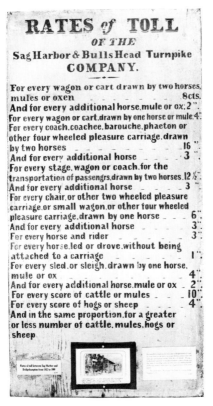

ABOVE
Turnpikes or toll roads were built for profit by private companies during the nineteenth century. These rates were charged for travel between Sag Harbor and Bridgehampton from 1852 to 1900.

BELOW
This whimsical weathervane was fashioned in 1870 in the shape of the sidewheeler Index. *It is a fine example of nineteenth-century Long Island folk art.*

THE STAGE SEWANHACKEY

Travel by stagecoach was not exclusively a Western custom, as illustrated by this 1852 painting by Henry Boese of The Stage Sewanhackey. *The building in the background is Brooklyn's City Hall.*

Sometimes travel by horsedrawn coach was less than elegant.

A later mode of transportation was by trolley car. Here is opening day in 1911 of the trolley service in Patchogue.

they dined, and after that, jog on to Babylon, where they put up for the night. A most delightful way this was to take a jaunt: there was no hurry, no fuss and bustle about it. . . . No mode of traveling ever suited our taste better; it was the very acme of enjoyment.

The next morning you left Babylon just after daylight, which in the summer was itself worth living for, journeyed on to Patchogue, where you got your breakfast between nine and ten o'clock, with a good appetite for it, we warrant you. You would get no dinner this day, nor would you feel the want of it after your late and hearty breakfast, but travel along slowly and pleasantly until you reached the rural postoffice at Fire Place, standing on the edge of a wood. Here, if you have a taste for the beautiful in nature, you would walk down the garden to look at the trout stream filled with the speckled beauties. . . .

Shortly after sunset, you would stop for the night, the second one of your journey, at a place called Quagg or Quogue. Here you might, after supper on a moonlight night in the beginning of August, if you were so fortunate as to be there at such a time, as we were, cross the meadows with a guide, and walk down to the sea-beach, where, with no sound but the beating of the waves upon the shore, swelling in from a waste of waters of three thousand miles, and making the earth tremble under your feet, with scarcely a breath of air to move the hair upon your forehead, and nothing in sight for miles upon miles but the white sand hills glistening in the moonbeams on one side, and this world of waters on the other, you would more than at any other time realize the immensity of creation, and your own comparative insignificance.

The following morning you would breakfast at Southampton, after passing through a pine forest, in a portion of which, from the early hour and blindness of the road, you would probably require a guide to go ahead of the horses with a lighted lantern. . . . Sag Harbor would be reached in time for dinner, after which the mail stage would travel on to its final destination at East Hampton, arriving there just before sunset on Saturday afternoon, thus occupying nearly three days to traverse a distance of one hundred and ten miles. But most pleasant days they were, and no one has ever tried this mode of journeying through Long Island who had pleasure in view, who did not wish to try it again.

It is difficult to reconcile Furman's romantic description of travel through a pastoral Long Island of 1835 with the fact that the gritty Long Island Rail Road already had been in existence for a year and, within a decade, would be running smoky, clangorous trains through the length of the same island.

The history of that railroad is a story of vision and grubbiness, of public service and venality, of unfettered imagination and unbelievable stupidity. It is replete with contradictions and ironies. The most striking: while the LIRR was conceived—without regard for Long Islanders—as simply the best way to get from New York to Boston, it became the most heavily traveled local railroad in the world.

The LIRR was born out of the desire for a rail link between New York and Boston that would eliminate the need to lay track across the hills,

ABOVE
Despite contentions by some commuters, some Long Island Rail Road trains, such as this one from the nineteenth century, have been retired from service.

BELOW
Long Island Rail Road locomotive #92 at the Cross Islands Cycle Path, Medford, 1897.

This Long Island Rail Road train presents a dramatic silhouette against the horizon.

The Long Island Rail Road constructed most of its own stations, but this one at Shinnecock was a former post office.

valleys, and rivers of Connecticut. As an alternative to such a direct but expensive route, planners and promoters decided to build a 95-mile line from Brooklyn to Greenport, at the end of Long Island's North Fork, where passengers and goods would be ferried across Long Island Sound to Stonington, Connecticut, a few miles west of the Rhode Island border. There, they would continue the journey to Boston on the existing Norwich & Worcester Railroad.

The principal engineer of the Brooklyn & Jamaica Railroad Company, which was formed in 1832 and later would be leased by the Long Island for the venture, assured prospective investors of the scheme's feasibility. He reported in 1834:

The public mind is quite familiar with speeds of twenty to thirty miles per hour, and numerous locomotives in various parts of the country are wheeling daily over their respective tracks, at these rates, without a murmur of alarm or disapprobation. I think it not unreasonable, therefore, to assume five hours as a fair average trip from Brooklyn to Greenport. . . . The ferry will then occupy two hours, but by making the ferry boat a convenient hotel, with proper arrangements for rest and refreshments, this will prove only an agreeable and profitable relaxation. The remainder of the trip to Boston will be performed easily in four hours and a half, so that only eleven hours and a half will be required for the entire journey from New York or Brooklyn to Boston.

There were several factors that would burst this bubble of optimism. But first, the railroad had to be put into operation. And this required a route from Brooklyn to Greenport. Three choices were considered: along the North Shore, approximating the present Route 25A; a few miles further south, approximating the present Route 25; and still further south, through the flattest and most barren areas. The last was selected because its topography made it the cheapest and easiest for laying track. It now constitutes the LIRR's Main Line.

Through a combination of construction and the leasing and purchasing of other lines, the road was completed by 1844. There were to be only two stops en route—at Hardscrabble (Farmingdale) and Punk's Hole (Manorville)—to take on fuel (wood) and water. When a delay in the shipment of rails from England threatened to delay the highly publicized opening, the track crew at Punk's Hole, mostly Irish immigrants, successfully substituted heavy timbers topped with iron strips.

The inaugural run took place on July 27, 1844, and featured a special three-section train filled with railroad and civic officials, stockholders, celebrities, and newsmen. Spurred by the occasion, the train covered the ninety-five miles in three and one-half hours instead of the scheduled five. Horses and wagons crowded the site of the celebration, and boats of all description crammed Greenport harbor. According to one description, it clearly was a day to remember:

A large tent was spread north of the tracks. . . . Four tables one hundred feet long were spread under the tent, and dinner was served to the parties who had come on the train and a few villagers. The provisions were brought from New York, and included forty baskets of champagne and half a case of brandy. As a natural consequence, many of the excursionists were so stupidly inebriated that it was necessary to put them on board the cars. . . . The whole affair was discreditable in the extreme.

That inaugural celebration seems to have marked a high point in relations between the railroad and Long Island. In the months and years that followed, the main feeling apparently shared by the line and the community was tension. The woodburning locomotives sent sparks showering into the air to fall on fields, woodlands, and barns, setting them ablaze and causing considerable damage to farmers' property, produce, and livestock. The farmers fought back in court and outside of it. They tore up sections of track and set fire to depots. They fired at armed guards hired to ride "shotgun" on the locomotives. They even sawed through the timbers on the Peconic River bridge, sending an escort engine crashing into the water.

There were other concerns, too. In the Deer Park area, named for the herds that roamed wild, when locomotives accidentally ran down the animals, the engineers placed their antlers on the cowcatcher and joined the villagers in a venison feast at which the engineer with the most "trophies" was crowned. Near Yaphank, an old woman, angry because the railroad refused to recompense her for running over her cow, poured a bucket of soap over the rails at a grade before the arrival of each train. After numerous trains failed to negotiate the hill, railroad officials agreed to pay the woman twenty dollars. And there was moral indignation, too, at the LIRR's violation of the Sabbath by scheduling Sunday "Milk Train" excursions; they finally were withdrawn.

But the railroad's most egregious miscalculations surfaced in 1848, when competitors laid tracks through Connecticut on the "impassable" route LIRR officials had eschewed. The new line offered an "all-rail" connection between New York and Boston, putting the Long Island into bankruptcy in two years. At that point the folly of having placed its own rails "through the most sterile and desolate parts of the Island" became apparent. Forced to rely on Long Islanders alone for its revenues, the railroad found that it had placed its tracks miles from most of the villages it would have to serve.

Through acquisitions of local lines and extensions of its own, the Long Island Rail Road finally established a transportation network that provided service to virtually all who might wish to use it. The quality and cost of that service have been something else, however, and for much of its life, the LIRR, fairly or not, has been characterized more with ridicule than appreciation.

But toward the end of the nineteenth century, under the direction of Austin Corbin, one of America's most imaginative and successful entrepreneurs, the Long Island Rail Road provided a glimpse of what might have been. Corbin, a Harvard Law School graduate who made a reputation and a fortune in banking, real estate, shipping, and transportation, was appointed receiver during one of the LIRR's bouts with bankruptcy in 1880, lifted it out of its distress within a year, and became its most productive president. Through far-sighted and prudent management, Corbin was largely responsible for extending lines, improving service, pruning liabilities, and carrying out needed rehabilitation projects.

However remarkable Corbin's accomplishments were, they represented only a prelude to what he envisioned for the railroad and Long Island. For it was Corbin's dream to refashion transatlantic steamship travel by creating new terminals in each continent: Fort Pond Bay at Montauk would replace New York Harbor, and Milford Haven in Wales would replace Southampton or London. The proposal would have embarked and debarked passengers sooner than under the system then (and now) in use, and transported them by train, rather than ship, to their destinations in New York and London.

Corbin was no idle dreamer, and, although he had wealthy and influential friends, he clearly had taken on an incredible task. It would require the approval of two nations over all the entrenched business and political interests that had a stake in the existing route. But for one who had

Throughout the nineteenth century, agriculture was the most important business on Long Island. Glimpses of farm life during that era have been recaptured at the Old Bethpage Village Restoration and are seen in these photographs taken during different seasons, both indoors and out. They show a general view of the community (ABOVE); a farm kitchen (BELOW); (OVERLEAF ABOVE LEFT) hogs being butchered; (BELOW LEFT) a sled; (ABOVE RIGHT) Noon Inn from Layton Store; (BELOW RIGHT) plowing a field.

resurrected the Long Island Rail Road, nothing was too awesome or intimidating.

From scores of engineers, accountants, lawyers, surveyors, maritime authorities, financiers, and political operatives, Corbin and his associates devised a plan that would cut about eight and one-half hours off travel time between London and New York in good weather, and possibly days in foul. If that seems relatively incidental in terms of a weeklong journey, Corbin had many other rationales. The most important benefit, he argued, was the elimination of the dangerous and time-consuming approach to New York Harbor past Sandy Hook, which was crowded with ships and in need of dredging.

The project did get off the ground, although it was not destined to fly. Legislation was introduced in Congress and the government ordered a survey. But Army engineers twice turned down the plan and legislative attempts were rebuffed. Still, Corbin went ahead. He extended the existing line from Bridgehampton to Montauk in 1895, and this commitment revived Washington's interest. The next year, with a new bill in the hopper, Corbin pressed his case in the halls and committee rooms of Congress. Just when passage seemed possible, Corbin was killed in an accident, and his associates, while sharing his hopes, lacked his charisma and zeal. The project died with its creator.

Ironically, Corbin's faith in Fort Pond Bay and the new trackage were justified just two years later when they were utilized in the emergency assembly of port facilities and an Army camp necessitated by the Spanish-American War. Rapid transportation between Brooklyn and the tip of the South Fork aided quick construction of Camp Wikoff at Montauk, where yellow fever victims were hospitalized and quarantined.

If it was Corbin's fate to live in a time and among people not yet ready to share his vision, so it was with Josiah Warren. An inventor, reformer, and philosopher, Warren founded the utopian community of Modern Times in what is now Brentwood. For a decade, around the Civil War era, it provided a sanctuary for what Warren and some one hundred followers described as "individual sovereignty" and what headline writers of the day called "free love." Based on the following account by a sympathetic visitor, the Reverend Moncure Daniel Conway, the headline writers seem to have been on the right track:

The arrangements of marriage were, of course, left entirely to the men and women themselves. They could be married formally or otherwise, live in the same or separate houses, and have their relations known or unknown to the rest of the village. The relation could be dissolved at pleasure without any formulae. Certain customs had grown out of this absence of marriage laws. Secrecy was very general, and it was not considered polite to inquire who might be the father of a newborn child, or who the husband or wife of any individual might be. Those who stood in the relation of husband or wife wore upon the finger a

Long Island Rail Road President Austin Corbin's dream of a time-saving transatlantic rail-ship route would have given passengers from Europe a look at the Montauk Lighthouse rather than the Statue of Liberty.

red thread; and so long as that badge was visible the person was understood to be married. If it disappeared, the marriage was at an end.

But Warren's philosophy transcended interpersonal and social relationships. A disciple of Welsh reformer Robert Dale Owen, who established the New Harmony commune in Indiana, Warren put his radical economic theories into practice in his Long Island community through a system in which labor was compensated with labor, not cash. For example, at the Modern Times "Time Store," the price of an item was based on its cost to the merchant, an amount which residents paid with money, plus the salesperson's time spent in serving them, an amount which they could pay with their own labor. The labor cost was calculated by turning on a large clock when service was begun and shutting it off when the transaction was completed.

For a while, everything went like clockwork and so idyllic was Modern Times, said Conway, that it could be found "either by railway or by rainbow." It was described as the most ideal and utopian of all communities in the United States, if not the world, because there was no dishonesty, disorder, or crime, and thus no policemen, prisoners, judges, or jail.

But there was no industry, either, and without a real economic base, together with the depression of 1857, the community began to come apart. Too many residents left to seek work outside, and by the end of the Civil War even Warren had to admit the failure of his experiment to reshape society.

This was a time when America began to look to itself for inspiration: to find it in ordinary people and commonplace activities. In art, nobody better exemplified this search than a homegrown Long Islander named William Sidney Mount, who was born in Setauket in 1807 and spent most of his life in Stony Brook. Roaming the roads of Suffolk, he produced a significant number of paintings depicting colorful scenes of rural life, most of which are displayed at The Museums at Stony Brook. Proudly unconventional, in his later years Mount created a studio in an enclosed, glass-roofed, horse-drawn wagon and traveled the countryside behind it, playing his violin.

In literature, a poet from Long Island became America's voice, describing its beauty, its strength, and its possibilities. Walt Whitman was born in 1819 in a West Hills house (now 246 Walt Whitman Road, Huntington Station) built by his father, moved to Brooklyn as a child, then back to Long Island as a young man to teach, report, publish (*The Long-Islander*, at age nineteen), edit (*Brooklyn Daily Eagle*, at age twenty-six), and write poetry that gained him worldwide recognition.

The most famous and universal American poet, Whitman drew heavily on his Long Island experience. In his reminiscences, *Specimen Days*, he recalled how "the successive growth stages of my infancy, childhood, youth and manhood were all pass'd on Long Island, which I sometimes

Among Long Island's most famous sons was artist William Sidney Mount (ABOVE), *who popularized the rural life of the Setauket-Stony Brook area in paintings such as the typical buildings of* Long Island Farmhouses (OPPOSITE ABOVE), *and* The Sportsman's Last Visit (OPPOSITE BELOW).

While Walt Whitman is regarded as a universal poet, Long Islanders still claim him as their own. Born in this house in West Hills, Huntington Station, he won worldwide acclaim but never forgot the "isle of the salty shore and breeze and brine."

feel as if I had incorporated. I roam'd, as boy and man, and have lived in nearly all parts, from Brooklyn to Montauk point."

He described his Paumanok (its aboriginal name) from the ocean to the Sound, through all the seasons: "The shores of this bay, winter and summer, and my doings there in early life, are woven all through L. of G." (*Leaves of Grass*, his most celebrated work).

And his recollections might have been written yesterday, not a century ago:

Sail'd more than once around Shelter island, and down to Montauk—spent many an hour on Turtle hill by the old light-house, on the extreme point, looking out over the ceaseless roll of the Atlantic. I used to like to go down there and fraternize with the blue-fishers, or the annual squads of sea-bass takers. . . . The soothing rustle of the waves, and the saline smell—boyhood's times, the clam-digging, barefoot, and with trousers roll'd up—hauling down the creek—the perfume of the sedge-meadows—the hay-boat, and the chowder and fishing excursions. . . .

He remained connected to his roots through his poetry many years after moving away, and wrote two poems about Long Island in 1888, as he approached his seventies, that are part of *Leaves of Grass*:

Paumanok

Sea-beauty! stretch'd and basking!
One side thy inland ocean laving, broad, with copious commerce, steamers, sails,
And one the Atlantic's wind caressing, fierce or gentle—mighty hulls dark-gliding in the distance.
Isle of sweet brooks of drinking-water—healthy air and soil!
Isle of the salty shore and breeze and brine!

From Montauk Point

I stand as on some mighty eagle's beak,
Eastward the sea absorbing, viewing, (nothing but sea and sky,)
The tossing waves, the foam, the ships in the distance,
The wild unrest, the snowy, curling caps—that inbound urge and urge of waves,
Seeking the shores forever.

One of the earliest creative Long Islanders, Whitman probably remains one of its most prominent offspring. For him, Long Island provided inspiration; for many of those who followed to his "fish-shape Paumanok"—painters and poets, writers and dancers, architects and musicians—it was Whitman, too, who inspired.

CHAPTER FIVE

City and Suburb

T he birth of the modern suburban phenomenon that has transformed the look and life of America can be pinpointed. It happened in 1823. In that year, in the *Long Island Star*, Hezekiah B. Pierpont, after having bought up Brooklyn Heights properties for two decades, advertised lots for sale "as a place of residence [providing] all the advantages of the country with most of the conveniences of the city." Anticipating the possibilities of commutation, he pointed out that "gentlemen whose business or profession require their daily attendance in the city, cannot better, or with less expense, secure the health and comfort of their families."

What Pierpont counted on was the safety and predictability of ferry service between Brooklyn and Manhattan following the success of Robert Fulton's *Clermont*, which had steamed up the Hudson River in 1807. Before the invention of the steamboat, winds, currents, and weather had rendered sailboats both dangerous and unreliable as ferries, making the East River a temporarily effective moat separating the populations on both its banks.

With the introduction of steam ferry service in 1814 and the growth of New York City, Brooklyn's future became irreversible: it would develop as an adjunct to Manhattan, but would itself be a city. By 1810, New York State, with a population approaching one million, and New York City, with a tenth of that, supplanted Pennsylvania and Philadelphia as the nation's most populous state and city. Long Island, with fewer than fifty thousand people, had about half the population of New York City, most of it concentrated in Suffolk County (21,000) and Queens County (19,000). Kings County (8,300), with the exception of its riverside communities of Brooklyn and Bushwick, remained largely rural as the towns of New Utrecht, Gravesend, Flatbush, and Flatlands grew imperceptibly.

The completion of the Erie Canal in 1825, which created a water route from the Atlantic to the Great Lakes, made New York's port a magnet for foreign and coastal trade, and, in turn, stimulated the development in Brooklyn of such shipping-related businesses as ropemaking and warehousing. This, together with an influx of European immigrants and freed black slaves, was reflected in an explosive population growth that saw the community doubling in size with each decade between 1800 and 1860. In 1834, over the opposition of New Yorkers who feared competition, Brooklyn officially became a city.

Pumpkins, which abounded on Long Island before the arrival of European settlers, still constitute one of the area's major crops. This field of glowing orange beauties is in Calverton.

By the middle of the nineteenth century, about half of Brooklyn's expanding population was foreign-born: Irish, escaping the potato famine; Germans, fleeing political persecution following the vain Revolution of 1848; and English, drawn by the lure of economic opportunity. Later, they would be joined by vast numbers of southern and eastern Europeans, particularly Italians and Jews, to form one of the country's most diverse populations—a catalog of the nationalities that comprised America's fabled melting pot.

With each wave of newcomers, ethnic institutions were formed to ease the transition by retaining elements of the past. Brooklyn became the City of Churches, providing houses of worship for Dutch Reformed, Episcopalians, Presbyterians, Roman Catholics, and Baptists. Occasionally institutions, including the churches, became caught up in the changing times: when the interracial congregation of the Sands Street Methodist Church became anxious over the proslavery attitudes of its pastor, black parishioners withdrew and formed the High Street African Wesleyan Methodist Episcopal Church.

By mid-century, growing concern over slavery began to intrude on the national drive toward material progress. Divisions over the issue began to appear between North and South, between Democrats and Whigs, between industrialists and farmers. Long Island did not escape the controversy.

Kings County, in particular, had a tradition of involvement with slavery, stemming from its settlement by the Dutch and its agricultural character. (In New York State, the Dutch were the most likely ethnic group to own slaves, and slavery was more compatible with farming than with other pursuits.) By 1790, black slaves constituted about one-third of the Kings' population, and the county's slaveholders were slow to release their charges voluntarily, although they complied with the state's mandated emancipation in 1827.

Among the most committed abolitionists was the Reverend Henry Ward Beecher, who used his pulpit at Brooklyn's Plymouth Church to condemn slavery as immoral and anti-Christian. "As a Christian nation, we have a right to interfere in this matter," he said in 1850. "We are not to cease our exertions until the victory is accomplished. I will not, as one man, cease my endeavors or hold my peace unless the vile monster is driven from the land."

Arrayed against the abolitionists was the area's Democratic Party apparatus, especially its newspapers, which courted the foreign-born vote by appeals to racial prejudice, and by stirring up unjustified fears that if freed, Southern slaves would travel North to take away their jobs. The election of 1860 marked not only the presidential candidacy of Abraham Lincoln, the first Republican, but a referendum in New York State to give equal voting rights to "people of color" by eliminating the requirement that they own property, a qualification not demanded of whites.

It was a bitter campaign in which a Democratic assemblyman from Brooklyn railed that "the proposition to put negroes on a footing of political equality with the white men is repugnant to the sense of the American people." The fact that the suffrage amendment could have added a maximum of only 1,250 black voters in Brooklyn did not deter the Democratic press from publishing white-supremacist, rabble-rousing editorials and articles. And they apparently carried some weight. Although Lincoln won the state, including Suffolk, he was soundly defeated in Brooklyn. The amendment lost statewide and was rejected by overwhelming margins on Long Island.

Lincoln was not a popular president; even within Republican ranks he was attacked as moving too slowly to end slavery. But the secession of the South and the firing on Fort Sumter in 1861 united Northerners, regardless of party. After the fighting broke out, the defense of the Union became paramount and there was strong support for its position in Brooklyn, as well as throughout Long Island.

Long Islanders who fought in the Civil War, such as young Henry W. Prince of Southold, found themselves in New York's 127th Monitors Regiment. And many, such as Prince and these eight Oysterponds (now Orient) volunteers photographed in Alexandria, Virginia, in 1863, were in Company H. Three of these eight were killed during the next two years.

One of the few monuments to Civil War veterans on Long Island is in Roslyn Cemetery, Roslyn.

At the beginning of the Civil War, there was no military draft; communities were expected to recruit through appeals to patriotism, aided by bonuses of fifty or one hundred dollars. In 1862, the President issued a call for 300,000 volunteers for three years, and the 127th New York Monitors Regiment was organized. The press leaped at the opportunity to participate, from the sidelines, as the following editorial in the *Suffolk Times* makes apparent:

The patriotism of our township has finally been aroused. Her sons are flocking to the recruiting offices, leaving the plowshare buried in the furrow, and the stately corn fields to some other harvester. . . . The good old town of Southold desires her sons to be volunteers for the army, and many of our best men have already rallied around the standard, "The Stars and Stripes." A company is now being formed. All who can carry a musket should now come forward. Let no man skulk from his duty!

Like tens of thousands of farmboys, Henry W. Prince of Southold buried his plowshare at the age of twenty-two to sign up with the 127th. His fears and hopes and frustrations, as expressed in his letters home, no doubt convey many of the feelings of fellow Yanks:

A soldier's life is very uncertain. If not wasted away with disease he may die in an instant by the bullet. I have been wonderfully blest since I became a soldier. Have enjoyed good health, have been able to march through cold &

heat & never failed to keep with the Regt. I feel that I have much to be thankful for, & I rejoice that I am able to defend our country. I trust I may see the day when Rebels will be reconciled to the Union & the best of Governments. I am sorry that we have so many Traitors at the North & even on L.I. They are a curse to the country. Talk about the negro being a curse to the country, I think it is the rebellious white man. I am glad the black man can fight for the downfall of Slavery.

In time, young Prince lost some of his earlier partisanship and ruminated about more universal concerns:

I want once more to get in good society. It will seem more like living. Soldiering is a rough coarse life, calculated to corrupt good morals & harden a man's heart. We have no female society to influence us for the better, but are surrounded by coarse vulgar companions. I could not feel contented if I were not a soldier trying to aid the government. As it is I strive to be a man & a son you will not be ashamed to own. Should I live to return probably I shall be coarse & unrefined but I trust I will be as good at Heart as when I left you & I hope better. I think I will never be ashamed of coarse clothes or plain food. We as a nation have been living too fast. Too much pride & care too much for dress. Methinks I have learned a lesson since I became a soldier.

Appeals to patriotism are invariably invoked by the old and answered by the young. Winslow Homer portrayed this youthful Union volunteer in 1864.

Sensitivity to the opinions on the home front is characteristic of soldiers, as Prince made clear:

The "Suffolk Times" has a good deal to say about the Southold Boys & our drunken officers. I wish he would say less, for the officers are mad, & a good many I think dislike Co. H on acct. of that piece in "Times." I believe it true that a number of our officers take too much whiskey, but to say all do is saying too much & to say they are beastly intoxicated is saying too much. Whiskey is a curse & it ought not to be allowed in the Army except for medicinal purposes. As the law now is, officers can get it but enlisted men cannot.

As the war began to wind down, Prince began to consider the future. Farming, particularly on Long Island, seemed to have lost much of its appeal:

I would be pleased to live on or near the homestead, as long as I live where it is convenient & for my interest, but you know Mother, Father has worked hard to make a living on a farm that he bought cheap. Now what chance is there for a poor man at present prices for land & manure on L.I.? I believe I have a little ambition. I desire to do a little good in this world & do something more than make just enough to eat & to clothe me. A hermit can do that. I don't desire riches, for happiness is not found in them.

Prince rose to the rank of sergeant during his three years' service, survived, and returned to Southold, where he farmed, clerked, became

a salesman, a merchant, and a banker. He married, had three children, prospered, and served his church and his town as well as having served his country. He was eighty-five years old when he died in 1925.

The Civil War had a mixed impact on Long Island. While siphoning off manpower, it triggered a demand for industrial and agricultural productivity. Orders for armaments, uniforms, ships, equipment, and foodstuffs stimulated the economy, particularly in areas close to New York City. At war's end, the western Island was ready to embark on the period of industrialization and urbanization that would soon embrace the reunified nation.

The most striking change took place in Brooklyn, where the spillover of commerce from Manhattan created a burst of business activity. But differences in size and in land costs between the two adjacent cities gave each its own character. Companies began establishing their executive and sales offices in Manhattan, but put their factories in Brooklyn. Passenger ships tied up at Manhattan piers, but cargo ships docked on the Brooklyn waterfront. Manhattan put on a white collar; Brooklyn's was blue.

The growth of industry in Brooklyn following the Civil War created a new and faster tempo. However, public transportation was slow, crawling along not quite at a snail's, but at a horse's pace. Conveyances called horsecars, drawn by two-horse teams over tracks on scheduled runs, transported as many as forty passengers to destinations as remote as Flatbush and Gravesend. While a major improvement over walking, the horsecars were, like the ferry system, inadequate to the fast-growing demands for speed and mobility.

This dissatisfaction set the stage for what was to become the most significant and dramatic transportation advance of the period, and one that would have far-reaching effects not only on the development and interdependence of Manhattan and Brooklyn, but on the relationship of New York and Long Island, of city and suburb. It was the construction of the Brooklyn Bridge and elevated railways.

A bridge across the East River had been discussed for many years before the State Legislature, responding to proposals from builder John A. Roebling, approved the project in 1867 and put him in charge. The concept was staggering: it was to be the world's longest suspension bridge, requiring the embedding of immense pillars in the bottom of a swift-flowing tidal waterway. Nothing like this had ever before been attempted on such a scale. It called for originality of design, of materials, of construction techniques; it represented the culmination of human efforts to conquer nature for the betterment of society.

It was completed in 1883 by Roebling's son, Washington, who took over upon his father's death from tetanus, and who himself suffered the bends while at work and was crippled for life. The achievement stirred the imagination of America—of poets, as well as engineers, merchants, and public officials.

In dedication ceremonies a century ago, the bridge was hailed as:

without a rival among the wonders of human skill. It is not the work of any one man or of any one age. It is the result of the study of the experience and of the knowledge of many men in many ages. It is not merely a creation; it is a growth. It stands before us today as the sum and epitome of human knowledge; as the very heir of the ages; as the latest glory of centuries of patient observation, profound study, and accumulated skill, gained, step by step, in the never-ending struggle of man to subdue the forces of Nature to his control and use.

From a practical standpoint, the bridge vastly increased the speed and volume of traffic between Brooklyn and Manhattan, created new commercial districts at both ends, and, most important to the development of Long Island, made commuting, and thus suburban living, feasible. The utility of the Brooklyn Bridge was enhanced considerably within a few years by the erection in 1885 of elevated railways—Els—that enabled steam, and soon electric, engines to transport passengers above the crowded streets at many times former speeds. The network of elevated railways, with connections to the cable cars that crossed the bridge, opened vast portions of Brooklyn to residential development and established a precedent for the eventual suburbanization of most of Long Island.

The Brooklyn Bridge, completed in 1883, changed the future of both Long Island and New York. It was regarded as the embodiment of man's ability to control nature.

Swelled both by immigration from Europe and migration from the surrounding area, Long Island's population passed the million mark in the 1890 census, with the overwhelming bulk of it—more than 80 percent—concentrated in Kings County, and virtually all of that in Brooklyn. If further proof were needed that Brooklyn had achieved urban status, it came in 1895 with the Great Trolley Strike. As the trolley owners employed strikebreakers to keep the cars rolling, and more than 6,000 transit workers fought to shut them down, violence erupted and the state militia had to bring it to an end.

One remnant of that bitter dispute, in which at least two workers were shot to death by militia troops, was the rallying song of the embattled strikers:

> Remember we are working men
>   and honestly we toil,
> And gentlemen, remember we
>   were born on Brooklyn soil,
> Nor can the pampered millionaires
>   the spirit in us break,
> The fame of our fair city
>   is clearly now at stake.

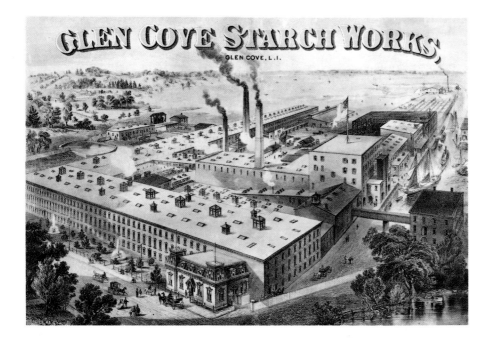

GLEN COVE STARCH WORKS,
GLEN COVE, L.I.

Although much of Long Island retained its rural character well after the Civil War, industries, such as this starch works in Glen Cove, began to appear.

The "fair city" was not to exist much longer in that form. Pressure to create Greater New York by consolidating adjacent areas with Manhattan had been building for several decades. So far as Brooklyn was concerned, the need for consolidation became compelling by the 1890s when it could no longer borrow money because it had reached the debt limit imposed by the State Constitution. But political considerations delayed what was a highly complicated process in itself. Of particular concern to Brooklyn's Democratic machine was the effect that the change might have on its power. However, legislative approval was finally obtained, and on January 1, 1898, Brooklyn, the Bronx, Richmond, and Manhattan, together with the western third of Queens, all became boroughs of New York City.

The remainder of Queens—the towns of Hempstead, North Hempstead, and Oyster Bay—was still part of Queens, but not part of New York City. This absurdity was remedied with their embodiment as Nassau County on January 1, 1899.

The tremendous growth of western Long Island following the Civil War had only a limited counterpart in the eastern portion. While some communities flourished by filling a particular need, such as shipbuilding in the case of Port Jefferson, or the huge Duryea Starch Company in Glen Cove, most of Suffolk and the part of Queens that would become Nassau retained a largely rural, agricultural flavor.

The Long Island Rail Road, frustrated in its plan to link New York with Boston, had on its hands hundreds of miles of track, locomotives, and freight and passenger cars. What it did not have was enough business; so it set about to create a demand for its services, and in the process, played a major role in the development of the Island.

There was, for example, milk. In the latter half of the nineteenth century, Long Island dairy farmers, benefiting from inadequate methods of refrigeration that kept upstate producers out of the picture, did a booming business by supplying milk quickly to the vast New York City market. Herds in the mid-Island area around Hicksville and Syosset made Westbury the most important milk-shipping station on the LIRR.

Further east, farmers clamored for the latest labor-saving equipment to increase production and get their vegetables on Brooklyn and Manhattan dinner tables. Potatoes, strawberries, cauliflower, cabbages, asparagus, cucumbers, and brussels sprouts were introduced, accepted, and cultivated with great success. To expedite service, the railroad introduced "piggybacking" decades before most major lines. This involved transporting farmers' wagons on flatbed cars, which then were ferried across the East River from the Long Island City terminal to markets in Manhattan.

While some Long Islanders were farming the land, others were reaping a harvest from the sea. The quiet bays along the Island's North and South Shores and between the flukes of its fishtail had been rich with oysters, scallops, and clams before the arrival of Europeans. The settlers had learned from the Indians to gather and prepare shellfish, and

While technology has altered considerably the look of farming on Long Island, produce has changed little during the past century. Still seen in Suffolk are potato pickers

passed along their techniques and appetites to succeeding generations. Consequently, after a few centuries of exploitation, the oyster beds were becoming depleted. By 1824, Blue Point, near Patchogue on Great South Bay, a community so renowned for oysters it had given them its name, was described as a "former" source of shellfish in an official report.

Local baymen, using rowboats and toothed tongs, were eking out only a meager living until the introduction of the dredge enabled them to scoop up huge quantities of oysters and to move on to other and deeper areas. But by 1870, the public beds in Great South Bay had become so exhausted that a law was passed barring the use of dredges there. It was only then that the baymen realized the threat of well-financed "planters," who for more than a decade had been systematically "seeding" embryo oysters on privately leased beds, property that was not affected by the anti-dredging ordinance. Unable to compete effectively, the baymen unsuccessfully sought legislation to restrict the planters. This led to feuding over territorial rights, pirating, and even some gunplay before the century ran out. The baymen lost, but the oyster industry grew, and the LIRR was used extensively, along with boats and wagons, to transport the shellfish to New York.

Another prime Long Island industry that developed during the nineteenth century and relied heavily on the railroad was duck farming. The familiar white fowl that wind up on menus almost everywhere as Long

OPPOSITE

A potato field in Bridgehampton (ABOVE LEFT); *farms in East Mattituck* (ABOVE RIGHT); *Greenlawn barns in winter* (MIDDLE LEFT); *the striking pattern of the Leuthardt barn in East Moriches* (MIDDLE RIGHT); *and farm hands hoeing a Jamesport field* (BELOW).

RIGHT

One way to attract attention was devised by this retailer at The Big Duck in Flanders.

OVERLEAF

What's a menu without Long Island duckling? Farms such as this one at Carmans River are where it all begins.

Island duckling got their start in 1873 from a clipper ship that had visited the Orient. Called Pekin ducks after their origin in China, they were brought to New York and made their first Long Island appearance on farms in the Speonk-Eastport area. The industry grew rapidly around Moriches Bay, and at its height was providing about 60 percent of the ducks raised in the United States. The ducks, which could look forward to a life span of about three months, were hatched in incubators, moved to brooders and then outdoors until reaching a weight of five or six pounds. Many of the Suffolk farms added railroad sidings to expedite shipping to markets in the city and further west.

The railroad also made a concerted bid for passenger business by promoting Long Island, initially as a summer playground and eventually as a place to live year-round. For the wealthy, the miles of beaches for bathing, woods for hunting, and fields for horseback riding had long made the Island an accessible recreational paradise. Those with money always had been able to leave the city easily to take advantage of the ocean off Brooklyn, at Coney Island and Manhattan Beach, and off Queens, at the Rockaways. Great hotels there and out in Suffolk at such places as Shelter Island and Babylon catered to ever-larger numbers of the affluent who were eager to flee the increasing waves of immigrants crowding the city.

In time, middle-class New Yorkers followed that route eastward, finding accommodations in private homes, which became "guest," "tourist," or "boarding" houses during the summer. After taking the train to Bridgehampton or Bellport, vacationers were met at the station by coaches, which conveyed them to a place of green lawns, shady trees, comfortable verandas and hammocks, and bountiful meals, all for well under ten dollars a week.

SEASON 1905
MANHANSET HOUSE
MANHANSET MANOR

SHELTER ISLAND   NEW YORK

ABOVE
The S. S. Sagamore *of the Montauk Steamboat Company carried visitors from New York to vacation spots on Long Island.*

LEFT
The Manhanset House on Shelter Island attracted thousands of vacationers at the turn of the century with advertisements such as this one.

BELOW
Before refrigeration, grand hotels such as the Manhanset House depended on ice cutters at work on a Shelter Island pond. Cakes of ice would be stored in icehouses throughout the summer.

OPPOSITE
Many of Long Island's grandest hotels were vulnerable to fire, such as the blaze that is destroying Shelter Island's Manhanset House in this 1910 photograph.

While the fascination that Long Island seemed to hold for many New York City residents was being exploited piecemeal by hotel and boarding-house operators, an immigrant boy, who had pooled energy, imagination, and a small inheritance into one of the nation's greatest fortunes, decided to do it wholesale. He was Alexander Turney Stewart and he had amassed his wealth as a Manhattan merchant. On the advice of architect John Kellum, in 1869 he bought more than 7,000 acres of the vast Hempstead Plains at fifty-five dollars an acre with the intention of building his own community. It was to be his, literally: he would build roads, homes, shops, a hotel, even a branch railroad line and station. And he would keep them all; everything, including the houses, would be for rental only. It was to be called Garden City.

Some of the initial reaction was ebullient. "Hempstead Plain, hitherto a desert, will be made to bloom as a rose," trilled *Harper's Weekly.* "It will be the most beautiful suburb in the vicinity of New York. God speed the undertaking." The project began to pall when Kellum, who had designed the community and was directing its construction, died. Work went on, but interest in renting Garden City's houses was limited; prospective residents wanted to own their own homes. When Stewart died in 1876 and failed to provide in his will for further development of

the village, the entire project almost collapsed. However, it managed to stay alive until changes in concept and operation, including the establishment of individual ownership brought about by the Garden City Company, stimulated new interest.

Along with Stewart Avenue, the most enduring tribute to Garden City's creator is the magnificent Gothic Cathedral of the Incarnation, seat of the Episcopal Diocese of Long Island, which was built in 1885 as a memorial to him by his widow. Its 220-foot spire towers over the pink sandstone structure on Cathedral Avenue and has served as a landmark to generations of Long Islanders.

To an elite group of New Yorkers, no public inducement to live on Long Island was necessary. Summer visits had confirmed the area's appeal for them, and they began purchasing vast wooded tracts on the near North Shore and even as far distant as Babylon for what would become some of the most palatial estates in America. Soon manor houses, modeled after those belonging to English royalty, began to rise behind high stone walls. Grand residences set back along miles of landscaped approaches were augmented by guest cottages, carriage houses, barns, stables, greenhouses, pools, ponds, and fountains.

The names of the owners comprised a list of corporate, financial, and social leaders equivalent to, if not indistinguishable from, the "Four

Hundred" of New York's high society: Vanderbilt, Grace, Mackay, Morgan, Hitchcock, Clark, Belmont, Whitney, Phipps, Guggenheim, Bostwick, Swope, Guest, Pratt, Harriman, Roosevelt, Kahn, Tiffany, and more.

Descriptions of their lifestyles seemed to outrival fiction. George C. Taylor, an eccentric millionaire who chose a bayside site in the Town of Islip for his country house, stocked his 1,500-acre estate with deer and game birds for sport, and maintained a herd of elk and peacocks for show. Clarence Mackay bought 650 acres on Harbor Hill, near Roslyn, to house his summer residence—the reproduction of a French chateau that reportedly cost five million dollars to build and landscape.

Along with their great wealth and stature, many of these men developed special interests in art, music, and sports. One of the most prominent was August Belmont, an ardent horseman, who indulged his avocation on 1,100 acres of what is now known as Belmont Lake State Park near Babylon. About half the property was cultivated to feed the horses and other livestock, another sizable portion was used for grazing and paddocks, and there were accommodations for fifty stable boys, as well as a building large enough for winter workouts. A 24-room mansion served as the country home; there was a 40-acre lake with a boathouse, and some thirty other buildings that housed squash courts, game rooms, carriages, ice, and dogs.

This early movement to the suburbs and beyond coincided with a new mood that had captured the American imagination during the close of the nineteenth century. It was a recognition of adult fun, of the value of play, of the importance of recreation in stimulating the spirit and revitalizing the body. It was the first time that the nation had permitted itself to discard the Puritan ethic sufficiently to enjoy leisure without guilt. And it was to lead to a new appreciation of Long Island.

CHAPTER SIX

Fun and Games

By the time America began learning how to play after the Civil War, Long Island was already one of its most popular playgrounds. Horse racing, the national pastime before baseball, had been a part of Long Island life for two centuries, appearing almost as early as the first colonists. Long Island's climate and geography lent itself to hunting, fishing, sailing, ice skating, and bathing. Its affluent sportsmen were quick to adopt imports, such as polo, golf, tennis, and later, motorcar and airplane racing. Its masses learned to cycle, took their bikes on Long Island Rail Road excursions, and marveled at the exploits of "Mile-A-Minute" Murphy.

It was as early as 1665 when the royal governor of New York, Richard Nicolls, became the figurative sire of today's two-dollar bettors by ordering the creation of a racetrack called New Market on the Hempstead Plains "for encouraging the bettering of the breed of horses, which, through great neglect, has been impaired." The sport proved an immediate success, and the approximate location of the track has been maintained through modern times with Aqueduct, Belmont, Jamaica, and Roosevelt Raceway.

By 1670, when Daniel Denton's *A Brief Description of New York* was published, racing and Long Island were as inseparable as stablemates. "Toward the middle of Long Island," he wrote, "lyeth a plain 16 miles long and 4 broad, where you will find neither stick nor stone to hinder the horses' heels, or endanger them in their races. Once a year the best horses in the island are brought hither to try their swiftness, and the swiftest rewarded with a silver cup, two being annually procured for that purpose."

In those days, and until after the Civil War, races involved only two horses. These match races usually consisted of 4-mile-long heats, the winner being the first horse to win twice. Since the heats were run consecutively on the same day, they represented an enormous test of endurance. They also created intense competition and, for the time, vast wagering. The competition and the wagering were increased further by regional rivalries, principally pitting horses from the North against those from the South.

The first of these North-South confrontations took place in 1823 at the Union Course, near Jamaica, between American Eclipse, an unde-

As long as there is bright sunshine to mellow the bite of a winter's day, there will be ice skaters on Long Island. The popularity of the sport has not been diminished by time, and skaters still whirl and spin on St. John's Pond by St. John's Episcopal Church in Cold Spring Harbor (ABOVE), Coindre Hall Park in Huntington (LEFT), and Centerport Mill Pond in Centerport (RIGHT).

feated 9-year-old New York stallion, and 3-year-old Sir Henry, owned by a southern syndicate. Interest was so high that a newspaper compared it to the presidential "balloting in the House of Representatives for Jefferson and Burr." The gate was estimated at 60,000 persons—extraordinary, considering that the combined population of New York City and Long Island was less than 220,000—and more than $200,000 changed hands when American Eclipse won the third and decisive heat by a length.

In 1845, when what proved to be the last regional rivalry was held on Long Island, a crowd of 70,000, "a larger collection of people than we have ever before seen at the Union Course," according to the *New York Tribune*, saw the South's Peytona beat the North's Fashion in "one of the most exciting races the North has ever known. . . ."

At the turn of the century, tracks were operating all over the metropolitan New York area. In Brooklyn alone, there was racing at Gravesend, Coney Island, and Sheepshead Bay, where Futurity Day was a celebrated event. Long Island's place in American racing was fixed in 1905 with the opening of Belmont Park on a 650-acre site in Elmont that included a railroad station, two thousand stalls, and a grandstand for nine thousand fans. Built by the Westchester Racing Association, under the leadership of August Belmont Jr. and William C. Whitney, it took two years to construct and featured clockwise, English-style racing at fall and spring meetings. Despite a disastrous fire that destroyed the grandstand and other buildings in 1917, racing continued, and a rebuilt facility, worthy of the appellation "Beautiful Belmont," was unveiled in time for legendary Man o' War to win the Belmont Stakes in 1920. That race, the final third of the Triple Crown, is regarded by many experts as

the most important test of 3-year-olds because of its mile and one-half distance.

Harness racing, in which horses pulled drivers in carts called sulkies, was popular, too, and a track was laid out in 1825 near the Union Course in what was then called Centreville and is now Rego Park. It was there, in 1847, that Albany Girl tried to run one hundred miles in ten hours, only to collapse after nine and one-half, just two and one-half miles short of her heartbreaking goal. Harness racing was the feature of the county fairs held annually at alternate sites in Hempstead, Jamaica, or Flushing until 1866, when a permanent location was fixed at Mineola. But the top trotters, such as Lady Suffolk, who broke the two-and-one-half-minute mile in 1845, disdained the fairs for more profitable circuits. It was almost a century later, during World War II, that Freeport attorney George Morton Levy put trotting into the big time and big money by presenting it under the lights at Roosevelt Raceway.

LEFT
Harness racing got an early start on Long Island at a track in what is now Rego Park. Later, it became a popular feature at the annual Mineola Fair, where this photograph was taken in 1936. The area now houses the State Supreme Court complex.

BELOW
Time has not altered the expressions of winning, losing, and anxious bettors, as confirmed by this early twentieth-century Colliers *magazine cover called "Opening of the Racing Season." It was done in 1905 by Charles Dana Gibson, famous for his "Gibson Girl" paintings.*

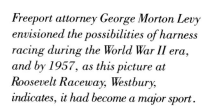

Freeport attorney George Morton Levy envisioned the possibilities of harness racing during the World War II era, and by 1957, as this picture at Roosevelt Raceway, Westbury, indicates, it had become a major sport.

These were the sports that drew the crowds in those times, but admission was rarely charged, and so the costs were borne by a few men of wealth. They were borne easily, it should be added, in those pre-income-tax days when people of means seemed to despair of ways to reduce their fortunes. Another way they found was yachting, and Long Island, with its sheltered coves, deep harbors, and broad Sound, provided all the opportunity they needed.

Estates were built along the Sound, where its ample but protected waters could not only be viewed but used. Docks and boathouses were as *de rigueur* as carriage houses and parlor maids. "Any man who has to ask about the annual upkeep of a yacht," John Pierpont Morgan reportedly asserted, "can't afford one." Morgan, clearly, never had to ask. And his superyacht *Corsair* was the figurative flagship of the sleek armada that luxuriated in Long Island Sound. The yachting crowd required watering holes as well as water, and so yacht clubs were created: the Seawanhaka Corinthian in Oyster Bay, and the New York Yacht Club's Station 10 in Glen Cove.

In the decades that followed the onset of the twentieth century, yachting became boating, and the size of the vessels, along with the net worth of their owners, shrank drastically. As the sport was democratized, sailboat racing became more widespread, power boating more popular, and yacht clubs catering to both preferences proliferated until membership in more than one hundred became available to Long Island's boat people.

Another sport that began with the rich—but stayed with them—was polo. It reached Long Island just before the turn of the century, having been introduced to Newport's high society a few years earlier. But Long Island's horsey set adopted polo—and vice versa—so that the game

One of the oldest and most unusual looking yacht clubs in America was the New York Yacht Club's Station 10 in Glen Cove. In 1950 it was loaded on a barge for towing across the Sound to Mystic Seaport, Connecticut.

soon became inextricably associated with the place. The Meadow Brook Club in Westbury, and the Rockaway Hunting Club in Cedarhurst were the places in which to play and to watch, as young men from exclusive families traded goals and good sportsmanship in a world of their own making.

Polo got its American start at Newport around the turn of the twentieth century, but it soon became a fixture on Long Island. This match was at the Meadow Brook Club in Westbury.

OVERLEAF
The waters off both shores of Long Island were a natural for yachting and boating of all kinds. Sail and power pleasure boats followed in the wake of the millionaires' superyachts and made Long Island Sound and the South Shore Bays a sailor's haven. A summer's day will find sailboats racing (ABOVE), sailboats at the Centerport Yacht Club on Northport Harbor (BELOW LEFT), pleasure boats under an early morning sun in Northport Harbor (ABOVE RIGHT), and power boats passing through the Shinnecock Canal (BELOW RIGHT).

Polo reached its zenith in the 1920s, and names such as Hitchcock, Guest, Bostwick, Iglehart, and Whitney dominated the sport and the headlines when the United States and Great Britain vied for the Westchester Cup, an event that brought the Prince of Wales to Long Island in 1924. The difference between performances, even the players agreed, was not so much athletic as equine. Good polo ponies were eagerly sought, although sometimes, as reportedly was the case with Winston Guest, they came as wedding gifts.

A similar sport, in the sense that its reputation far exceeded the number of its participants, was fox hunting. Scathingly described by Oscar Wilde as "the unspeakable in full pursuit of the uneatable," fox hunting achieved prominence on Long Island among those who prized everything English. Beginning in 1877, pink-coated hunters galloped

behind the hounds on North Shore estates, or, later, at the Meadow Brook, Rockaway Hunting, and Queens County Clubs. But progress ended fox hunting in its traditional style (with live foxes) when the construction of divided highways permitted routes to the foxes that were denied to their pursuers. Some hunts are still conducted, but the hounds chase the trail of an anise-scented bag, a change that might meet with Wilde's approval.

For the well-to-do who preferred hunting from less precarious perches, Long Island's location on the Atlantic migratory flyway provided ducks and geese in sky-darkening numbers. Like birds of a feather, wealthy hunters flocked together in exclusive organizations such as the Long Island Shooting Club, which traced its origins to the antebellum days as "an association of gentlemen who had enjoyed trapshooting in England." A decade or two later, in 1858, August Belmont formed the Suffolk Club at Carmans River in South Haven, and in 1865 the Southside Sportsmen's Club was organized on the Connetquot River at West Sayville by a group that included William K. Vanderbilt, W. Bayard Cutting, Pierre Lorillard, Charles Tiffany, and John G. Heckscher.

On the North Shore, the Brooklyn Gun Club, which in 1893 changed its name to the Wyandanch Club in honor of the Indian sachem, provided happy hunting grounds along the Nissequogue River in Smithtown for New Yorkers who could "skip off the evening train, have the morning shoot of the following day and return for business the day after." Other New Yorkers traveled out to Captree Island in the Great South Bay, where members at the Wa-Wa-Yanda Club, mostly politicians, pursued not only game but "the cultivation of friendly feeling, social enjoyment and rational amusement."

Further east, a socially correct group created the Flanders Club at the turn of the century to shoot ducks in Peconic Bay. Their cherished isolation was interrupted in 1920 by the protests of the Long Island Fish and Game Protective Association, which contended that a new state law benefited "clubs of wealthy sportsmen rather than the residents of Long Island and those who are unable to join exclusive organizations." The concern of local hunters was a statute banning from Peconic Bay battery shooting, an extremely effective method of hunting amid decoys from a heavily weighted boat floating very low in the water. They charged discrimination on the grounds that the Flanders and Southside members used improper techniques on their private ponds, such as baiting with corn, while the public was prevented from utilizing equivalent gambits, such as shooting from batteries.

Eventually, protective game laws were enacted prohibiting these and other tricks, although the clubs generally maintained that they had practiced conservationist policies. In time, too, most of the clubs' holdings were taken over by the county or state to become public recreational

OPPOSITE ABOVE
One of Long Island's early appeals to wealthy New Yorkers was its abundance of wild waterfowl. These ducks are enjoying life on a Smithtown pond.

The exclusive hunting clubs of bygone days have become public parks. Connetquot River State Park in West Sayville was once the Southside Sportsmen's Club (OPPOSITE LEFT), and the Canada geese feeding on the lawn of the Nissequogue River State Park in Smithtown could not have done so without risking their lives when it was the Wyandanch Club (OPPOSITE RIGHT).

Duck hunters setting decoys at Patchogue in 1900 (ABOVE). Decoy-making requires skill, patience, and artistry, as these examples from the nineteenth-century collection at The Museums at Stony Brook demonstrate. William Bowman executed Yellowlegs and a Hudsonian Curlew (BELOW LEFT), while the Black-bellied Plovers were the work of Obediah Verity (BELOW RIGHT).

areas. Flanders is in Sears Bellows County Park, Suffolk is in Southaven County Park, Southside is in the Connetquot River State Park, and Wyandanch is in the Nissequogue River State Park.

Fishing, of course, had long been identified with Long Island; first in terms of survival, then for its commercial value. Now it, too, became a sport in both salty ocean and Sound, and in freshwater rivers and ponds as well.

Golf came to America through Long Island, but its passage was so inconspicuous, according to Samuel Parrish, one of its sponsors, that

Long Island's waters have harbored seafood of all varieties. These commercial fishermen are tarring their seines at Orient in 1916.

almost two years passed before it was discovered. It was 1891 when a Scottish-Canadian golfer named Willie Dunn was brought to Long Island by Edward S. Mead and William K. Vanderbilt Jr., who had watched him play in France. Dunn designed a twelve-hole course at Shinnecock Hills, which resembled the terrain of Scotland where the sport already was popular. Using 150 Indians from the Shinnecock reservation, the course was built almost entirely by hand, and some Indian burial mounds were left intact to serve as bunkers.

Incorporated the same year, Shinnecock Hills became the first golf club in Long Island and one of the first in America. Its clubhouse, whose white-columned porches overlook both the Atlantic Ocean and Peconic Bay, was the work of the noted architect Stanford White and opened in 1892. Site of the 1986 United States Open, Shinnecock Hills had hosted the second U.S. Open in 1896. Parrish recalled:

In the beginning, so quietly and unobtrusively was golf introduced into this country that it was some time after the Shinnecock Clubhouse had been built and the game was being played in the "Hills" in all its red-coated, white-collared and monogrammed brass-buttoned splendor (a picturesque but for many years past an abandoned feature of the early days of golf, I still have the buttons; the moths the coat) before the game became sufficiently well known to attract the slightest notice from the newspapers. . . .

From 1893 on, however, a veritable craze swept over the country, and the Shinnecock Club became the Mecca for golfing pilgrims from all sections of the country, seeking information before starting in to construct their own links.

Although professional golf tournaments have followed the sun through the southwest in recent times to permit year-round competition, Long Island has hosted some important matches through the years, including three other Opens, one of which Bobby Jones won in 1923 at the Inwood Country Club, and another Gene Sarazen captured in 1932 at Flushing's Fresh Meadow Country Club. The Island's generally flat or rolling topography has lent itself to the sport, and some one hundred public and

ABOVE

The stately Shinnecock Hills Golf Club, designed by famed architect Stanford White, became one of America's first when it opened in 1892. It is the site of the 1986 United States Open.

BELOW

Long Island has been the scene of many notable golf tournaments, such as this one at Deepdale Golf Club, Lake Success, in the 1950s. Player in the center wearing black is champion Sam Snead.

private courses—many with lengthy weekend waiting times—testify to its popularity.

American tennis and Forest Hills were virtually synonymous for more than a half-century until the nation's most prestigious tournament, the United States Open, was moved in 1978 to another Long Island location at Flushing Meadows. Despite this association, Long Island was neither the place where tennis made its American debut, nor the location of the first National Championships. The game first was played on Staten Island, having been brought there from Bermuda in the late nineteenth century by an American tourist named Mary Outerbridge, and Newport was the scene of the first National Championships in 1881.

The Championships, strictly amateur at that time, arrived at Forest Hills in 1915, when the West Side Tennis Club moved to the suburbs from the West Side of Manhattan. Eight years later, with the club's name still intact, the 14,000-seat stadium and familiar Tudor-style clubhouse, which served so long as the focus of tennis in America, were constructed. It was there on the grass at center court that the champions of earlier eras—Bill Tilden, Don Budge, Jack Kramer, Helen Wills, and Alice Marble—served and stroked their way to fame, if not fortune.

While all sports no doubt provide some benefit, a few transcend their purpose to affect society in unintended and, occasionally, significant ways. One such was the homely sport of bicycling. Like many other nineteenth-century innovations, the bicycle came to America from England. The year was 1876 and the bicycle, a strange device with a huge front wheel, was looked on largely as a novelty. But in 1880, an organization was formed that would provide the leadership and political pressure to begin transforming a haphazard arrangement of rough country roads into an integrated system of smooth highways. Named the League of American Wheelmen and called the L.A.W., it exerted a profound influence on New York State and, particularly, Long Island.

With the development toward the end of the century of the "safety" bicycle and the pneumatic tire, replacing the awkward earlier style with its uncomfortable hard rubber, cycling gained tremendous popularity and gave city dwellers a personal interest in road improvement. The effect of the L.A.W. was considerable, as it pointed out in 1895:

Within the last year our State Division has distributed ten thousand illustrated pamphlets, describing the best methods of making and maintaining country roads; it has secured the passage of a law for the erection of guide boards at country road crossings; it has aided in the raising of funds for the construction of the cycle path from Prospect Park to Coney Island (the nation's first); it has successfully opposed the obnoxious bills introduced in the legislature at Albany for the unfair curtailment of wheelmen's rights on the public highways and streets . . . and has issued five thousand tour books for the use of wheelmen and horsemen describing the most delightful and popular tours in the United States.

OPPOSITE ABOVE
A trout fisherman in hip boots tests his skill and luck in the Connetquot River.

OPPOSITE BELOW
Golfers playing into the fall can appreciate the colors of autumn leaves at Bethpage State Park.

BELOW
Helen Wills, who dominated American women's tennis during the Twenties, winning the national singles championship seven times in nine years, is about to serve on an East Hampton court in this 1928 Childe Hassam work.

The impact of this campaign soon became apparent as Kings and Queens Counties embarked on an extensive macadam road-building project, while Suffolk licensed cyclists and used the revenues to construct bicycle paths from Smithtown to Port Jefferson, Riverhead to Greenport, and Amityville to Amagansett, with a network of interconnecting lanes.

By 1898, the craze had so taken hold that the Long Island Rail Road was running specially equipped cars solely to transport bicycles. It also published a guide called *Cyclists' Paradise*, extolling the beauties of the Island and offering tips on the best ways for wheelmen (and wheelwomen) to appreciate them. For example:

Every condition on Long Island is favorable to the cyclist. The record-breaking scorcher finds in the south shore road an ideal century course, smooth, level and almost a straight stretch; the road rider who enjoys hill-climbing with the long compensating coasts, finds these conditions fulfilled on the north shore with a hard roadbed eliminating danger and increasing exhilaration, while the tourist finds on each of the three main roads points of great beauty. The side runs are full of agreeable surprises, with a marvelous diversity of topography.

The brochure contained a map of Long Island's cycling paths and even included an advertising message from the phone company, which contended that "no Paradise for cyclists or any one else would nowadays be complete without telephone service."

Weekends saw thousands of bike riders fanning out on the LIRR's

specials to explore the Island's villages, beaches, woods, and waterways, and to spend their evenings at approved restaurants, their nights at approved hotels, and their money at both. The railroad's promotional talents reached their peak in July, 1899, when it constructed a mile-long wooden runway between the tracks near Farmingdale to test the claim of a cyclist named Charles M. Murphy that he could pedal a bike at the speed of sixty miles per hour. Accompanied by reams of publicity and thousands of spectators, the stunt involved racing behind a timed LIRR train. In just 57.8 seconds, "Mile-A-Minute" Murphy became Long Island's latest hero.

Another sport that produced far-reaching consequences for Long Island and for the nation was auto racing. At the opening of the twentieth century, Europe was far ahead of the United States in the design and construction of cars, particularly high-performance racing vehicles. The new sport was very popular among wealthy spirited young men, who justified their involvement on the grounds that it stimulated serious interest in the development of automobiles and roads.

One of the most involved was William K. Vanderbilt Jr., who raced his Mercedes on both sides of the Atlantic and was determined to upgrade American automobiling. In 1904, he proposed a 300-mile race for international competitors on public roads between Lake Success and Jericho, offering the winner the Vanderbilt Cup—thirty pounds of silver designed by Louis Comfort Tiffany.

The announcement was not received with universal enthusiasm. Many local residents and farmers were concerned about the effect of 100-mile-per-hour speeds on North Hempstead and Jericho Turnpikes, as well as the connecting back roads that would constitute the track. But the event was approved by the Nassau County Board of Supervisors and the Automobile Club of America, and when it was held later that year, the French entry won, a feat that was duplicated in 1905.

By 1906, the race had become established, attracting more than 200,000 fans from throughout the country, many of whom jammed not only the shoulders but the roadways themselves, and two of whom were killed and scores narrowly missed by the careening racers. As a result, the Automobile Club of America withdrew its support for future racing on Long Island's public roads.

In response, Vanderbilt and his associates decided to construct a private, landscaped, 50-mile roadway from Queens deep into Suffolk, not only to accommodate the Vanderbilt Cup Race, but to be used as a public toll road and to test automobile products. The financial Panic of 1907 stalled investors, delaying the project and canceling that year's race. But enough of the world's first concrete highway was completed during the next twelve months to permit incorporating a 9-mile stretch in the 1908 competition. Mounting casualties on the public road portion of the Vanderbilt Cup races over the next few years brought mounting

ABOVE
The Tiffany-designed Vanderbilt Cup Trophy drew worldwide interest to motorcar racing on Long Island.

OPPOSITE ABOVE AND BELOW
The spectacular Vanderbilt Cup Race in 1906 had spectators on telephone poles and roofs watching the cars from Europe and America skid along country roads. When spectators jamming roadways became casualties, the races had to be abandoned.

pressure to end the "slaughter," and the event was abandoned after the 1910 meet.

But the Long Island Motor Parkway lived on. Eventually forty-eight miles long, the first high-speed, limited-access, paved roadway stretched from Horace Harding Boulevard in Queens to Lake Ronkonkoma; it included sixty-five bridges and twelve toll lodges, cost millions of dollars to build, and was used by 150,000 cars annually during the 1920s. The toll, a steep two dollars in 1908, dropped to one dollar and a half in 1912, one dollar in 1917, and forty cents in 1933.

The development of Long Island's extensive public parkway system by Robert Moses made the narrow 22-foot-wide toll road obsolete and, unable to sell it or pay its taxes, Vanderbilt finally turned it over to the counties for $500 and cancellation of a $90,000 tax bill. Surviving is a 13-mile section between Dix Hills and Lake Ronkonkoma; four toll lodges, originally designed by architect John Russell Pope after French country homes and subsequently converted to private use; and fading memories.

As some early twentieth-century daredevils were making history on Long Island's roads, others were creating it above. For while the distinction of being aviation's birthplace belongs to Kitty Hawk, North Carolina, the site of the Wright Brothers' first flight in 1903, the Island can authoritatively claim to be aviation's cradle. Within six years of the Wrights' feats the skies over the Hempstead Plains became the scene of rickety aircraft, fearless pilots, and broken records. Pioneer airman Glenn H. Curtiss got the Long Island aviation industry off the ground on July 17, 1909, when he flew his Golden Flier for fifty-eight minutes over Mineola and Westbury to win $10,000 and the Scientific American Trophy for the first flight of at least twenty-five kilometers (fifteen and one-half miles) by an American. Valentine W. Smith of Far Rockaway recalled:

Contemporary motorists relive the past in their antique auto on a drive along a tree-lined road in Remsenburg.

This airplane looked like an enlarged box kite. The driver's seat projected out in front and the engine with the propellor, set to push forward, was at the back. It was an ideal morning with no wind stirring, and at sunrise Mr. Curtiss wheeled the machine to the east side of the Fair Grounds, and went up a little higher than the tree tops, and circled around for half an hour [sic]. At the end of that time the plane fairly collapsed from the excessive strain, but he had remained in the air just long enough to win the prize of $10,000.

The New York Aeronautic Society had commissioned Curtiss to build and fly that plane, and during the next few weeks one of its members, Charles F. Willard, learned enough under intensive instructions from Curtiss to complete the first "extensive" cross-country flight on August 13: twelve miles from Mineola to Hicksville, where he made a safe forced landing. By year's end, the first airplane built on Long Island, a biplane designed by Frank Van Anden of Islip, and the first monoplane, built by Dr. Henry W. Waldon, were test-flown satisfactorily at Mineola.

These feats and dozens more dazzled crowds who rode, walked, or drove out to the flat, treeless Plains in the ensuing months to view the exploits of the newest American craze—the flying machine. There was a new record for flying passengers (three), the first pilot to cross Long

ABOVE

By covering twenty-five kilometers (fifteen and one-half miles) over the Hempstead Plains in his Golden Flier on July 17, 1909, aviation pioneer Glenn H. Curtiss won ten thousand dollars and put Long Island in the flying business.

BELOW

Jimmy Doolittle, who was to win fame in World War II for leading a daring carrier-based bombing raid on Tokyo, was a lieutenant when he was photographed with this early Curtiss seaplane; he won the Schneider Cup in it.

Women were not far behind in taking up flying. Harriet Quimby, drama editor of Leslie's Weekly, *was an early aviatrix who learned to fly at the Moisant Aviation School in Garden City.*

Island Sound (Clifford B. Harmon), the first attempt at aerial gunnery (Infantry Lieutenant Jacob Fickel fired two bullets into a ground target from a plane flown by Curtiss), the first air-to-ground radio transmission ("Another chapter in aerial achievement is recorded in the sending of this wireless message from an airplane in flight"), and the first American woman pilot (Dr. Bessica Faith Raiche).

The sport, as it then seemed to be, was so new and the accomplishments so rapid that rarely a week went by without some record being set or broken. And it was all done with such flair. As many as ten thousand Long Islanders would visit the flying fields on weekends to "toot their automobile horns vigorously whenever a daring airman would make even the briefest flight," remembered one spectator. "If a flier bobbed his plane up and down in the air in daredevil fashion, the crowd would applaud vigorously."

Long Island's role in aviation received worldwide acknowledgment in the fall of 1910, when the International Aerial Tournament was held at the Belmont Park Racetrack. The Wright Brothers and Curtiss attended but did not compete, as aviators from England and France challenged those from the United States in a variety of events that included tests of speed, distance, and altitude. The weeklong meet attracted as many as seventy-five thousand daily spectators—at two dollars a ticket—to watch "The Heavenly Twins," Arch Hoxsey and Ralph Johnston, vie for the $5,000 altitude prize by spiraling into the sky until their gas tanks ran dry, their engines sputtered, and they were forced to glide their Wright biplanes to earth. Johnston won and set a new record of more than nine thousand feet.

A year later, the next International Aerial Tournament also was held on Long Island, this time at the Nassau Boulevard Airfield in Garden City. It was noteworthy for two events that foreshadowed the different directions in which air power would affect the twentieth century. One involved pilot Earl Ovington, who made the first air mail delivery by flying six miles and dropping a bag of 640 letters and 1,280 postcards near the Mineola Post Office. The other involved Lieutenants Thomas D. Milling and Henry H. Arnold, who, using the only two planes owned by the Army, spotted troops concealed in the Long Island woods to demonstrate the military potential of aircraft.

It was 1911, and the time for playing games was beginning to run out. America had learned to have fun. But soon there would be other lessons to master. In three years World War I would erupt; in five years the Hempstead Plains would become the site of a military flight training school at Hazelhurst, later Roosevelt Field; in six years an adjacent Army base called Mitchel Field would be created; and in thirty years Lieutenant Henry H. (Hap) Arnold would command the U.S. Army Air Corps during World War II.

Over Here,

The Hempstead Plains, which would figure prominently as the site of military bases in both world wars, was introduced to the sounds of pounding boots and bugle calls long before the beginning of the twentieth century. It had heard officers' commands and soldiers' curses during the American Revolution, the War of 1812, the Civil War, and, as the location of Camp Black, during the Spanish-American War, as well. Besides Camp Black near Mineola, Long Island's involvement in that brief conflict in 1898 was notable chiefly for Camp Wikoff, at Montauk, and Theodore Roosevelt, whose extraordinary participation as organizer of the volunteer "Rough Riders" cavalry regiment made history and headlines.

Roosevelt, the most famous Long Islander and the only one to become President, enjoyed a long and pleasant association with the area, having first visited it as a child. After being graduated from Harvard in 1880, he bought 155 rolling, wooded acres in Oyster Bay, kept 95 of them, and began construction of a 23-room house to be called Sagamore Hill. The name was taken from Roosevelt's boyhood days, when he was told by a local bayman that the hills once had been occupied by a Matinecock Indian sagamore, or chief.

The rambling Victorian house, typical of the period and yet exceptional like its owner, was conceived by Roosevelt, designed by the New York firm of Lamb and Rich, and built for him and his young bride, Alice Lee. "I wished a big piazza," he said, "where we could sit in rocking chairs and look at the sunset; a library with a shallow bay window looking south, the parlor or drawing room occupying all the western end of the lower floor." But Alice never watched a sunset from the piazza. She died at the age of twenty-two, before the home's completion, following the birth of their first child, Alice.

Roosevelt's mother died the same day, and it was three years before he occupied Sagamore Hill with his second wife, a childhood playmate named Edith Carow. The intervening time, which was to alter markedly the direction of his life, was spent ranching in the rugged Badlands of the Dakota Territory, where the 25-year-old widower sought distraction from his grief.

LEFT
Teddy Roosevelt's trophies adorn this restored room at Sagamore Hill. Roosevelt became an adherent of rugged living after spending a couple of years in the American West following the deaths of his first wife and mother. He later went on African safaris.

BELOW
Roosevelt's idea to form the "Rough Riders" to fight in the Spanish-American War—an offshoot of his youthful experiences in the West—had a crucial impact on his political future.

OPPOSITE
Charismatic and endowed with keen political instincts, "T. R." reaped a rich harvest from the publicity that attended articles such as this 1899 cover story in widely read Scribner's magazine.

During the next decade, Roosevelt, a Republican who had been elected to the New York State Assembly at the age of twenty-three, unsuccessfully ran for mayor of New York City and served as a U.S. Civil Service commissioner, New York City police commissioner, and Assistant Secretary of the Navy before resigning in 1898 to form the celebrated "Rough Riders." That group of dashing mounted riflemen was an offshoot of Roosevelt's Dakota days, having been recruited largely from among Western plainsmen and cowboys. The regiment was a great source of pride to him and he wrote a friend that "you would enjoy seeing the mounted drill, for the way these men have got their wild half-broken horses in order is something marvelous."

The Rough Riders, like the other American troops in the Spanish-American War, were afflicted more by disease than by the enemy. Attacked principally by yellow fever, they were unable to combat it in the sultry Cuban climate amid deplorable sanitary conditions. To isolate the disease victims from the general population, it was decided to set up a military hospital at Montauk Point. The development of Fort Pond Bay and extension of the Long Island Rail Road as part of Austin Corbin's grandiose transatlantic port scheme facilitated rapid construction of Camp Wikoff, as the base was named, and enabled troop and hospital ships to dock there rather than going through New York or Brooklyn.

The ships began unloading ailing soldiers even before the camp was ready, as Roosevelt noted:

COL. ROOSEVELT

Tells the story of **THE ROUGH RIDERS** in Scribner's Magazine. It begins in January and will run for six months, with many illustrations from photographs taken in the field.

JANUARY SCRIBNER'S

NOW READY   PRICE 25 CENTS

For the first few days there was great confusion and some want, even after we got to Montauk the men in the hospital suffered from lack of almost everything, even cots. But after the first few days we were well cared for and had abundance of all we needed, except that on several occasions there was shortage of food for the horses, which I would have regarded as even more serious than a shortage for the men, had it not been that we were about to be disbanded.

Once organized, Camp Wikoff satisfactorily handled 25,000 troops, losing only 126, and Roosevelt approved heartily of its operation. "On the whole," he said, "the month we spent in Montauk before we disbanded was very pleasant."

For Roosevelt at least, the ensuing months were pleasanter still, as his combat adventures made a lasting impact on his political career. His charisma, daring, shrewd sense of publicity, and luck combined, within three years of the war's conclusion, to make him a national hero, governor of New York, Vice-President of the United States, and, on the assassination of William McKinley, the nation's youngest President at the age of forty-two.

But this dizzying rise to prominence did not dilute Roosevelt's love of Sagamore Hill nor his desire to spend time there. It became his summer White House and the place he most prized for cavorting with his six children and numerous young relatives. No affairs of state could divert the President from those commitments. One afternoon when he was discussing tariff rates there with a visiting statesman, a group of boys appeared, announcing: "Cousin Theodore, it's after four."

"By Jove," he said, "so it is. Why didn't you call me sooner? One of

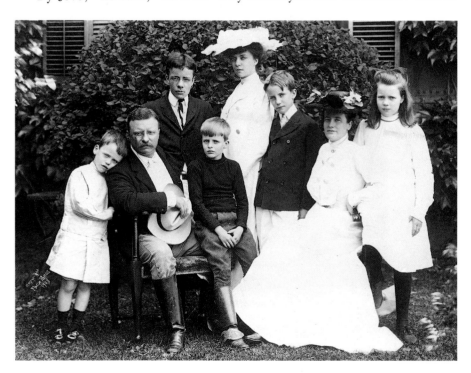

you boys get my rifle." Then, turning to his distinguished visitor, he explained: "I must ask you to excuse me. We'll finish this talk some other time. I promised the boys I'd go shooting with them at four o'clock and I never keep boys waiting."

His proclaimed dedication to the "strenuous life" was carried out at the Oyster Bay estate by riding, hiking, chopping wood, and rowing. Often, these activities were combined during outings at adjacent Lloyd Neck, where, after a 6-mile row, the President and his young chums would hike to a campsite at which he would prepare dinner. Later, around the campfire, he would relate tales from his rich outdoor experiences out West and in Cuba, or recall classics from literature and history.

"I love all these children and I have great fun with them," he wrote. "And I am touched by the way in which they feel that I am their special friend, champion and companion."

Sagamore Hill proved to be the ideal home for a man dedicated to nature and to accumulating the mementos of global excursions. Inside the spacious home, every aspect of Roosevelt's amazingly active life found a niche, from statues of cowboys to elephant tusks and moose heads; few residences ever so revealed their occupants' interests.

Despite his wide travels, Roosevelt was a familiar figure on Long Island, particularly during presidential campaigns. When he was denied the Republican nomination for a third term in 1912 and formed the Bull Moose Party to advance his progressive platform, he got support from his Nassau neighbors, many of them leading Republicans.

"We joined the movement only because we felt Teddy had been cheated at the Republican Convention and many of us idolized the man," explained Sanford Davison, one of the founders of a local "Roosevelt Progressive" club. Although he ran strongly for a third-party candidate, Roosevelt failed to carry his home county in that election, losing in Nassau to Democrat Woodrow Wilson by about 500 votes, while outdistancing incumbent President William Howard Taft, the Republican nominee.

"T. R." continued to live at Sagamore Hill throughout his rich 60-year life, and was buried beneath a simple headstone in nearby Young's Cemetery, Oyster Bay Cove, in 1919.

The vast, flat, treeless prairie called Hempstead Plains, which early settlers found so desirable as a pasture for cattle and sheep, was deemed ideal by early airmen for a flying field, and, whenever war loomed, received top priority as a military training base. Thus, after the Spanish-American War, the tents of Camp Black were replaced by the aircraft hangars of fledgling aviators—until 1917, when the United States declared war on Germany and the Army converted a year-old National Guard base there to Hazelhurst Field.

Named for Leighton W. Hazelhurst, the first noncommissioned officer killed in an aviation accident, the Mineola facility served as the site of a training school for Army and Marine Corps pilots under the tutelage of pioneer fliers called the "Early Birds." Among the trainees was Quentin Roosevelt, youngest of Teddy Roosevelt's four sons, and, according to his father, "the brightest of the children." A few months before the armistice ending World War I, Quentin was killed in a combat mission over German lines. "He died," his father said, "as the heroes of old died; as brave and fearless men must die when a great cause calls." In Quentin's honor, Hazelhurst was renamed Roosevelt Field in 1918.

Just to the south of Hazelhurst-Roosevelt, across Stewart Avenue, that same year an installation called Aviation Field No. 2 became Mitchel Field, after former New York City mayor John Purroy Mitchel, who was killed during aviation training in Louisiana. Used as a training center then, it would achieve its greatest service as an air base during World War II.

In the late summer of 1917, adjacent to the western edge of Mitchel Field, an Army base named for Brigadier General Albert L. Mills was echoing simultaneously to the sound of carpenters' hammers and marching feet. The feet belonged to National Guardsmen from every state in the Union, who were called up to form the 42nd (Rainbow) Division, the first American infantry troops to be sent overseas in World War I. Supervised by Douglas MacArthur, who was to gain fame as the Pacific commander of U.S. forces during World War II and as United Nations commander during the Korean War, these doughboys were virtually adopted by the villagers of Garden City, Hempstead, and Mineola before spearheading American Expeditionary Force assaults in France.

As the troops poured in, local residents and merchants were overwhelmed. "Literally thousands of men thronged the streets," recalled Hempstead historian Felix Reifschneider, "sat on the roofs of trolleys and perched on the steps and bumpers, and packed the taxis besides. Every home made the boys welcome and hospitality was unbounded. Eight new restaurants were built and new stores sprang into existence on all sides."

In Garden City, which was almost totally residential, volunteers pressed to do their bit in entertaining the young soldiers. "One of the biggest jobs at Camp Mills," *The Evening Sun* pointed out in September, 1917, "is the care of visitors. It is estimated that fifty thousand people visited the Rainbow Division last Sunday. The whole problem has been taken out of the hands of the military authorities and handed over to a group of women in the area."

As many as 30,000 doughboys jammed Camp Mills before they began shipping out in December. There were tensions and barroom brawls, but there was affection, too. And after the war, veterans of the Rainbow Division erected a monument to their 2,950 dead and 13,290 wounded in a small park in Garden City on Clinton Road, south of the LIRR tracks.

OPPOSITE ABOVE LEFT
Tent life at Camp Mills, 1917.

OPPOSITE ABOVE RIGHT
A review of the 42nd (Rainbow) Division at Camp Mills, Garden City, 1917.

OPPOSITE MIDDLE LEFT
Camp Upton at Yaphank was the first stop for tens of thousands of draftees during World War I. It was constructed in less than three months during the summer of 1917 and received soldiers by early September.

OPPOSITE MIDDLE RIGHT
Doughboys learned how to fight with bayonets as part of their basic training at Camp Upton. The 77th Division trained here before going overseas.

OPPOSITE BELOW LEFT
Relaxing after a vigorous day of drilling, World War I soldiers listen to a phonograph at the Long Island Army camp.

OPPOSITE BELOW RIGHT
Its proximity to New York City made Camp Upton a popular place to be stationed. On weekends, doughboys often would be met by their wives for some fun in the city.

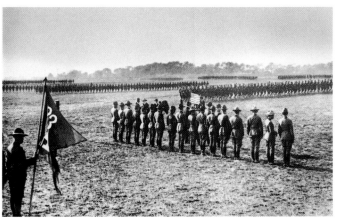

After the November 1918 armistice, Camp Mills became a major demobilization center, as troops from Europe and many parts of the United States passed through its gates for almost a year en route to civilian status. Among those who did not was Lieutenant William Bradford Turner, an infantryman from Garden City whose heroism won a posthumous Congressional Medal of Honor, one of only ninety-five awarded to soldiers during the entire war.

During the hectic months after America's entry into World War I in the spring of 1917, a Suffolk counterpart to the scene at Camp Mills was being enacted near Yaphank, on a tract now housing the Brookhaven National Laboratory. There, on more than 10,000 acres of flat, swampy, mosquito-ridden land, as many as 15,000 skilled workers and laborers struggled through the hot, wet summer to build barracks for 37,000 soldiers, mostly draftees, who would never forget Camp Upton.

The construction of that Army installation, named after a Civil War general named Emory Upton, was a marvel of logistics and supervision since almost all the workmen had to be fed and housed on the isolated site. Special railroad sidings were laid to facilitate the shipment of lumber and other materials, and a large number of private detectives had to be hired to cope with the influx of crooks who swarmed over the camp. Criminality was so rampant that a U.S. District Court was established at the base while it was being built and it tried more than 1,000 cases in about two months.

Troops began arriving little more than two months after construction started, and by the end of the following month, 30,000 men were being trained at Camp Upton. Among them were members of the 77th Infantry Division, which, composed largely of Long Islanders and New Yorkers, was soon to fight valiantly in the crucial Argonne Forest Battle in France.

One of Upton's more famous trainees was songwriter Irving Berlin, who put together a revue called *Yip! Yip! Yaphank!* that entertained not only his buddies but Broadway audiences. Berlin's experience at the camp led him to compose "Oh, How I Hate to Get Up in the Morning," which survived the war to become a popular song.

Because of its isolation, providing social activities for the soldiers became a major problem. One solution was to let them out, and a shuttle train was run from the camp to the Long Island Rail Road's main line so the men could spend their weekends in New York. It also enabled thousands of relatives and friends to ride in from the city and other parts of the Island for Saturday and Sunday visits.

Like Camp Mills, Upton was converted to demobilization after the war, and tens of thousands of overseas veterans were processed there before returning to their homes. Processed there, too, were thousands of mules that the Army had decided to dispose of at auction. After being sold, they were lassoed, had their government brands removed, were herded into railroad cars, and dispatched to their new owners.

World War I brought varied appeals for enlistments through recruiting posters for the U.S. Navy by artist Howard Chandler Christy.

During the World War II production of This Is the Army, *Irving Berlin sits on a cot and reminisces about his World War I experiences at Camp Upton.*

In 1921, everything else at Camp Upton was auctioned off: barracks, stables, hospitals, warehouses, garages, engines, heating and refrigerating plants, electric substations, telegraph poles, wiring, even lavatories. Structures were moved or torn down and dismembered for parts and lumber. Hundreds of carloads of material were shipped around the country. Successful bidders had sixty days to remove their purchases. And then all was gone. The place became almost as it had been. An era not only had ended, it had disappeared. But the Twenties had arrived. And Long Island was ready to roar.

CHAPTER EIGHT

Fast Times

Through a gazebo, Old Westbury Gardens appears even more elegant. Its unique landscaping draws thousands of visitors annually.

Long Island and the Jazz Age were made for each other. On the North Shore, there was the Gold Coast: millionaire playboys, sophisticated ladies, champagne tastes, lush life. Off the South Shore —three miles off—there was Rum Row: illegal liquor-laden ships, evasive contact boats, machine-gun-toting "go-through guys," watchful Coast Guard interceptors.

It was the Roaring Twenties, and for Long Island it was an era described by unbelievable facts and unforgettable fiction. Glittering parties were held on lawns so extensively lit that the Long Island Lighting Company had to be notified to prevent an overload; dinners for 1,500 guests were held in just one of a mansion's 86 rooms; gardens were so large and delicate that they required the care of 50 workers; housekeepers were so demanding that they supervised the placing of fresh flowers in 200 vases each day.

And in a room over a garage in Great Neck, Francis Scott Key Fitzgerald began to memorialize it all with his novel, *The Great Gatsby*:

There was music from my neighbor's house through the summer nights. In his blue gardens men and girls came and went like moths among the whisperings and the champagne and the stars. At high tide in the afternoon I watched his guests diving from the tower of his raft, or taking the sun on the hot sand of his beach while his two motor-boats slit the waters of the Sound, drawing aquaplanes over cataracts of foam. On week-ends his Rolls Royce became an omnibus, bearing parties to and from the city between nine in the morning and long past midnight, while his station wagon scampered like a brisk yellow bug to meet all trains. And on Mondays eight servants, including an extra gardener, toiled all day with mops and scrubbing-brushes and hammers and garden-shears, repairing the ravages of the night before. . . .

At least once a fortnight a corps of caterers came down with several hundred feet of canvas and enough colored lights to make a Christmas tree of Gatsby's enormous garden. On buffet tables, garnished with glistening hors d'oeuvre, spiced baked hams crowded against salads of harlequin designs and pastry pigs and turkeys bewitched to a dark gold. In the main hall a bar with a real brass rail was set up, and stocked with gins and liquors and with cordials so long forgotten that most of his female guests were too young to know one from another.

Fitzgerald saw in Long Island the stuff that the American Dream was made of, captured its elusiveness on pad with pencil, lived its false promise with his wife, Zelda, as America's Golden Boy and Girl, the gorgeous, talented, irresponsible embodiment of the Roaring Twenties. His experiences and observations were derived from a nineteen-month stay between 1922 and 1924 in a rented stucco house at 6 Gateway Drive, Great Neck Estates. It is still there, in what would constitute the "West Egg," or noveau riche, portion of Gatsbyland, which readers of the book would recognize never quite compared with the very rich milieu of "East Egg" (Sands Point), the home of Gatsby's love, Daisy Buchanan, and her husband, Tom.

Scott and Zelda partied among the rich and mighty at the estate of Herbert Bayard Swope, sportsman and publisher of the *New York World*, and formed a close relationship with writer Ring Lardner, a Great Neck neighbor whom Fitzgerald later eulogized as "that fine medallion, all abraded by sorrows that perhaps we are not equipped to understand." Other literary and theatrical personalities who brightened Great Neck neighborhood soirees in the Twenties included Lillian Russell, Groucho Marx, Leslie Howard, Will Durant, P. G. Wodehouse, George S. Kaufman, Oscar Hammerstein II, and Ernest Truex.

Celebrities abounded on the North Shore then; nor was there any shortage of estates: more than five hundred were occupied during that era, most of them within sight of the Sound or secluded behind high walls in the Old Westbury-Brookville-Muttontown-Locust Valley area. Like ancient emperors, America's corporate and financial rulers scoured the globe for styles, materials, and treasures to live in and with.

Rome's Borghese Gardens were figuratively transported to Glen Cove to enhance Winfield, the showplace of F. W. Woolworth. Built in the Italian Renaissance style, it boasted a marble staircase that, at an estimated two million dollars, probably was the most costly ever constructed. Entry was along a lengthy driveway past the gardens, Roman statuary, and a magnificent pool. The house itself contained fifty-six rooms, including bedroom suites reflecting different historic periods.

Reaching back far further in time to decorate his premises, William K. Vanderbilt II placed columns from the ruins of ancient Carthage at the entrance to his 43-acre summer estate overlooking Northport Bay in Centerport. (The other seasons were spent at his estate in Lake Success, or at his homes in New York and Miami.) The mansion complex and adjacent Hall of Fishes marine museum, both preserved and now open to the public, are Spanish Revival in design and reflective of the Vanderbilts' lavish tastes and wide interests.

The most ornate rooms are one containing an organ whose 2,000 pipes are concealed behind an eighteenth-century tapestry, and Mrs. Vanderbilt's luxurious bathroom-dressing room that has a tub cut from a block of pink Venetian marble and is decorated with gold-plated fixtures.

ABOVE

The chronicler and embodiment of the Jazz Age, F. Scott Fitzgerald lived with his wife, Zelda, in this rented stucco house at 6 Gateway Drive, Great Neck Estates, in 1922 and 1923, absorbing the Gold Coast ambience.

BELOW LEFT

In a plain room above the garage at the rear of the Great Neck Estates home, Fitzgerald began writing The Great Gatsby, *regarded by many as a classic depiction of Roaring Twenties' manners and morals. His friendships with the wealthy and famous gave him access to the lifestyle he described in the novel.*

BELOW RIGHT

Enjoying the good life he wrote about, F. Scott Fitzgerald, Zelda, and their daughter, Scottie, pose aboard a liner in 1926. Scottie later wrote that as a child she thought everyone's parents lived like hers.

The Hall of Fishes did double duty: its roof served as the first tee for the estate's 10-hole golf course, while its interior housed more than 17,000 specimens of marine life collected by Vanderbilt during three decades of worldwide exploration, much of it aboard his 265-foot yacht, *Alva.*

For wealth *and* achievement, few families can compare with the Whitneys, whose ventures in finance, transportation, politics, diplomacy, society, and sports are legendary. The accomplishments began with William C. Whitney, who fashioned a transportation network, accumulated vast wealth, fought the corruption of Boss Tweed, built an estate in Old Westbury, and fathered two sons, Harry Payne Whitney and William Payne Whitney.

ABOVE
In a less serious vein, John Held Jr. was Fitzgerald's artistic counterpart in chronicling the Jazz Age. This watercolor, painted for Life *and entitled* Milkman, Good Morning, *conveys the sophisticated irresponsibility of the times.*

BELOW
The naughty spirit of the Twenties was captured in this humorous illustration entitled Bathing Beauties *by artist James Montgomery Flagg for* Judge *magazine.*

OPPOSITE ABOVE
The Vanderbilt mansion in Centerport, designed by Warren and Wetmore, was augmented by columns from the ruins of Carthage at its entrance, and a golf course.

OPPOSITE BELOW
Interior of the Hall of Fishes at what is now the Vanderbilt Museum in Centerport. William K. Vanderbilt II collected 17,000 specimens of marine life, which are on display here.

The sons branched off but shared a strong interest in Long Island and in racing. Harry Payne remained in the Old Westbury area, married the former Gertrude Vanderbilt, founder of the Whitney Museum of American Art, and raised horses. Their son, Cornelius Vanderbilt (Sonny) Whitney, continued the family involvement in racing and became one of the nation's foremost horsemen. The estate, once comprising some 1,000 acres, largely has become the Old Westbury Golf and Country Club and, along with its striking Tudor-style racing stables, the New York Institute of Technology.

William Payne, who dropped the William, and Helen Hay Whitney, known in her day as "the first lady of the American turf," were the parents of John Hay (Jock) Whitney, who, while going on to a distinguished career as ambassador to the Court of St. James's and publisher of the *New York Herald Tribune*, perpetuated his mother's stake in racing. With his sister, Joan Whitney Payson, he operated the famed Greentree Stable, which bore the same name as his 500-acre estate off Shelter Rock Road in Manhasset. Secluded behind a modest wooden fence, Greentree has remained intact and includes just about everything: indoor tennis courts and swimming pool, conservatory, stables, barns, chicken house, and guest cottages.

The problem of keeping in touch with the family was minimized by Charles Pratt, who, like the Rockefellers, amassed a fortune through Standard Oil. Pratt began buying up property on the Sound near Glen Cove around the turn of the century, and by the Twenties his clan was living on a dozen or so adjacent estates comprising more than 1,000 acres. There even were facilities used in common, such as the stables, garages, and gardens called Pratt Oval, and an indoor tennis and squash complex that has been converted into the Glen Cove YMCA. At one time, Herbert L. Pratt occupied the mansion called The Braes that is now the Webb Institute of Naval Architecture; George D. Pratt resided in the 49-room Tudor revival structure named Killenworth, now a Soviet residence for members of its diplomatic corps; John Teel Pratt was home in the nearby red brick Georgian mansion that has become a retreat for business executives called Harrison House; and Harold Erving Pratt feted social leaders at Welwyn, whose red-tiled roof sheltered a tennis complex and stables and now is part of a Nassau County wildlife preserve.

Not to be outdone, the Morgan family owned two islands, East and West, off what is now Lattingtown. East Island belonged to J. P. Morgan, son of the original robber baron and in some respects his father's son. Access to his 52-room Georgian mansion was across a stone bridge and past a guardhouse that was "supposedly" manned around-the-clock. Supposedly, since on a night in 1915, while Morgan was entertaining the British ambassador, a German sympathizer armed with a revolver and seething with anger at the financier's aid to the Allies, got into the house and, attempting to kill Morgan, succeeded in wounding him. Morgan recovered, but the would-be assassin committed suicide in jail while awaiting trial.

Before and after that incident, violence was as alien to East Island as poverty. Morgan so prized serenity that he grazed a herd of cattle on the front lawn because the scene enhanced his sense of tranquillity. East Island was connected to West Island by a causeway and to their owners by consanguinity: J. P.'s son, Junius Spencer Morgan, built his home, called Salutations, as the Twenties were coming to a close. Among its appurtenances were a dollhouse, used by the Morgan children, that was a miniature Salutations, and a large bank of kennels that housed Mrs. Morgan's show dogs.

Another family that found familiarity bred content was the Guggenheims, Daniel and Harry, heirs to a copper fortune. Daniel arrived first in Sands Point in 1917, purchasing Castlegould, a 300-acre property that included a Tudor-Jacobean mansion built in 1912 for Howard Gould, son of notorious stock manipulator Jay Gould. Howard Gould's wife, actress Viola Katherine Clemmons, had wanted a copy of Ireland's Kilkenny Castle, but he had other plans, and the only resemblance to Kilkenny can be found in the design of the large stables. Mrs. Gould's desires apparently were unfulfilled on several counts, since she obtained a legal separation following a lurid two-year court battle that included allegations involving her relationship with William F. (Buffalo Bill) Cody.

Daniel Guggenheim named the structure Hempstead House, because it overlooked Hempstead Bay, and furnished it in a style befitting a member of one of the nation's wealthiest families. In 1923, when his son, Harry, married his second wife, Caroline Morton, Guggenheim gave him 90 acres of the estate as a wedding gift. Harry immediately set about constructing a medieval Norman manor house on the water, which he called Falaise. Instead of emulating his father's taste, the younger Guggenheim sought to impress through quality rather than size. This appeal to connoisseurship resulted in a second-generation Gold Coast mansion that made Falaise smaller and more livable than Hempstead House, and that made it notable for its transplantation of European art and architectural fragments such as columns, doors, sculpture, and carvings.

Like most Gold Coast estates, its guest list was impressive, drawn from its owner's varied interests, which in this case included horseracing (1953 Kentucky Derby winner Dark Star), publishing (*Newsday*), diplomacy (ambassador to Cuba), art (Solomon Guggenheim Museum), and the advancement of aviation and rocketry. Guggenheim regularly entertained architect Frank Lloyd Wright, financier Bernard Baruch, rocket pioneer Robert Goddard, and presidential aspirant Adlai Stevenson.

One of Falaise's most famous visitors was Charles Lindbergh, who needed a quiet place to write after returning from his epic transatlantic flight in 1927. The result was *We*, a best-selling account of that spectacu-

OPPOSITE ABOVE
Falaise, owned by Daniel Guggenheim's son, Harry, was designed by Frederick Sterner and built on ninety acres that the younger Guggenheim had received as a wedding gift. Co-founder of Newsday, *he lived here with his wife, Alicia Patterson,* Newsday's *first editor and publisher. The estate is now part of Nassau County's Sands Point Preserve.*

OPPOSITE BELOW
Old Westbury Gardens, the former estate of John S. Phipps, was designed by London architect George Crawley and contains paintings by Gainsborough and Reynolds, and furniture by Chippendale.

ABOVE
The Georgian estate of J. P. Morgan on East Island, off Lattingtown, was accessible only by a bridge protected by a guardhouse. But in 1915, a would-be assassin got in.

RIGHT
Castlegould, built for Howard Gould, son of financial manipulator Jay Gould, was bought later by Daniel Guggenheim. Architect Augustus Allen designed the support buildings, including the stables, which resemble Ireland's Kilkenny Castle.

BELOW
Hempstead House, the main structure on the Castlegould estate, was designed by Hunt & Hunt and named by Guggenheim for its site overlooking Hempstead Bay.

lar feat. Falaise, which Guggenheim shared with Alicia Patterson, his third wife and *Newsday*'s first editor and publisher, was given to Nassau County after his death in 1971, and is open to the public as part of the Sands Point Preserve.

The preserve also includes Hempstead House, which, following Daniel Guggenheim's death, served as an asylum for British children seeking to escape the bombing of London during the early years of World War II, as a facility for the Institute for Aeronautical Sciences, and as a U.S. Navy Special Devices Training Center (where atomic research was conducted), before coming under county aegis.

Other places where the lavish style of the Twenties still can be absorbed include two of Long Island's most magnificent showplaces: Planting Fields, the estate of William Robertson Coe in Oyster Bay, and Old Westbury Gardens, the John S. Phipps estate. Both are renowned for their matchless landscaping, and the structures themselves are outstanding examples of architecture and decor. Coe brought the gate from Carshalton Park in England to guard the entrance to Planting Fields, while at Old Westbury Gardens, paintings by Thomas Gainsborough, Sir Joshua Reynolds, John Constable, and John Singer Sargent hang in rooms furnished with the works of eighteenth-century English cabinetmaker Thomas Chippendale.

Fire, maintenance costs, taxes, and developers' enticements were responsible for the destruction of most of the Gold Coast palaces, including what may have been the most spectacular of all, the estate of banker Otto Kahn in Cold Spring Hills, Huntington. Kahn, whose zeal for social activity matched his drive for wealth and power, sought the highest point on Long Island for his contemplated residence and, on finding it occupied, purchased another site and had it elevated. On it, he built a 126-room, turreted castle, golf course, and formal gardens that made the estate world-famous. The grounds and building later became the Eastern Military Academy, until it went bankrupt in 1979.

Another estate that became an educational institution was Broad Hollow, the home of F. Ambrose Clark and now the State University of New York College at Old Westbury. One of the dynamic personalities of the time, Clark was a noted horseman who not only owned, but trained and rode thoroughbreds on his 500-acre estate. Also an owner of the Singer Sewing Machine Company, he hosted luncheons for 500 guests in his white-pillared, 42-room colonial mansion. But when he decided to throw a party for the visiting Prince of Wales in 1924, Clark evidently felt that the facilities were inadequate, for he had an oak-paneled ballroom built for the occasion.

No longer standing is the French chateau at Harbor Hill, Clarence Mackay's 600-acre Roslyn estate and the site of what may have been the grandest party of them all. Held in honor of the Prince of Wales during his weeklong visit to attend the 1924 International Polo Matches at

Taxes and maintenance costs forced the closing of many of the great Gold Coast estates, some of which have become public institutions. Metal sculpture, titled Sidewinder, *by Allen Bertoldi, decorates the former Childs Frick estate in Roslyn, now the Nassau County Museum of Fine Art* (ABOVE). *Once Broad Hollow, the F. Ambrose Clark estate, designed by Rogers & Zogbaum, is now the State University College at Old Westbury* (MIDDLE). *The Dairy Barn, which once supplied milk to the Whitneys in Old Westbury, currently fills other needs for New York Institute of Technology students as an activity center* (BELOW).

Westbury, the reception was attended by 1,200 guests, who dined on lobster piled six feet high, danced to the music of Paul Whiteman, and inhaled perfume sprayed from the magnificent garden fountains. The winding, mile-long entrance drive was lit by thousands of blue electric bulbs strung through the trees that lined it, and a huge American flag, composed of still more red, white, and blue lights, glowed over the chateau's gabled roof.

The fact that this extraordinary affair was held during Prohibition underscored public contempt for that law; among the celebrants were government officials, judges, diplomats, clergymen, and military leaders. But on Long Island there also was appreciation for the constitutional amendment banning the importation, manufacture, transportation, or sale of intoxicating liquors. Bootlegging became a prime industry in Nassau and Suffolk during Prohibition's 14-year life.

After the Eighteenth Amendment went into effect in early 1920, vast quantities of liquor continued pouring into the United States; of course it did so in a new way. Large yachts and schooners picked up 3,000-case loads from the French islands of St. Pierre and Miquelon, south of Newfoundland, or from many islands in the Caribbean, and anchored off the Long Island coast just beyond the 3-mile limit of federal jurisdiction. There—on what became known as Rum Row—immune from law enforcement, they hung signs from their masts announcing their wares, and awaited the arrival, at dusk, of the contact boats, swift, silent, converted Jersey skiffs which sought to evade the Coast Guard and speed the liquor to shore. With lookouts posted to warn of the approach of patrols, the transfer of the cargo took place according to a well-defined ritual that was fast-paced with a style all its own. To protect against gangsters or undercover agents, sellers often required buyers to confirm their "legitimacy" by producing matching halves of torn dollar bills. With such preliminaries disposed of, prices were agreed upon, orders placed by shouts from ship-to-ship, rolls of bills tossed onto the seller's deck, and cases of liquor loaded aboard the pitching skiffs.

After that, skill and luck determined if the goods were delivered or the rumrunners caught. The contact boats, generally powered by automobile engines with underwater exhausts to minimize sound, hoped to race

ABOVE
Made to order for the Roaring Twenties is this couple in their snappy 1927 Buick Sports Roadster.

OPPOSITE
Rumrunners brought illicit liquor to secluded East End beaches such as this during Prohibition. Long Island was a beehive of bootlegging activity as contact boats picked up whisky from ships waiting on "Rum Row" outside the 3-mile limit of federal jurisdiction, and smuggled it ashore.

back to beaches or secluded docks in Montauk, Fire Island, Cutchogue, Freeport, Greenport, Shelter Island (which still has its Bootleggers' Alley), and other waterfront communities. The darkness helped and so did fog, for the skippers were veteran seamen who knew the local waters well. They soon developed evasive techniques to augment their navigational skills and the swiftness of their small boats. Sometimes they might use an identical but empty vessel to lead the Coast Guardsmen on a false chase, or toss the liquor overboard after attaching the cases to buoys for subsequent retrieval, or as a reluctant, but frequently successful, gambit —commit bribery. Occasionally, when all else failed, the rumrunners simply heaved their cargo into the sea to escape arrest. When that happened, particularly if it occurred close to shore accompanied by the roar of gunfire, alert beachfront residents might rush out to salvage the abandoned liquor.

There were huge profits to be made, and it did not take long for criminals to recognize that the size and complexity of the operation called for businesslike organization. Quicker than one could say "Al Capone," organized crime was born. Investing money in every phase of the illicit business, the newly formed mobs even had their contact boats built by the same shipyards that made the Coast Guard craft, enabling them to obtain the specifications of the government ships; they could then install engines capable of outdistancing them.

But the Coast Guard was regarded by the rank-and-file bootleggers as a far less formidable foe than the "go-through guys." These were professional robbers and killers who, riding the speediest boats and carrying deadly Thompson submachine guns, would "go through anything" to get what they wanted. What they wanted were the fat bankrolls used to buy the contraband, and to get them, like an updated version of the murderous pirates who roved Long Island waters in an earlier century, they would pull over the contact boats and rob them at gunpoint. The contact-boat crews were especially vulnerable; normally they went unarmed in order to mitigate their sentences if caught and convicted of rumrunning.

One of the most popular eastern Long Island bootlegging terminals was Greenport, ideally located because of its access to the open sea, to the secluded coves of Shelter Island and the North and South Forks, and to Jericho Turnpike, which led to New York. On shipment nights, the community's dock area literally would be taken over by mobsters who stood guard while the cargoes of illegal liquor were unloaded from the contact boats and placed aboard trucks for the predawn run to the city. Finding loaders was no problem: most townspeople able to lift and carry cases were eager to do so for twenty dollars—the equivalent of a few days' pay. Once ready to move, the convoy fell into position: a line of trucks sandwiched between escort cars filled with armed gangsters.

The precautions were not exaggerated. Rival gangs and hijackers would lie in wait along Jericho Turnpike and other major routes to ambush the

Prohibition evaders and agents played an ongoing game of cat-and-mouse throughout the existence of the Prohibition law. (OPPOSITE ABOVE) This one-time private yacht, Edith, *from which customs agents are unloading contraband booze, was carrying $75,000 worth of illegal liquor when it was stopped by Coast Guardsmen. (OPPOSITE BELOW) One dirty trick that did not quite work involved hiding 3,000 bags of bottled whisky amid the coal aboard this coal steamer.*

BELOW
The Prohibition laws were violated so openly that they inspired songs. This is the cover of the sheet music for "Everybody Wants a Key to My Cellar," a number popularized by Bert Williams.

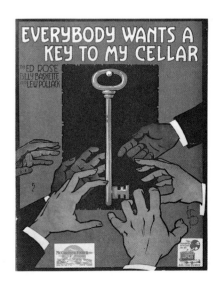

caravans by blocking the road with stalled vehicles or ramming them with empty cars. There would be warning gunfire and, if the hijackers encountered resistance, violence; stealing the trucks and their contents was a high-stake, high-risk business.

Obviously unable to complain to the authorities, the bootleggers devised new methods to make their deliveries. One was to send high-powered cars, outfitted with false bottoms to conceal the liquor and with shock absorbers to prevent sagging, at breakneck speeds on Vanderbilt's private Long Island Motor Parkway. Local police and federal agents also had to be evaded, but with corruption widespread, payoffs frequently insured a lack of interference. In instances where some officials, notably Nassau District Attorney Elvin N. Edwards, sought to carry out the unpopular law, little public support existed.

Most of the antibootlegging pressure on Long Island came from the churches and the Ku Klux Klan; the latter, having been revived nationally in 1915 after its seeming demise in 1869, enjoyed extensive backing. In Nassau and Suffolk during the early Twenties, one out of every eight residents was a member of the Klan. Espousing "law and order" along with vicious attacks on Catholics, Jews, the foreign-born, and blacks, the Klan strongly pressed for enforcement of Prohibition and eagerly provided manpower to assist officials in patrolling highways and performing other parapolice work.

When a special constable named Ferdinand Downs was killed by bootleggers in Southampton, the Klan made a major issue of the crime and called for 10,000 members to attend his funeral. Although that goal was not reached, more than 2,000 mourners did show up to demonstrate their indignation, along with paying their last respects. More significantly, after Patrick Ryan, a Catholic from New York City, was charged with Downs' killing, he contended that he could not get a fair trial locally and succeeded in gaining a change of venue to Kings County. In granting the motion, a State Supreme Court justice said: "There exists in Suffolk County great hostility toward Roman Catholics and a feeling of bias, prejudice and passion exists and is expressed against the defendant whenever men congregate."

The Klan's anti-Semitism was not limited to speeches. After a Jewish druggist in Freeport was cleared by police of having attacked a little girl in the summer of 1924, the Klan ordered him to leave town and, when he refused, kidnapped him on a village street and left him in Hicksville. The victim, Ernest Louis, then sold his store and moved, explaining that the harassment had destroyed his business.

Although in recent years the Klan's national activities have been directed primarily against blacks, in the Twenties on Long Island it was the foreign-born who were regarded as a threat to the "American way of life." They constituted more than 20 percent of the Nassau and Suffolk population, while blacks comprised only about 2 percent. Antiblack activists concentrated on preserving existing housing patterns, which meant, for example, seeking to keep blacks out of predominantly white Roosevelt, or insuring that blacks in Freeport lived only in the Bennington Park section.

Freeport was a stronghold of KKK sentiment, and the organization had little difficulty in demonstrating boldly or in gaining an audience. On September 20, 1924, an estimated 30,000 spectators lined the village streets to watch a parade of 2,000 Klansmen and Klanswomen led by Freeport Police Chief John M. Hartman. Floats called on the citizenry to "Teach the Bible in Public Schools," "Protect American Womenhood," and maintain "Clean Politics." In Suffolk, 25,000 men, women, and children attended a Klan rally near Central Islip in the summer of 1923 to hear a minister describe Jews and Catholics as dangerous to the United States and to witness the initiation of 1,500 new members.

There was remarkably little opposition to the Klan's cross-burnings and other hate-mongering activities by public officials. What protests did arise usually came from victimized groups, such as when the Knights of Columbus and synagogue members criticized the Freeport school board for accepting a flag and flagpole from the Klan.

By 1926, the KKK had begun to decline in influence on Long Island. This was evident in local elections in Greenport, Babylon, and Sag Harbor, where anti-Klan candidates were successful, a fact noted in *The New York Times:* "Long Island seems to be recovering from its belief in the Ku Klux Klan. . . . Thus has good sense returned to Long Island, and its people have resumed the display of their accustomed intelligence."

The Klan's promotion of nativism held some appeal on Long Island, particularly to old-line families—the white Anglo-Saxon Protestants who resented the intrusion of newcomers and feared the threat they represented to their traditional domination of the area's institutions. So long as Catholics and Jews had only been sprinkled among the population, these feelings had been kept relatively in check, although aspects of anti-Catholicism and anti-Semitism came to America with the first settlers. But the immigration expansion that began with the Irish and Germans in the mid-nineteenth century and became an explosion with the Italians, Poles, Russians, and Jews in subsequent decades, triggered far more active hostilities.

Catholics became part of Long Island's history as early as 1683, when the Duke of York, a Catholic, appointed Catholic Thomas Dongan to replace the tyrannical Edmund Andros as royal governor of New York. Long Island's first Mass probably was celebrated by Dongan's chaplain, Jesuit Father Thomas Harvey, when the governor arrived in Sag Harbor en route to his new post.

The Catholic influx was sporadic in the beginning. In the 1750s, a few French immigrants from Nova Scotia, called Acadians, made their

The Klan focused its Long Island campaign of hatred on the foreign-born, Catholics, and Jews in those days.

way to Long Island after a stay in New York and settled in various Suffolk villages. But so few Catholics were living in the Thirteen Colonies at the time the United States was formed, that when the first diocese was established in Baltimore in 1789, it embraced the entire nation. As Catholics, primarily from Ireland, began to enter the country in greater numbers, three more dioceses, including one for New York, had to be created in 1808.

On Long Island, Catholic communities developed at both ends. In Brooklyn, this led to the formation in 1823 of the Island's first Catholic church, St. James, at the present site of St. James Cathedral in the Borough Hall section. In eastern Suffolk, after several years of prayer meetings, Catholics in Sag Harbor purchased a former Methodist church in 1838, and converted it into what apparently was Long Island's second Catholic church and Suffolk's first. This was accomplished with financial support from a prominent Protestant, offsetting considerable antipathy from other Protestants.

The Catholic population was augmented during the following decade when large numbers of Irish were employed to lay Long Island Rail Road track from Brooklyn to Greenport. Swelled significantly by migration following the destruction of the potato crop in Ireland, the Catholic community had grown large enough by 1853 to warrant the creation of the Diocese of Brooklyn, consisting of Kings, Queens (which then included Nassau), and Suffolk Counties.

The next hundred or so years became the most significant in Catholic history on Long Island. Vast numbers of Italian and Polish immigrants poured into Brooklyn and Queens toward the turn of the century and watched their children and grandchildren populate Nassau and Suffolk during the post-World War II exodus to the suburbs. From representing a vulnerable minority on Long Island in the mid-nineteenth century, Catholics became a powerful majority in the mid-twentieth, a circumstance reflected by the establishment in 1957 of a new diocese for Nassau and Suffolk. Seated at St. Agnes Cathedral, the Diocese of Rockville Centre now has more than one million communicants, making it the nation's largest after Brooklyn.

For many Italians, Long Island provided the opportunity to transplant the ambience of their native land to the estate of a Gold Coast magnate. As the nineteenth century came to a close, some of New York City's most affluent families had decided to live or entertain on Nassau's North Shore and they needed skilled landscapers and gardeners to help them emulate the sumptuous showplaces of Europe. One of the places they drew on for expertise was the Italian town of Durazzano, whose residents flocked to America and settled in the rural community of Westbury. They worked on the estates, planting trees and shrubs, hedges and flowers. Those who were not required on the estates soon found employment in the flourishing nursery business, particularly with a leading firm named Isaac Hicks and Sons. Immigrants from Italy also settled in Long Island villages such as Glen Cove, Oyster Bay, and Inwood, going into construction work or, later, becoming barbers, shoemakers, and tailors.

Although, like most immigrants, Italians tended to be clannish and preoccupied with their own institutions and societies, they soon discovered that their interests would be ignored by the Protestant hierarchy unless they learned to exert political pressure. In Westbury, for example, Italian-Americans were furious during World War II when the village board, citing Italy's Axis status, curtailed the annual festival honoring Our Lady of the Assumption, the community's most colorful ethnic celebration. When the war was over, they channeled their anger and frustration into politics and soon found they could gain representation within the power structure and, ultimately, control of it.

The postwar rush to the suburbs found Americans of Italian descent buying homes in such areas as Franklin Square, Elmont, East Meadow, Levittown, Hicksville, Deer Park, Copiague, North Babylon, and Commack. By 1980, they clearly had become the predominant ethnic group on Long Island and were exercising significant political influence in Nassau and Suffolk, both in elective positions and behind the scenes.

Another major ethnic group that encountered difficulties on Long Island both because of their foreignness and their Catholicism was the Poles. They also arrived in substantial numbers toward the turn of the century, finding work as farm laborers, often in the employ of German immigrants who had settled a generation or two earlier.

In time, they gravitated toward eastern Suffolk, where they purchased land, grew potatoes, and populated Riverhead, which they dubbed "Polish Town, USA." Attempts to keep the ethnic heritage alive are concentrated at St. Isidore's Church, erected there in 1907 and named for the

patron saint of farmers. The Nassau counterpart is St. Hedwig's Church in Floral Park, built in 1903.

Jews were among the earliest Europeans to seek a home in Long Island and, consistent with the treatment they have received throughout their long history, met with resistance and hostility. A group of twenty-three Jews who had fought with the Dutch and earned permission to trade in New Netherland were challenged on their arrival in 1654 by New Amsterdam Governor Peter Stuyvesant. Directed by his superiors to grant the Jews admission to the Dutch territory, which included Long Island, Stuyvesant acquiesced, but imposed severe restrictions on their rights to own property, open stores, worship publicly, and perform skilled labor. One of the group, Asser Van Swellem Levy, demanded, persisted, and eventually won equal rights for himself and his co-religionists.

Levy made his summer home in what is now Long Island City, bought property elsewhere on Long Island, and saw his son's family settle in East Hampton in 1730. In 1750, another Jewish pioneer, Aaron Isaacs, a Sag Harbor merchant, married Mary Hedges of East Hampton, became a convert to Christianity, a father, and, later, grandfather of John Howard Payne, author of "Home Sweet Home."

During the nineteenth and early twentieth centuries there were pockets of Jews who appeared in the most unlikely Long Island communities. In Sag Harbor, for example, they went to work at the Fahys Watch Case Company and built Temple Adas Israel in 1898, the oldest existing synagogue in Nassau or Suffolk. In Lindenhurst, then called Breslau by its German founders, they worked in a button factory or used the village as the hub for peddling in western Suffolk. In East Setauket, they were employed in the J. W. Elberson rubber factory and formed the Congregation Agudath Achim, now the North Shore Jewish Center.

Jews, who settled in New York City in vast numbers on their arrival from Europe, generally remained in the five boroughs until the 1920s. When they did move, many made their homes within relatively easy commuting distance of the city, in such communities as Great Neck, the Five Towns (Woodmere, Hewlett, Cedarhurst, Lawrence, and Inwood), Lynbrook, Freeport, Hicksville, and Long Beach. But it was not until the post-World War II migration that they moved in sufficient numbers to comprise almost 20 percent of Long Island's population, and become its second largest ethnic group, after Italians.

German immigrants came to Long Island earlier than most Europeans, settling in the Hempstead Plains in the 1850s to coax vegetables out of the dry fields. Completion of the Long Island Rail Road to Hicksville prompted a real estate mini-boom there as newly arrived Germans came out from New York City and Brooklyn, liked what they saw, and began buying lots and homes.

In the ensuing decades, German farmers moved into many areas of western Nassau, such as Floral Park (named for its nurseries), New

In East Setauket, Jewish employees of a rubber factory established Agudath Achim Synagogue, now the North Shore Jewish Center.

Hyde Park, Elmont, Freeport, and Franklin Square. Their institutions, particularly the Lutheran Church, soon followed, and today more than one hundred Lutheran churches serve Long Island congregations of German and Scandinavian extraction. One of the area's best-known Lutheran facilities is the Mill Neck Manor School for Deaf Children, which occupies the stately English Tudor mansion formerly owned by Robert L. Dodge.

Of course, the earliest Europeans to colonize Long Island were the Dutch and English. Although refugees from religious oppression in the Old World, they became the arbiters of religious orthodoxy in the New. The Long Island Dutch worshiped in the Dutch Reformed Church as far back as 1654, when their leader, Peter Stuyvesant, directed the Reverend Johannes Theodorus Polhemus to organize three congregations in what is now Brooklyn. Two of the three are still functioning as part of the Reformed Church in America, although after the British took over Long Island from the Dutch in 1664, Dutch immigration eased, Dutch influence waned, and the growth of the Dutch Reformed Church was slowed.

The Puritan sect, which developed in opposition to the Church of England, dominated the English settlements on Long Island, as it had in New England. The initial religion to be brought from Europe to the Island, its first churches, in Southold and Southampton, were established in 1640. The Presbyterian and Congregational denominations evolved from the Puritans and continue to be active throughout Nassau and Suffolk.

Religion and politics were inextricable during colonial days, as church leaders helped write and enforce civil laws to support their religious tenets. Thus, church attendance was made compulsory at the risk of fines, corporal punishment, or even banishment.

In reaction to the harshness of the Puritans, other sects gained adherents during the eighteenth and nineteenth centuries, giving Long Island a religious pluralism with the addition of Methodists, Baptists, Episcopalians, and, despite severe harassment, Quakers. For the Episcopal Church, particularly, the growth of parishioners on Long Island has special meaning. It led to the Island's designation as a diocese, adorned by the Gothic Cathedral of the Incarnation in Garden City, which serves as the seat.

But the story of religious evolution on Long Island is replete with contradictions. The Puritans fled persecution in England only to inflict it on "non-believers" in their new homeland. This insistence on conformity led to the growth of denominations which espoused less stringent behavior and appealed to more liberal worshipers. Yet, it was many of these very churches that later supported attacks on twentieth-century "outsiders," the immigrants whose religious beliefs differed from their own.

That bigotry and intolerance lurked just below the surface of Long Island society became evident from the broad implicit support given to the Ku Klux Klan. And it is difficult to examine the period without recognizing the reluctance of Long Islanders to confront the prejudice and mean-spiritedness in their midst. It was a sordid chapter that revealed the depths to which the American character can descend.

Still, before the decade ran out, a brief, simple, yet extraordinary event would enable the nation to redeem its spirit. It was an exploit seized upon by the public to symbolize the traditional values—courage, grit, decency, self-reliance, humility, and faith—that they regarded as uniquely American.

It began on the misty morning of May 20, 1927, when a lanky, 25-year-old mail pilot from the Midwest left Long Island in an overloaded plane called the *Spirit of St. Louis* seeking fame and the $25,000 prize offered for the first nonstop flight between New York and Paris. The challenge of crossing the Atlantic had captured the attention of the world, and the dramatic takeoff was described by Russell Owen, correspondent of *The New York Times*, as follows:

A sluggish, gray monoplane lurched its way down Roosevelt Field yesterday morning, slowly gathering momentum. Inside sat a tall youngster, eyes glued to an instrument board or darting ahead for swift glances at the runway, his face drawn with the intensity of his purpose.

Death lay but a few seconds ahead of him if his skill failed or his courage faltered. For moments, as the heavy plane rose from the ground, dropped down, staggered again into the air and fell, he gambled for his life against a hazard which had already killed four men.

And then slowly, so slowly that those watching it stood fascinated, as if by his indomitable will alone, the young pilot lifted his plane. It dipped and then rose with renewed speed, climbing heavily but steadily toward the distant trees.

The spirit of unconquerable youth had won, and "Slim" Lindbergh was on his way to Paris.

Thirty-three and one-half hours later the shy, boyish aviator landed in Paris to a hero's welcome, detonating a binge of pride throughout the United States. Lindbergh's daring and modesty had provided an ideal antidote to the cynicism and self-indulgence of the Jazz Age. But the memory would have to last, for Americans soon would be searching vainly for something to cheer about. The stock market was going up only so it would have farther to fall. Prosperity still was booming, but the Great Depression was just around the corner.

CHAPTER NINE

Turning the Corner

Robert Moses, the controversial master builder who altered the face and pace of Long Island with his parks and parkways, poses in 1965 with Harry Guggenheim, Newsday's first president, in front of a painting depicting some of his innumerable construction projects.

Ironically, Long Island's failure to develop its commerce and industry spared it from a worse fate during the Great Depression. Still largely residential and agricultural, Nassau and Suffolk were less vulnerable to the effects of economic collapse than their urbanized neighbors. And Suffolk, even better suited than Nassau by its geography and history to exploit the land and the sea, was able to weather the crisis more easily.

Yet, it was a time of travail, particularly for commuters and construction workers whose livelihoods were jeopardized by paralysis and bankruptcy in manufacturing, wholesaling, retailing, and building. For despite the small-town character that permeated much of the Island east of Queens, the first third of the twentieth century was a period of transition, especially in Nassau, and of movement away from the traditional farm economy of the past toward the suburban growth of the future.

The two principal factors boosting Long Island's development at this time were railroads and roads. The opening of Pennsylvania Station in 1910, and the electrification of Long Island Rail Road service to Hempstead in 1908 and to Babylon in 1925, had enhanced greatly the ease of commuting by train to jobs in New York City. By 1930, 30,000 Nassau residents were doing just that.

While the railroad was moving commuters into the city, and thus inducing New Yorkers to consider moving to Long Island, an inadequate system of roads on the Island was having just the opposite effect on potential residents. City dwellers, including those from Brooklyn and Queens, seeking a restful Sunday in the country during the 1920s, found instead a bumper-to-bumper ordeal over the few narrow, potholed roads that connected Nassau and Suffolk with the rest of the nation. These conditions apparently had the tacit support of many Long Islanders who perceived that any improvement in road transportation would send unwelcome multitudes pouring into their midst from New York. Consequently, there was little encouragement—and massive resistance— when Robert Moses sought to implement his vision of a vast checkerboard of Long Island parks and an interconnected system of parkways through which to reach them.

Moses, a controversial combination of idealist and manipulator, public servant and personal power seeker, left an ineradicable imprint on Long Island, probably affecting more lives in more ways than any individual in or out of local government. Legendary by middle age because of his enormous accomplishments, Moses' reputation subsequently became tarnished, his policies called into question.

This decline apparently reflected a change in public attitudes toward the efficacy of automobile travel. Moses, as the most forceful proponent of more bridges, more expressways, and more parkways, once had been praised as Long Island's "Colossus of Roads." But as his emphasis on private—as opposed to mass—transit failed to alleviate traffic problems, his status fell as motorists' tempers rose. And this disenchantment with his judgment was accompanied by increasing distaste for his authoritarian manner and prickly personality.

Moses' presidency of the Long Island State Park Commission, a post from which he was to wield lifelong influence, came about in 1924 through Governor Alfred E. Smith, who had a profound effect on his appointee's career. Moses soon transformed this paper office—the only Long Island state park at that time was an unused portion of beach on Fire Island—into one of New York's most powerful governmental agencies. But not without struggle.

One of Moses' first goals—to convert the former East Islip property of George C. Taylor from a private hunting preserve to a public park—met potent opposition from the wealthy, influential sportsmen who enjoyed its use. It was only through Smith's backing, along with a $262,000 cash gift from philanthropist August Heckscher, that Moses was able to win a crucial legal victory, establish the state's right to appropriate property in such instances, and create Heckscher State Park.

A key incident in the protracted battle came when one of the landed gentry complained to the governor that if Moses succeeded, the area would be "overrun with rabble from the city." A fiercely proud product of New York's Lower East Side, Smith snapped, "Rabble? That's *me* you're talking about!" He gave Moses his total support. Later, Moses ran into similar hostility from elite North Shore estate owners who sought to block his proposed Northern State Parkway because it would run through their land. This time, however, a "compromise" was worked out. The result—the Northern State Parkway that took a suspiciously erratic course in the vicinity of the Old Westbury estates.

If Moses occasionally backtracked or sidestepped, his direction otherwise was straight ahead; his only velocity—top speed. In 1929, he saw Heckscher State Park open in June, the Southern State Parkway in July, and the Wantagh Causeway and Jones Beach in August. Each year brought new plans, new groundbreakings, new completions. In 1934, Bethpage State Park and Bethpage State Parkway were built; in 1935, the Meadowbrook Causeway; in 1936, the Heckscher State Parkway Spur.

ABOVE
Only the light poles look familiar in this 1930 photograph of the Southern State Parkway near Valley Stream. The absence of a divider, and a makeshift sign banning commercial traffic seem particularly out of place.

BELOW
In 1931, Robert Moses, second from right, was heading the Long Island State Park Commission, and Franklin D. Roosevelt, wearing his favorite Panama hat, was governor of New York. Occasion was the cornerstone-laying of Northern State Parkway.

There was other major highway construction, too. While the parkways barred trucks and skirted the villages, Nassau County concentrated on improvements to roads bearing commercial traffic between communities: the first section of Sunrise Highway was opened in 1928, and Merrick Road, Jericho, Hempstead, and North Hempstead Turnpikes were widened and paved.

This was a period of tight money, of Depression. And these vast public projects provided jobs. One of the most extensive uses of the New Deal relief rolls involved Bethpage State Park, where jobless architects

During the Depression, inexpensive camping at Heckscher State Park was a particularly popular way to vacation. This was the scene there in August, 1933.

were hired to plan the clubhouse and 1,800 unemployed workers to build it along with auxiliary units, four 18-hole golf courses, and the polo field. The government operation even involved the take-over of an idle factory to make new furniture for the clubhouse.

For laborers, there was heavy construction work on roads and drainage systems, post offices, military installations, and a new courthouse complex at the site of the old Mineola Fair on the south side of Old Country Road. And out-of-work white-collar employees were used to take an inventory of structures for the American Historic Buildings Survey, draw up a countywide lot and block map, paint murals on the walls of the old Nassau County courthouse on Franklin Avenue in Garden City (frequently misidentified as the Mineola courthouse), and establish a junior college—Nassau Collegiate Center—in the former Curtiss aircraft factory in Garden City.

At the same time, Nassau and Suffolk bankers were hard-pressed to keep going. Failures at the Bank of North Hempstead in Port Washington and the Long Beach Trust Company, and the imminent closing of the First National Bank of Rockville Centre, precipitated the formation in early 1932 of the Nassau County Clearing House. Meeting in emergency sessions, representatives of 60 banks cushioned the impact of First National's closing by working out protective arrangements with the Bank of Rockville Centre. After President Franklin D. Roosevelt declared a national "Bank Holiday" in March, 1933, to forestall panicky withdrawals by fearful depositors, Nassau emerged with several closings but without financial chaos. In Suffolk, the situation was even less severe. Although 6 of about 50 commercial banks failed to reopen on schedule, they did eventually, and without the loss of a single dollar.

In addition to the effects of unemployment and bankruptcy, the Depression stopped Nassau's real estate and housing boom in its tracks. Residential construction in such burgeoning villages as Rockville Centre and Freeport declined so drastically that the value of new homes built during the entire year of 1934 was less than that put up in a single month a decade earlier.

In Suffolk, too, real estate values plunged, and undoubtedly the biggest loser was the biggest plunger, a flamboyant, multimillionaire-speculator named Carl Fisher. The creator of Miami Beach, Fisher sought to duplicate his success at Montauk, which he envisioned as the "Miami Beach of the North." In 1926, he spent $1,000,000 to build the 200-room Montauk Manor, constructed a glass-roofed indoor tennis complex, yacht club, polo field, movie theater, and golf course, and adorned his superplayground with a seven-story office building. But a devastating hurricane later that year caused expensive damage to Fisher's Miami Beach holdings, and the 1929 stock market crash cut deeply into his remaining assets so that by the early 1930s he could not prevent his Montauk Beach Development Corporation from going into bankruptcy. All that remains of the dream are two of Montauk's most familiar landmarks—the Manor and that strange-looking, out-of-place, seven-story building.

The hurricane that struck southern Florida in 1926 never reached Long Island, but in 1938 another one did, and those living on Long Island then will never forget it. It came with little warning in the afternoon of September 21 and hit the Westhampton Beach area with terrible ferocity. Abnormally high tides, topped with huge breakers, sent 50-foot waves

A Long Island landmark and monument to an unfulfilled dream is the Montauk Manor Hotel. Built in 1926 at a cost of $1,000,000, it was intended as the capstone of developer Carl Fisher's "Miami Beach of the North," but fell victim to the Depression.

OVERLEAF

Jones Beach, one of the earliest of Robert Moses' projects, opened in the summer of 1929 and became popular immediately. By the Fourth of July, 1952, when this photograph was taken, the only space left was in the ocean.

roaring across the dunes, crushing hundreds of homes, tossing cars as if they were cartons, ripping new inlets into Quantuck and Shinnecock Bays, and killing at least 70 people, including 28 in Westhampton Beach alone. Power and telephone lines were out for days in some eastern Suffolk villages, travel was impossible as roads lay buried under several feet of water, sand, and mud, and many of the houses left standing were damaged beyond repair. Winds were clocked in excess of 100 miles per hour, and few communities were unscarred by the disaster.

The 1938 hurricane struck the South Shore of eastern Long Island with devastating force as this scene of destruction in Westhampton demonstrates. More than 70 people were killed during a few hours on September 21.

Besides being assailed by nature, Long Island was the scene those days of another kind of affliction. In the summer of 1937, stunned villagers watched as swastika-wearing, jack-booted members of the German-American Bund marched behind a brass band through Yaphank to Camp Siegfried, a 45-acre site of Nazi demonstrations and propaganda. Streets were named for Hitler, Goering, and Goebbels; bungalows were festooned with Nazi paraphernalia and photographs of the German dictator and his lieutenants; and books such as *Mein Kampf* and anti-Semitic pamphlets were offered for sale.

The Bund, formally the Amerikadeutscher Volksbund, had infiltrated and then taken over the German-American Settlement League, Inc., an organization that operated a communal settlement near a Yaphank lake. Under the leadership of Fritz Kuhn, a German engineer who aspired to

ABOVE

Members of the German-American Bund, an organization that openly admired the policies of Adolf Hitler in the period before the United States entered World War II, greet guests arriving at the Yaphank railroad station with the official Nazi salute. The Bund took over a settlement on a lake near Yaphank, called it Camp Siegfried, and indoctrinated children in Hitlerian rites and beliefs.

BELOW

American Nazi leader Fritz Kuhn, right, confers with some of his lieutenants in Franklin Square after returning from a visit to Germany in 1938. Kuhn, who preached racial and religious hatred at Sunday meetings near Yaphank that drew crowds of 50,000 people, was convicted of grand larceny and forgery in 1939.

become an American führer, the summer campsite was transformed into a miniature Germany, a place where sympathizers of the Third Reich could eat frankfurters, drink beer, and expose their children to Nazi indoctrination, martial training, and racial and religious hatred.

By the summer of 1938, Camp Siegfried was attracting as many as 50,000 spectators on a Sunday afternoon to watch close-order drill to the sound of German Army marches and hear Kuhn extol this "Aryan paradise and part of Germany in America." But the end of paradise was already in sight. Several members of the German-American Settlement League were charged with failure to file membership lists with the state government, and, perhaps worst of all, the Suffolk County Alcoholic Beverage Control Board refused to renew Camp Siegfried's beer and wine license. By 1939, Kuhn, convicted of grand larceny and forgery, was seeking converts in Sing Sing Prison. The Bund hung on through the courts until the United States declared war on Germany and seized the organization's assets.

Although Long Islanders expressed curiosity and displeasure in the mid-1930s about the Nazis in their midst, they showed only limited concern about those in Germany and the impact they soon would have on everyone's life. The Depression was still making its presence felt, and whatever political interest Long Islanders had was focused largely on the domestic scene.

On Long Island, particularly in Nassau, politics in the modern era has been determined by fear of one machine and acceptance of another. Nassau's electorate has reacted to the possibility of control by New York's *frequently* corrupt Democratic organization by preferring the control of its own *occasionally* corrupt Republican organization. It was imminent rule by New York City at the turn of the century that led to the county's formation. At a Mineola meeting called in 1898 to create Nassau by withdrawing from Queens the towns of Hempstead, North Hempstead, and Oyster Bay, a resolution was adopted unanimously. Containing what since has become for Republican candidates an obligatory swipe at the reputedly omnivorous octopus to the west, the resolution asserted that independence for Nassau was essential "to carry into effect the desire of the people to have a county free from entangling alliance with the great city of New York."

In the early years of the twentieth century, Republicans and Democrats swapped domination of the Nassau County Board of Supervisors—then composed of the chief executives (supervisors) of the three townships—as the Democrats stressed GOP "extravagance" and the Republicans warned of the "Tammany tiger." But within a few years, a wealthy oysterman and state assemblyman from the Five Towns, named G. Wilbur Doughty, became the man to deal with in western Nassau. Doughty's anti-New York City credentials were impeccable: he actually had gotten Inwood, his hometown, taken out of Queens and placed in Nassau.

In 1912, the GOP was split throughout the nation by the decision of former President Theodore Roosevelt to frustrate the presidential reelection bid of his one-time favorite and fellow Republican William Howard Taft. Roosevelt did it by running for President himself as an independent under the banner of the Progressive (Bull Moose) Party. Republicans everywhere were forced to choose between their party's incumbent candidate, Taft, and the popular ex-President who was campaigning against him. Nowhere was this controversy more divisive than in Nassau, where Roosevelt lived and enjoyed the support and friendship of prominent Republicans. When the election returns came in, it was clear that both Roosevelt and Taft had lost to Democrat Woodrow Wilson. What became evident only later was that Doughty had *really* won. The internal GOP strife helped Wilson to carry Nassau county, and enabled Doughty to take over the leadership of the stricken local Republican organization.

Shrewd and tough, Doughty assured his dominance by getting the State Legislature to require that representation on the Board of Supervisors be proportional, according to the relative population of the towns. This gave the Town of Hempstead, which happened to be Doughty's bailiwick, an additional seat, which he immediately filled with himself. Now armed with both public office and political power, he had little difficulty in asserting his will. Doughty formed an alliance with Andrew (Uncle Andy) Weston, a successful contractor and Republican leader, that brought Weston millions of dollars in highway and bridge contracts, usually without competitive bidding, as well as an indictment in 1922 for handing in false claims. The indictment was quashed.

Weston went on to become a millionaire-builder whose projects ranged from the Canadian border to the Alabama swamps. Doughty survived his own indictment in 1920, charging that he had tipped off gambling houses of impending raids (it was quashed), and groomed his nephew, J. Russel Sprague, a Lawrence police justice, to succeed him

When Doughty died in 1930, Sprague was ready and took over as Hempstead's supervisor-at-large, but he had to endure five years of infighting before he could assume his uncle's party mantle. In overcoming older and more experienced Republican politicians (Sprague was a comparatively young 43 when Doughty died), he had the considerable clout of Weston behind him. Created very much in Doughty's mold, Sprague did nothing to interrupt the beneficial arrangements that the contractor had enjoyed with his uncle. Materially, as well as politically, the Sprague-Weston relationship paid off for both. In later years, with Weston's help, Sprague made more than $500,000 on a $2,000 investment through secret harness-racing stock manipulations.

Pragmatic but farsighted, Sprague had a talent for organization and a feel for the future. His skills became apparent in the 1936 elections. The Republicans won handily in Nassau, despite losses almost everywhere else in the nation because of President Franklin D. Roosevelt's landslide conquest of Alfred M. Landon.

The 1936 election also marked the passage of the Nassau County Charter, a blueprint for modernizing county government by consolidating authority and responsibility under one official, to be called the county executive, and centralizing into new county departments many of the services formerly handled by towns and villages. It was a substantial personal victory for Sprague. He had championed the charter over the objections not only of Democrats but of many fellow Republicans who were concerned about the effect on tradition, local rule, and, of course, patronage. Once again the "Tammany tiger" was paraded into the Nassau arena and did its job: in leading the fight for adoption, Sprague described the charter as "a positive guarantee against future annexation to New York City without consent of our own people."

The charter went into effect in 1938 and, perhaps predictably, Sprague became Nassau's first county executive, a post to which he was reelected four times before retiring in 1952. Normally reserved and businesslike in appearance as well as manner, he had a politician's knack of projecting charm when necessary, a quality that made him a formidable candidate in addition to being a consumate boss.

Under Sprague's direction, Nassau's Republican organization gained a nationwide reputation for unanimity and efficiency. Loyalty was demanded and rewarded, although Sprague could forgive former political enemies, provided they were Republicans, when it suited the party's and his own purposes. He gained substantial status from his relationship with Thomas E. Dewey, although the former racketbuster failed—with Sprague's backing—in his 1938 attempt to unseat Democratic Governor Herbert Lehman and in his 1940 bid to become the GOP candidate for President. But Sprague's faith was vindicated when Dewey was elected governor in 1942 and swept the Republican presidential nomination on the first ballot in 1944. A decade later, in 1952, now wielding even wider influence as a Republican national committeeman, Sprague was an early passenger on the bandwagon of Dwight Eisenhower, when the popular general became the first Republican President in twenty years.

National politics did not diminish Sprague's interest in local party

BELOW
J. Russel Sprague, left, first Nassau county executive and the party leader who made the county's Republican organization the envy of politicians throughout the nation, accompanies New York Governor Thomas E. Dewey, the 1948 GOP presidential candidate, on a campaign swing through New Jersey.

OPPOSITE
Prematurely pleased with early returns on election night in 1950, W. Kingsland Macy, left, Suffolk Republican power and two-term congressman, later learned that he had lost his reelection bid to a little-known Democrat named Ernest Greenwood. With Macy, who continued wearing high, starched collars long after they had gone out of style, is Surrogate Edgar Hazelton of Huntington.

matters. Foreseeing the need to broaden the Nassau Republican organization's traditional Anglo-Saxon, Protestant hierarchy, he opened leadership posts to others, especially Italians, who were destined to become the county's largest ethnic group.

While the Doughty-Sprague dynasty was determining the political direction of Nassau, a colorful, old-fashioned, vengeful Republican boss was doing the same for Suffolk. Unlike his Nassau counterparts, however, W. Kingsland Macy was not reared for politics; his interest arose from a dispute with Robert Moses. Scion of a wealthy Nantucket whaling family, Macy was brought to Islip at the age of three, went through Groton and Harvard, ran a wholesale grocery firm, and was a partner in a Wall Street brokerage house before being politicized by the controversy over Moses' plan to transform the hunting preserve on the former George C. Taylor estate into a park.

Macy's zest and leadership in that fight led to an invitation in 1926 to become Suffolk County Republican chairman. He accepted and promptly buttressed his new role by purchasing a string of eight weekly newspapers. A committed conservative in ideology and dress, he favored high, starched collars and vitriolic exchanges. But he did not shun publicity and engaged in highly visible hostilities with Democrats and Republicans alike: from Franklin D. Roosevelt and Alfred E. Smith to Fiorello LaGuardia and Thomas E. Dewey.

As county and, in 1930, state GOP chairman, Macy attacked the scandalous administration of New York Democratic Mayor James J. Walker, and he was instrumental in launching the Seabury Commission investigation that paved the way for Walker's resignation. Macy's zeal and ambition were exceeded only by his inability to forgive or forget, a characteristic that led to an ongoing feud with Dewey and his own descent into political oblivion.

Dumped as state chairman in 1934, Macy was appointed to a 12-year term on the Board of Regents in 1941 and became enraged when Dewey, then governor, sought in 1948 to limit the board's power. Macy was determined to eliminate the popular governor from the state scene by frustrating Dewey's renomination in 1950, reportedly by making Dewey the Republican candidate for U.S. Senator.

On the eve of the 1950 GOP state convention, Lieutenant Governor Joe R. Hanley, who had been expected to run for governor, wrote a letter to Macy stating that Dewey had promised to clear up Hanley's personal debts if Hanley ran for the Senate and allowed Dewey to seek reelection. The letter wound up in Democratic hands and its blunt language stunned even professional politicians. "Today I had a conference with the governor in which certain unalterable and unquestionably definite propositions were made to me," Hanley stated. "If I will consent to take the nomination for the United States Senate, I am definitely assured of being able to clean up my financial obligations. . . ."

Macy denied leaking the letter to the Democrats and later won a libel suit against the *New York World-Telegram and the Sun* for an article contending that he had threatened to make the "Hanley letter" public unless he got the Senate nomination himself. Macy unsuccessfully had sought such a nomination in 1940 and 1944.

However, the Democrats gave the letter wide circulation during the 1950 campaign, in which Dewey was reelected governor and Hanley was defeated for the U.S. Senate. But the biggest loser was Macy. Running for a third term in Congress to a seat he had won by an overwhelming margin in 1948 from a district that had a 7-1 Republican advantage, Macy lost by 138 votes out of 152,500 to a little-known former schoolteacher named Ernest Greenwood.

The extraordinary outcome was attributed to the "Hanley letter" and disclosures by *Newsday* of widespread gambling and other irregularities in Macy's Suffolk jurisdiction. Macy announced his retirement as Suffolk Republican chairman, then changed his mind, and was defeated 411 to 6 by County Clerk R. Ford Hughes at a county committee meeting. The unforgiving, one-time GOP power suffered his final humiliation in 1953, when a vindictive Dewey refused to reappoint him to the Board of Regents.

For *Newsday*, the end of "King" Macy's reign represented a major victory, the culmination of a lengthy and bitter campaign to oust a longtime political boss whose conservative policies frequently clashed with those of the young, progressive, and brash newspaper. It was a particularly sweet triumph for Alicia Patterson, *Newsday*'s first editor and publisher, who had been portrayed in Macy's weeklies as an evil witch named "Malicia" and had been called before a congressional committee at Macy's behest to answer unsubstantiated charges that *Newsday* had financed Greenwood's campaign.

Newsday's arrival was rather inconspicuous. Born in a converted Hempstead garage, its first issue of 32 pages was run off (on secondhand presses) on September 3, 1940, for a circulation of 15,000, who paid three cents to read it. The garage had housed the short-lived *Nassau Daily Journal*, which Harry F. Guggenheim, Miss Patterson's third husband and *Newsday*'s first president, had purchased for $50,000 because, as he told the former playgirl, "everybody ought to have a job; people who make a business out of pleasure seldom are happy."

The feisty tabloid's survival and unimagined success was a tribute not only to Miss Patterson's daring, imagination, and tenacity, but to her passion for newspapering, a drive unknown to most of her socialite friends who assumed that *Newsday* was simply a rich woman's toy. ("How nice of your husband to give you such a pleasant wedding present," one told her.) What they did not realize was that as the fifth generation of a newspaper-publishing family and daughter of the founder of the New York *Daily News*, she long had dreamed of running a paper and hoped it would be her father's. (The hope evaporated in 1945, when her father,

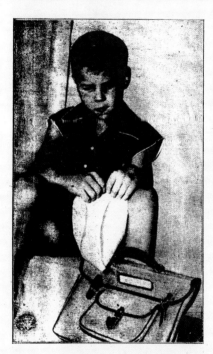

Joseph Medill Patterson, changed his will after a dispute over President Roosevelt whom she admired and he detested.)

Extraordinary events would shape the future of the newspaper, which, in turn, would have its own impact on the future of Long Island. Surviving World War II, with its paper, gasoline, and manpower shortages, was to prove even more crucial to *Newsday* than anyone might have imagined, for that positioned the newspaper to take advantage of the mass postwar movement of potential readers to the suburbs.

Although Miss Patterson's first editorial promised that "our first, second and final object is to present the news," in its early days the paper seemed poised on the brink of advocacy. If readers sometimes confused its news stories with its editorials, they never misunderstood its intent. Some of its early campaigns may have found unyielding authorities and even unsympathetic subscribers; but when young, uncertain, impatient veterans and their families later poured onto the Island, they appeared to sense an ally in this cocky, unconventional newcomer that seemed so eager to challenge virtually anything and anyone.

By starting a Suffolk edition in 1944, *Newsday* became the first Long Island newspaper to publish for both Suffolk and Nassau residents. This gave it a unique bicounty role that no governmental or public interest agency was filling; its concern transcended divisions and borders—it saw the two counties as a single Long Island.

When *Newsday*'s first issue rolled off the presses in 1940, Miss Patterson joined a small and hardly secure group of Long Island editors who could trace their heritage to David Frothingham, a young Massachusetts printer responsible for the Island's first journal, the *Long Island Herald*, whose initial issue was published in Sag Harbor on May 10, 1791. Although it printed little local news, the *Herald* was hardly reluctant to tackle controversy, and ran sharply worded editorials accusing President John Adams of operating the young democracy as if it were a monarchy. The paper also published some foreign and domestic news reprinted from other newspapers, as well as essays, poems, and local advertisements.

Frothingham closed the *Herald* on December 17, 1798, and, at the urging of Republican Aaron Burr, took over the New York City *Argus*. By switching papers, Frothingham achieved public notoriety, but journalistic fame, for his conviction under the newly enacted Sedition Act. The suit was brought by Federalist Alexander Hamilton over a letter published in the *Argus* in 1799 accusing him of having sought to suppress a Republican paper called *Aurora*. Frothingham was fined and imprisoned.

Sag Harbor was the scene of much of Long Island's early journalism. In 1804, Alden Spooner, a resident of Connecticut and descendant of *Mayflower* Pilgrim John Alden, began work at the *Suffolk Gazette* as its sole employee. "It will appear curious to any printer," he wrote, "to be told that I printed the *Suffolk Gazette* about two years, without the assistance of any person whatever—not even a boy! I was editor, printer, publisher, clerk and errand boy."

In 1811, Spooner bought a Brooklyn paper called the *Long Island Star*, which had been founded two years earlier. A weekly, like most of the early papers, it underwent a series of name changes and became a semi-weekly and a daily while remaining in the Spooner family until 1863, when it was discontinued. Among the *Star*'s employees was a teenager named Walt Whitman. He had been an apprentice in the composing room of another Brooklyn paper, the weekly *Long Island Patriot*,

One of Long Island's earliest newspaper publishers, Alden Spooner is shown in a portrait painted in 1832 or 1833 by Hubbard L. Fordham, about the time that Spooner hired young Walt Whitman as a printer's devil for his Long Island Star. *Spooner had bought the* Star, *which was published in Brooklyn, in 1811; it remained in the Spooner family until 1863.*

where he began working at the age of twelve. Spooner reportedly considered Whitman, who was obviously a late bloomer, as "an idle boy," and, according to one version, said that "if he had been stricken with fever and ague, the boy would have been too lazy to shake."

Despite such disparagement, Whitman, at nineteen, went on to found *The Long-Islander* in Huntington, which he left after about two years, although the paper still exists. Its first issue was noted by the *Enquirer*, a Hempstead weekly, which said that "from its columns we judge that its publisher (Mr. W. Whitman) has spared no pains to make it acceptable to the reading community."

In 1846, when he was twenty-six, Whitman became editor of the *Brooklyn Daily Eagle*, an influential daily established five years earlier. Under Whitman, the *Eagle* generally took a liberal line that reflected the Democratic-Republican philosophy, advocating humanitarian principles and civic improvement. As editor, Whitman covered news events, wrote editorials, and reviewed books, plays, operas, concerts, lectures, and art exhibits. The *Eagle* became a Brooklyn standby for another century, but Whitman was fired some two years later over his support of the Wilmot Proviso, which opposed the extension of slavery into any territories acquired through the Mexican War. After losing his job, the man who was to become one of America's greatest poets was hired as editor of the *Brooklyn Freeman*, a free-soil newspaper that he quit a year later when its editorial policy changed.

Although several daily newspapers, including Horace Greeley's *New York Tribune* and *The New York Times*, were in circulation before the Civil War, Long Island did not get its own daily until after World War I. Founded on March 7, 1921, in Rockville Centre by James E. Stiles, who had begun publishing weeklies in 1914, the *Nassau Review* began with 8 pages; by 1927, fed by the real estate boom, it became *The Nassau Daily Review*, with 24 pages and a circulation of more than 10,000.

The only local daily until *Newsday*'s arrival in 1940, Stiles' standard-size paper, by then the *Nassau Daily Review-Star*, found itself surpassed in circulation within two years by the upstart tabloid. Paralyzed by a lengthy strike in 1947, the beset *Review-Star* was bought by chain publisher S. I. Newhouse and merged in 1953 into his *Long Island Daily Press*, a Queens-based operation. In the 1960s, the now established tabloid overcame a brief challenge from *The Suffolk Sun*, a Cowles Communications paper put out in Deer Park for three years before it closed shop in 1969. Newhouse in 1977 folded the *Press*, leaving the Long Island newspaper field open to *Newsday*.

If Long Island has proved economically inhospitable to some newspapers, it has provided a healthy climate for much of the aircraft industry. When American involvement in World War II became increasingly likely, the nation began its military preparedness program. And it looked to the "Cradle of Aviation" for help.

The Grumman Aircraft Engineering Corporation helped the United States win the battle of the Pacific during World War II with record-breaking production of its carrier-based Wildcats, Hellcats, and Avengers. Pictured are fuselages of the F6F Hellcats on the Bethpage assembly line. Grumman turned out a total of 12,275 of the folded-wing Hellcats, including a record 605 during the month of March 1945.

By the end of the 1930s, there were about 5,000 people working in Long Island airplane plants, a figure that soared to almost 90,000 during the war. In 1939, about 700 employees of the Grumman Aircraft Engineering Corporation, formed in 1929 by Leroy Grumman and Leon (Jake) Swirbul, were turning out fighters and scout bombers for the Navy from the company's new plant in Bethpage; in nearby Farmingdale, at what had been the Seversky Aircraft Corporation, 1,500 employees of the recently formed Republic Aviation Corporation were making pursuit planes for the Swedish government and the U.S. Army.

After the Japanese bombed Pearl Harbor on December 7, 1941, these two manufacturers went into an all-out production schedule that, combined with the effectiveness of their planes, has been credited with changing the course of the air war over both the Pacific and Europe. For Grumman, the F4F Wildcat, its successor the F6F Hellcat, and the TBF-1 Avenger, with their folding wings, became not only the Navy's standard carrier-based fighters and torpedo bombers, but legends.

During the first five months of 1944, only 71 Hellcats were lost in destroying 444 Japanese planes in air combat and another 323 on the ground. A month later, during the battle of the Marianas, Hellcats shot down 346 enemy aircraft in one day—the war's greatest aerial victory—while losing only 30 of their own. And one Navy squadron reported that it had lost only one Avenger in sinking 14 enemy ships. It was such performance that endeared the company to American pilots and led Vice Admiral John S. McCain to tell a Washington labor conference that "the name 'Grumman' on a plane or part has the same meaning to the Navy that 'Sterling' on silver has to you."

What Grumman was doing to the Japanese in the Pacific, Republic was doing to the Nazis in Europe. Its P-47 Thunderbolt fighter-bomber knocked the Luftwaffe out of the sky at the rate of better than four-to-one. By war's end, Republic had grown to be the world's largest producer of fighter aircraft. More than 23,000 workers—60 percent of them women—had turned out over 9,000 Thunderbolts at the expanded Farmingdale complex, while another 6,000 were made at factories in Indiana. At Grumman, the record was even more astonishing. With 25,000 employees, the company put better than 17,000 planes into the hands of the Navy. To keep production at top speed, Grumman provided a nursery school, job counseling, and even a trucking service that repaired workers' cars and ran errands for them. By giving employees bonuses for keeping production costs down, the corporation pioneered a new type of incentive system that reduced the per-plane price of the Hellcat from $50,000 to $35,000 (a saving to the Navy in 1944 of more than $127 million).

Over Europe, P-47 Thunderbolts, made in Farmingdale by the Republic Aviation Corporation, took a heavy toll of Nazi aircraft and armored vehicles. These P-47N models, a long-range version, were flown principally in the Pacific. Republic was the world's largest producer of fighter planes.

There was also the Sperry Gyroscope Company, whose 32,000 workers made bombsights, automatic pilots, radar equipment, and other flight-related instruments at plants in Lake Success and Garden City. More than 4,000 employees worked for the Fairchild Camera and Instrument Corporation, and other thousands were hired by the Long Island aviation industry's largest subcontractor, the Liberty Aircraft Products Company in Farmingdale.

The overwhelming majority of Long Island war workers had never seen an assembly line. Many of the housewives never had a job before, but they poured into the factories, learned skills, and altered their lifestyles. Altered, too, was the landscape and character of Long Island. The war effort had changed forever its rural-residential ambience, splattering the flat fields with vast factories, exposing its recesses to commuting city dwellers, and creating a pent-up demand for its living space that would erupt in succeeding decades.

Long Island's location made it particularly sensitive to fears of bombing and submarine and naval attack; while there was a lot of excitement and some anxiety, no action was taken. Anti-aircraft batteries were set up in remote areas of Nassau's South Shore and Suffolk's East End, but never fired at an enemy. Civilians volunteered as aircraft spotters, learned how to distinguish between a German Messerschmitt and a British Spitfire, but did not see either. Still, the beaches bore grim reminders that the war was being fought only miles away. Gobs of oil, charred timbers, and bits of life jackets floated onto the sand from torpedoed ships. Coast Guardsmen patrolled the many miles of shoreline.

One of them was Seaman 2/c John C. Cullen. Shortly after midnight on June 12, 1942, he left the Amagansett Lifeboat Station in a thick fog to begin walking his three-mile post. Unarmed, in accordance with regulations, he had gone only a few hundred yards when he spotted three figures on the beach. The 21-year-old Coast Guardsman challenged them, and the men said that they had been fishing when their boat ran aground. Cullen told them that they would have to accompany him to the Coast

LEFT AND BELOW
*One of World War II's most
extraordinary episodes took place on
a beach near Amagansett, where four
Nazi saboteurs were put ashore by
submarine in 1942. Two Coast
Guardsmen and a U.S. Navy officer,
center, examine the place where
explosives were buried. Four other
agents were dropped off in Florida.
All but George Dasch* (SECOND FROM
BOTTOM) *and Ernst Peter Burger*
(BOTTOM) *were executed. Other eyes,
belong to Edward Kerling, Werner
Theil, Heinrich Harm Heinck, and
Richard Quirin.*

Guard station and file a report. At that point, a fourth man, dragging a large canvas sack, walked out of the surf.

Suspicious, Cullen turned to go but was stopped by one of the men who first threatened him and then, after a discussion in German with his companions, offered him a bribe. Cullen quickly took the money and ran back to his station to report the incident to skeptical officers. Within minutes, Coast Guardsmen were combing the beach and within hours, after first a pack of German cigarettes and then crates of explosives and German uniforms were unearthed, one of the most extensive spyhunts in American history was under way.

The four men were Nazi saboteurs who had been landed off the Amagansett beach by the U-202 in a fantastic and daring plot to destroy hydroelectric and aluminum plants, bridges and canal locks, railroad tracks and terminals, and New York City's reservoirs. Four other agents, assigned similar missions, were put ashore in Florida five days later.

The scheme had been worked out with a thoroughness worthy of Ian Fleming. "In the next six weeks," the eight were told during their first day of training, "you will become new men, with new identities, confirmed by birth certificates, draft cards and driver's licenses. When you destroy a machine or a factory or blow up a bridge, your work will not look like an accident. It will be sabotage and it will look like sabotage and the Americans will know that we are among them!" Carefully drilled, the eight English-speaking saboteurs were given $175,000 in American currency, clothes bearing American labels, explosives disguised as lumps of coal and blocks of wood, incendiary bombs enclosed in pen and pen-

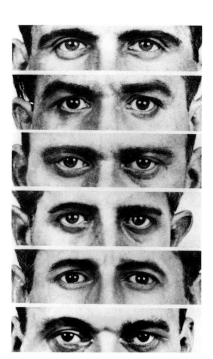

cil sets, and handkerchiefs with the names of contacts written in invisible ink.

By the time the Coast Guard, Army, Navy, and FBI figured out what was happening, the four agents who had come ashore on Long Island were in New York City hotel rooms, having taken the 6:51 A.M. Long Island Rail Road train from Amagansett to Pennsylvania Station. What might have happened if their leader, George Dasch, had not surrendered to the FBI in Washington a week later, is speculation. What did happen was that his seven accomplices were rounded up, tried, convicted, and, in the case of six, electrocuted. Dasch and Ernst Peter Burger, an SS lieutenant colonel, testified for the government, were sentenced to prison, and, in 1948, sent back to Germany. Cullen, a Long Islander, was awarded the Legion of Merit and a special citation from President Roosevelt.

While Operation Pastorius—as the Nazis named the plot in wry homage to Franz Pastorius, considered America's first German immigrant—was surely the most spectacular war story to be enacted on Long Island, the hundreds of thousands of men and women stationed in Nassau and Suffolk undoubtedly have their own recollections.

Long Island was filled with members of the armed forces. Camp Upton was reactivated, the Army Air Corps trained pilots and ferried planes to Europe from Mitchel Field and Westhampton, which had been converted from a commercial airport. Camp Hero at Montauk housed long-range artillery, the Montauk Manor had sailors from the torpedo-testing unit at Fort Pond Bay, and the United States Merchant Marine Academy at Kings Point trained officers for the maritime service.

When World War II ended in 1945, the Navy station at Lido Beach, which began turning sailors to civilians at the rate of 2,000 a day, symbolized Long Island's rush into peacetime. The pace was frantic; everyone was so anxious to resume their lives, to return to normalcy. What nobody realized was that within a decade Long Island would be changed more drastically than at any time in its history.

CHAPTER TEN

Taking Stock

T|he most terrible conflict in human history had ended and where there had been fear and suffering there now was hope. On Long Island, the biblical admonition to turn swords into plowshares was being followed with near-literal obedience. In Nassau at Lake Success, the temporary headquarters of the United Nations was being set up in a plant where the Sperry Gyroscope Company had made bombsights. In Suffolk at Yaphank, the Brookhaven National Laboratory, designed to develop the peaceful use of atomic energy, was rising at Camp Upton, where soldiers had been trained to kill in two world wars. And in cramped city apartments and crowded parents' houses, young veterans and their families wanted to pursue their hopes, too: a home of their own, a room for the kids, a yard for the dog, and a share of the American dream.

The war effort's demands for men and materials had all but stopped homebuilding. With the war's end, the demands came from the home-hungry. Listening intently was William J. Levitt, the 38-year-old president of Levitt & Sons, Inc., a firm with building experience and a bold idea. The experience had been gained in constructing a few prewar homes in Rockville Centre and the "Strathmore" developments on the North Shore. And the idea took shape in Norfolk, Virginia, along with thousands of rental units that the company built there for wartime shipyard workers. Together with his father, Abraham, an attorney, and brother, Alfred, an architect, Levitt had devised mass-production methods that enabled them to drastically reduce the time, and thus the cost, of home construction.

The Levitts pioneered the automobile assembly-line theory in the building industry, but instead of bringing car frames to teams of skilled specialists, they brought the teams of specialists to the homesites. More than 15,000 workmen would do the job: carpenters, masons, plumbers, electricians, painters, and landscape gardeners. Heavy machinery operators, using Levitt equipment, would dig trenches for foundations; Levitt cement mixers using Levitt cement would follow, pouring rows of concrete slab foundations. Precut piles of lumber would appear magically in front of each site at the appropriate time; so would squads of carpenters who specialized in framing, sheathing, roofing, and shingling. When it was perfected, the technique would complete thirty-five homes in a single day at prices $2,000 below those of competitors. But the Levitts needed special considerations: they did not provide basements;

More people meant more cars, and more cars meant more traffic. Twice a day, commuters who take the Long Island Expressway to New York increase their blood pressure at the Belt Parkway interchange in Douglaston.

223

they used unconventional "radiant" heating; they did not hire union labor; they demanded that appliance manufacturers sell directly to them; they did not permit customers a choice of colors; and the only non-Caucasians allowed to occupy Levitt homes had to be "domestic servants."

Not all of these conditions were known when *Newsday* headlined on May 7, 1947: 2,000 $60 RENTALS DUE IN L. I. PROJECT. The project, carrying a $16,000,000 price tag and financed by the Federal Housing Administration, was proposed for a 500-acre tract of flat, treeless potato fields south of Hempstead Turnpike in a sparsely settled area called, with little justification, Island Trees. The plan was greeted with near hysterical enthusiasm; within three weeks, Levitt received more than 6,000 written applications, and he promptly announced the purchase of enough property to accommodate another 2,000 units.

The only hitch was a Town of Hempstead building code provision that required basements. With *Newsday* unashamedly lobbying for elimination of the requirement, more than 800 veterans and their wives, many carrying babies, jammed the town hall and overflowed into the street when the board met for a hearing on the issue. It took only twenty minutes for the officials to repeal the provision unanimously. To have done otherwise would have courted disaster. Shouted one uniformed ex-GI: "Cellar or no cellar doesn't mean anything to me or anyone else here. We want the houses!" Roared another: "No cellar beats one room in an attic where you freeze to death for $45 a month!"

Construction began immediately on the four-room Cape Cod models with refrigerators, ranges, washing machines, and expandable attics. Four months later, the first 200 families moved in. Three months after that, Levitt gave the new community a new name: Levittown. That prompted the formation of Levittown's first civic organization, defiantly named the Island *Trees* Community Association. There were other complaints, too, especially when Levitt hiked the rent to $65 and upped the "absolute maximum" purchase price from $6,990 to $7,990. But people rented and bought.

Before he was finished, Levitt had built 17,447 homes, nine community swimming pools, a community hall, playgrounds, ballfields, village greens, and shopping centers. He planted more than 500,000 trees and set aside property for houses of worship—enough for a community of more than 83,000 people, which it became.

And Levittown became far more. It set the pattern for other developments on Long Island and for other Levittowns elsewhere: in Pennsylvania, New Jersey, Maryland, even Europe. It opened the door of affordable housing to war veterans and opened the floodgates to a mass exodus from the city. It was the symbol of postwar suburban growth and the stereotype of postwar suburban lifestyle.

In the Fifties, the growth seemed unending. Long Island's population, 604,103 in 1940, increased almost 60 percent by 1950, and then more

OPPOSITE

It did not take long for Levittown to grow. What the former potato fields of the section called Island Trees looked like after some of Levitt's 17,447 homes had been constructed is evident from the air.

BELOW

When people come, can shopping malls be far behind? Not in the Long Island of the Fifties, as this night scene at Roosevelt Field confirms. The Roosevelt Field mall was one of the nation's first attempts at one-stop shopping.

than doubled to nearly 2,000,000 by 1960. The influx was felt first in Nassau. Its population went up 65 percent in the Forties and 93 percent in the Fifties, before settling down, when space ran out, to a slim 10 percent in the Sixties. The rush to Suffolk came a bit later. Its population jumped 40 percent in the Forties, 142 percent in the Fifties, and 69 percent in the Sixties.

The pace was phenomenal. People needed goods and so the shops followed them out. But there was little space for stores in the established villages, little room for parking, and besides, most of the new people were living outside the old communities. So the new shops clustered themselves together near the new people, provided parking fields, and became shopping centers. The really big shopping centers enclosed themselves like cocoons and became shopping malls: Roosevelt Field, Smith Haven, Sunrise, and Walt Whitman.

More people meant more services: more schools, more roads, more trains, more sewage disposal, more hospitals, more electric power. Eventually, most of these needs would be met, but only after bitter controversy, extraordinary costs, and patent mismanagement. Poor planning, faulty construction, inefficient administration, or even tragedy or scandal became almost routinely associated with Suffolk's Southwest Sewer District, Nassau's County Medical Center, the Long Island Rail Road, and LILCO's Shoreham Nuclear Power Station.

Concern about elementary and secondary education had been a Long Island tradition since colonial and Revolutionary times, but it took centuries for higher education to become available. Not until 1912, when the Legislature established a New York State School of Agriculture at Farmingdale, did Long Island have its first public college. And students interested in careers other than farming had to wait until 1929, when Adelphi College, founded 33 years earlier as a women's institution in Brooklyn, moved to Garden City, where it became Long Island's first liberal arts school. During the depth of the Depression, in 1935, in neighboring Hempstead, the estate of a wealthy lumberman named William Hofstra was turned into a branch of New York University. Its name, Nassau College-Hofstra Memorial-New York University, hardly was the stuff from which fight songs are made. It did, though, separate from its parent institution two years later to become Hofstra College.

However, in the frantic Fifties, a desperate need arose for educational facilities at all levels. Between 1948 and 1954, elementary and high school enrollment on Long Island more than doubled, and by 1960 had doubled again. One of the most extraordinary examples, as might be expected, was Levittown. In 1947, the Jerusalem School District consisted of a 3-room schoolhouse and 47 pupils. Ten years later, its successor, School District 5, was educating 16,300 students in 14 buildings. Dramatizing the change is the Jonas F. Salk Junior High, a 40-room, $3,000,000 structure built opposite the original school on Jerusalem Road.

In higher education, the pattern was similar. Existing institutions expanded and new ones were born. Adelphi and Hofstra became universities, each annually educating more than 11,000 undergraduate and graduate students. Nassau's first college, the state agricultural school at Farmingdale, was absorbed into the state university system in 1948 and made a two-year agricultural and technical college.

But these developments did not begin to meet the area's burgeoning needs. And so new facilities arose, many on the luxurious estates that adorn Nassau's Gold Coast. Long Island University opened its C. W. Post Center on the Brookville property of cereal heiress Marjorie Merriweather Post in 1955 and its Southampton College campus in 1963; New York Institute of Technology welcomed students to its Old Westbury campus on the former C. V. Whitney estate in 1964, while on the nearby fields of F. Ambrose Clark, the State University of New York College at Old Westbury began its program three years later.

The largest and one of the Island's most prestigious centers of learning is another unit of the State University of New York, at Stony Brook. Originally located in Oyster Bay in 1957 as the State University College to prepare high school mathematics and science teachers, it became a University Center in 1960, and moved to its present 1,000-acre campus in 1962. During the next 20 years, its faculty grew from 175 to 1,000 and its student body from 1,000 to 16,000. Its Health Sciences Center, which became Long Island's tallest building in 1976, includes the 540-bed University Hospital and School of Dental Medicine.

The demand for local, low-cost education led to the creation of two-year community institutions in both counties. Nassau Community College opened in 1960 in the county courthouse complex as part of the state university system and is now located at what was Mitchel Air Force Base. Suffolk Community College, also started in 1960, has campuses in Selden, Brentwood, and Riverhead.

Self-education on Long Island owes it origins to East Hampton's Reverend Samuel Buell, who, as early as 1753, organized the Philogrammatican Library. Six years later, Huntington followed, as the Reverend Ebenezer Prime became custodian of a library society there. While many communities in both counties established public libraries before World War II, the population explosion of the 1950s triggered a corresponding demand for facilities, particularly in areas of recent growth. This was met in the two counties through the formation of the Nassau Library System and the Suffolk Cooperative Library System, which provide consulting, processing, purchasing, and distribution services, and expedite the transfer of books from the shelves in one community to the readers in another. They also have benefited the public by helping various libraries to build collections in particular fields, and then make them available to all.

The rush to the suburbs probably had its most traumatizing effect on motorists, who found they could not rush anyplace. While the Fifties and Sixties may have been the "go-go" decades in the financial world, that was not the name Long Island drivers had for them. Existing roads simply were incapable of handling the tremendous upsurge in vehicles, and new highways, notably the Long Island Expressway, merely lured more commuters into the daily bumper-to-bumper grind.

It is perhaps on the LIE during the morning and evening rush hours that suburbanites are most likely to wonder how worthwhile the move from Brooklyn and Queens really was. Then, and when they contemplate their tax bills, according to an extensive study of suburban attitudes published by *Newsday* in 1973, are Long Islanders most distressed with their lot. The survey found that the cost of keeping up a home and the amount of time involved in getting to work were the major dissatisfactions with suburban living. Such concrete concerns, Long Islanders indicated, were far more distressing to them than some of the frequently voiced complaints of social critics, such as the monotony of suburban pace, the sameness of suburban residents, and the lack of cultural stimulation on the suburban scene. Residents told interviewers that far from being bored with suburban life, they liked very much what they had found.

In addition to describing themselves as "very happy" or "happy"—not an uncommon occurrence except, perhaps, when the respondents are prison inmates—more than 90 percent of the Long Islanders said that they would recommend their communities to friends as a place in which to live. "It really bothers me," a Yaphank housewife said, "the way they call it 'suburbia' and make it sound so dreary. We think it's just fine."

The suburbanites also encountered little difficulty in making friends or in coping with the relative isolation of their new environment. Substantial majorities disagreed with the statement that "I don't have as many friends here as I would like," said that their neighbors were very friendly, and, reinforcing that contention, reported visiting often with friends.

One mother in her late thirties remembered being quite concerned about moving to Dix Hills from her Queens apartment. "In the city neighborhood where I came from, everyone was very friendly," she recalled. "And I was very apprehensive, thinking it would be very lonely out here and that I would be stuck in the house all day with nothing to do. But when we settled in and I looked around, I found that many of the other women also came from a city environment and were just as anxious to make new friends. One thing I found was that in the city you never asked someone to go to the store with you or pick something up, since it was very convenient to go by yourself. But now that you need a car to get to the store, neighbors will tell you when they're going—to see if you want a lift or if there's anything they can get for you. That kind of cooperation makes for a very friendly atmosphere."

The contention that culturally the suburban landscape bears a striking resemblance to a desert received little support from the Long Islanders interviewed in the *Newsday* study. Almost two-thirds said that they were satisfied with the availability on Long Island of plays, concerts, and lectures, although a similar proportion expressed dissatisfaction with the quantity of museums and art galleries. The significance of these responses is somewhat suspect, however, since it was found that the more interest a respondent had in the arts, the more likely the respondent was to feel that facilities were inadequate on Long Island. Further, there was a question of awareness. One person, after admitting never having visited a museum or art gallery anywhere, assumed that since there were plenty of shopping malls on Long Island, enough galleries must have been provided, too.

The overall contentment with suburban life found by the survey was augmented by an absence of interest in the urban milieu. The Long Islanders told interviewers that they rarely went to New York City to shop, for entertainment and cultural events, or for any other reason. Only about 10 percent said that they visited at least once a month.

Such findings led to the conclusion that Nassau and Suffolk were emerging as a distinct suburban society with its own attitudes and values, one that no longer looked to New York for its needs and fulfillments. It also led to speculation that certain city dwellers had a clear propensity —socially, culturally, politically—for suburban living and that they eventually moved to the suburbs, leaving behind those with a more urban orientation.

If this speculation were valid, it would account for the political conversion that people seemed to undergo when they moved from primarily Democratic New York City to primarily Republican Long Island. Many explanations have been given for what appeared to be a switch in party affiliation. Some observers attributed it to the desire to conform, some to the change that came with acquiring property, and others to the persuasive powers of the Republican organizations in the two counties. The study found simply that New Yorkers who moved to Long Island were more likely to be Republicans than New Yorkers who remained.

While this finding may not have touched off any celebrations at Nassau or Suffolk Democratic headquarters, it did not keep voters in either county from crossing party lines to elect Democrats to top posts. In 1958, Suffolk voters approved a charter providing for a county executive similar to the arrangement that had governed Nassau since 1938. And in 1959, Suffolk elected as its first county executive a Democrat who had never held political office, H. Lee Dennison, and elected a predominantly Democratic Board of Supervisors as well. Dennison won by only 559 votes that time, but he was twice reelected to four-year terms by substantially larger margins. There was little doubt that his success was based on personal popularity: Democrats lost control of the 10-member board, and were in the minority on the 18-member county legislature that replaced it in 1970.

In 1961, Nassau elected its first Democratic county executive, Eugene H. Nickerson, who went on to win reelection twice, in 1964 and again in 1967. Under the direction of county chairman John F. English and under the spell of the Kennedy and Johnson administrations in Washington, the Nassau Democratic Party pulled one political upset after another and seemed to have the once omnipotent Republican machine in disarray. Misjudgment, internal power struggles, and evidence of corruption and conflicts of interest plagued the GOP in both counties during the chaotic postwar decades. It would take years of grassroots effort, particularly by Nassau Republican leader Joseph M. Margiotta, before the party would reestablish the dominance in local politics that had characterized it

The need for housing, shopping, sewage disposal, and other services to meet demands of the postwar population explosion created temptations that some public officials could not resist. In 1970, Newsday won its second Pulitzer Prize for meritorious public service in exposing widespread corruption among public officials in Suffolk.

OPPOSITE

The Islanders (in white uniforms), shown here (ABOVE) in action against the Detroit Red Wings at the Nassau Veterans Memorial Coliseum in 1980, became the toast of the National Hockey League after winning the Stanley Cup that year. Dennis Potvin and Clark Gillies (BELOW) hoist the symbol of supremacy after the playoffs, a scene that was repeated in 1981, 1982, and 1983.

In the Sixties, Seventies, and Eighties, Long Islanders excelled in a variety of professional sports. In basketball, Julius (Dr. J.) Erving, who grew up in Roosevelt and went on to star with the Nets before they left Long Island, soars up for a basket against Denver at the Nassau Coliseum in 1975 (ABOVE). In football, Jim Brown of the Cleveland Browns dominated the National Football League after starring at Syracuse University and, before that, at Manhasset High School, where he is shown at practice in 1951 (RIGHT). In boxing, Gerry Cooney of Huntington was a leading heavyweight contender after his first round knockout of Ken Norton (BELOW) at Madison Square Garden in 1981.

limit to what can be done without jeopardy to the land and the sea and the air.

There still are places on Long Island that have been unchanged through time, that retain their pristine quality. Steven Englebright, director of the Museum of Long Island Natural Sciences at the State University at Stony Brook, points out that beneath the seemingly useless pine barrens in central Suffolk, rain still enters the ground without running across a parking lot, without first being filtered through our cultural activities. He warns that if we want to continue our current lifestyle on this finite island, we must assure our water supply by saving our woodlands.

Once a region of surpassing natural loveliness and ecological harmony, Long Island has been victimized by exploitation and betrayed by indifference. Each generation of Long Islanders bears, along with the power for destruction, the responsibility for protection. Those parts of our Island that remain unspoiled are not only our most vital resource, they are our most precious heritage. But, as history constantly reminds us, a glorious past is no guarantor of a viable future.

Long Island can still boast sparkling waters and verdant hills, summer beaches of shell-sprinkled sand and winter ponds frozen over with glittering coats of blue-white ice. There still are spring meadows redolent with the scent of sweet grasses, and fiery autumn leaves that cling to wind-whipped trees. It is still a place of beauty and promise, worth preserving. And it is ours.

Long Islanders are facing some difficult decisions that may well determine the direction of Nassau and Suffolk. One involves Shoreham, an old place that has been given new meaning as the site of the Long Island Lighting Company's controversial Nuclear Power Station. Another involves unchecked development, which threatens the ecological future of the Island and could end forever scenes such as this in Mt. Sinai.

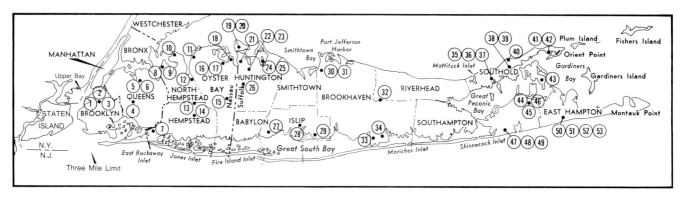

1 Brooklyn Museum	18 Sagamore Hill (Oyster Bay)	34 William Floyd Estate (Mastic Beach)
2 Brooklyn Children's Museum	19 Joseph Lloyd Manor House	35 Old House (Cutchogue)
3 Lefferts Homestead (Brooklyn)	(Lloyd Neck)	36 Wickham House (Cutchogue)
4 King Manor House (Jamaica)	20 Caumsett State Park (Lloyd Neck)	37 Schoolhouse (Cutchogue)
5 Bowne House (Flushing)	21 Whaling Museum	38 Southold Historical Society Museum
6 Quaker Meeting House (Flushing)	(Cold Spring Harbor)	39 Southold Cemetery
7 Rock Hall (Lawrence)	22 Heckscher Museum (Huntington)	40 Horton's Point Lighthouse (Southold)
8 U.S. Merchant Marine Academy	23 The Arsenal (Huntington)	41 Oysterponds Historical Society
(Kings Point)	24 Vanderbilt Planetarium (Centerport)	(Orient)
9 American Merchant Marine Museum	25 Vanderbilt Museum (Centerport)	42 Webb House (Orient)
(Kings Point)	26 Walt Whitman House	43 Mashomack Preserve (Shelter Island)
10 Sands Point Preserve	(Huntington Station)	44 Custom House (Sag Harbor)
11 Garvies Point Museum (Glen Cove)	27 Sagtikos Manor (West Bay Shore)	45 Whaling Museum (Sag Harbor)
12 Old Westbury Gardens	28 Bayard Cutting Arboretum (Oakdale)	46 Whaler's Church (Sag Harbor)
(Old Westbury)	29 Suffolk Marine Museum	47 Southampton Historical Museum
13 Cradle of Aviation Museum	(West Sayville)	48 Old Halsey Homestead
(Garden City)	30 Museums at Stony Brook	(Southampton)
14 Black History Museum (Hempstead)	31 Museum of Long Island Natural	49 Parrish Art Museum (Southampton)
15 Old Bethpage Village	Sciences (Stony Brook)	50 Home Sweet Home (East Hampton)
16 Planting Fields Arboretum	32 Brookhaven National Laboratory	51 Mulford House (East Hampton)
(Oyster Bay)	(Yaphank)	52 Clinton Academy (East Hampton)
17 Raynham Hall (Oyster Bay)	33 Manor of St. George (Mastic Beach)	53 Hook Mill (East Hampton)

Long Island is the largest island in the contiguous 48 states, comprising 1,723 square miles (4,463 sq. km.). It is 118 miles (190 km.) long, from 12 to 20 miles (19 to 32 km.) wide, and is separated from the mainland by the Narrows, the East River, and Long Island Sound, while bounded on the south by the Atlantic Ocean. Long Island is divided into 4 counties: Kings (also the borough of Brooklyn) and Queens, both of which became part of New York City in 1898, and Nassau and Suffolk. The total population, according to the 1980 census, was 6,728,074, which would make Long Island the tenth most populous state. Kings had the most people, 2,230,936, while Queens had 1,891,325, Nassau had 1,321,582, and Suffolk had the fewest, 1,284,231. Together, Nassau and Suffolk's population totalled 2,605,813 in 1980, more than that of 19 states. Nassau is divided into 2 cities, Glen Cove and Long Beach, and 3 townships, Hempstead, North Hempstead, and Oyster Bay. Suffolk is divided into 10 townships, Huntington, Babylon, Smithtown, Brookhaven, Islip, Riverhead, Southold, Southampton, East Hampton, and Shelter Island.

Some Places to Visit

BROOKLYN

Because many museums and historical sites operate on seasonal or special schedules, prospective visitors should telephone in advance.

BROOKLYN MUSEUM, at 188 Eastern Parkway (Washington Avenue and Grand Army Plaza), is one of New York's major cultural and historical institutions, containing extensive collections and exhibits. The interior of an early Dutch farmhouse—the Jan Martense Schenck house (c. 1675)—is furnished with Dutch period items; there are furnished rooms from the colonial to modern periods; and archaeological and ethnographic material relating to the various peoples of the world.
    HOW TO GET THERE: From the Long Island Expressway, take the Brooklyn-Queens Expressway (Interstate 278) south to Flatbush Avenue to Brooklyn Museum.
    FOR FURTHER INFORMATION: 212/638-5000.

BROOKLYN CHILDREN'S MUSEUM, at 145 Brooklyn Avenue (at St. Mark's Avenue), was founded in 1899 as the world's first museum for children. It contains "hands on" technological devices, as well as a wide range of scientific, cultural, and historical exhibits, including a windmill, greenhouse, steam engine, and plant and animal habitats.
    HOW TO GET THERE: From the Long Island Expressway, take the Brooklyn-Queens Expressway (Interstate 278) south to Atlantic Avenue, take Atlantic Avenue east to Brooklyn Avenue, take Brooklyn Avenue south four blocks to St. Mark's Avenue and museum.
    FOR FURTHER INFORMATION: 212/735-4432.

LEFFERTS HOMESTEAD, at Prospect Park, a restored early Dutch colonial dwelling containing period furnishings, was partially burned during the Battle of Long Island in 1776, rebuilt, and moved to its present site.
    HOW TO GET THERE: See Brooklyn Museum.
    FOR FURTHER INFORMATION: 212/965-6560.

CENTERPORT

VANDERBILT PLANETARIUM, at 180 Little Neck Road, features changing astronomy programs dealing with such phenomena as the beginning and end of the earth and using an advanced projector in the Sky Theater. There are special shows for children of different ages.

VANDERBILT MUSEUM, the Spanish Revival-style summer mansion of William K. Vanderbilt II, contains ornate rooms and scientific exhibits. Nearby is the Hall of Fishes that houses a collection of 17,000 marine specimens brought by Vanderbilt from around the world.
    HOW TO GET THERE: From the Long Island Expressway, take Route 110 (Exit 49N) north to Route 25A, then west on Route 25A to Little Neck Road in Centerport, then north on Little Neck Road to Vanderbilt Planetarium and Museum.
    FOR FURTHER INFORMATION: Planetarium: 516/757-7500; Museum, 516/261-5656.

COLD SPRING HARBOR

COLD SPRING HARBOR WHALING MUSEUM, on Main Street (Route 25A) opposite Turkey Lane, is located in this picturesque village of art galleries, boutiques, and real estate agencies. It contains four rooms of such whaling memorabilia as a whaleboat, harpoons, scrimshaw, and a diorama of this important whaling port in its 1850 heyday.
    HOW TO GET THERE: From the Long Island Expressway, take Route 110 (Exit 49N) north to Route 25A, then west to the museum. There is a public parking lot a short distance west of the museum on the south side of Route 25A.
    FOR FURTHER INFORMATION: 516/367-3418.

CUTCHOGUE

OLD HOUSE, off Main Street, as its name suggests is old, really old. Built in 1649 in Southold by John Budd, it was moved to Cutchogue in 1660, and is thought to be one of the oldest houses still standing in New York State. It is furnished with seventeenth-century items.

VILLAGE GREEN COMPLEX nearby includes the 1740 Wickham house, one of the oldest remaining North Fork farmhouses, and the 1840 Schoolhouse. Both are furnished appropriate to their period.
    HOW TO GET THERE: Take the Long Island Expressway to its eastern end, then Route 58 east to

Route 25, and continue east on Route 25 into the village, where it becomes Main Street. Turn south on Case Lane to the sites.

FOR FURTHER INFORMATION: 516/734-6532.

EAST HAMPTON

"HOME SWEET HOME," at 14 James Lane, is the seventeenth-century saltbox home of John Howard Payne, actor, playwright, and composer of the song "Home Sweet Home." It is decorated with furniture from various periods and includes an extensive collection of lusterware.

MULFORD HOUSE, next door at 12 James Lane, was built in the late seventeenth century and is one of the oldest homes on Long Island. It carries the name of the family that occupied it for more than 200 years, rather than Captain Josiah Hobart's, who constructed it.

CLINTON ACADEMY, across the village green on Main Street, is the state's oldest secondary school, having been opened in 1784. No longer operational, it was regarded as an early preparatory school for Yale University.

HOOK MILL, at the north end of Main Street, was built in 1806 and restored in 1939. Its interior reveals a fascinating complex of windmill machinery.

HOW TO GET THERE: From the Long Island Expressway, take County Road 111 (Exit 70) south to its end, then Route 27 east to East Hampton Village, where it becomes Main Street.

FOR FURTHER INFORMATION: 516/324-0713; 516/324-6850.

FLUSHING

QUAKER MEETING HOUSE, at 137–16 Northern Boulevard (near Main Street), built in 1694, is the oldest meeting house on Long Island and the oldest in the nation to be in regular use. During the Revolutionary War, the British used it as a hospital, barracks, and storehouse. There is a Friends' cemetery in the backyard.

HOW TO GET THERE: From the Long Island Expressway, take Main Street (Exit 23) north to Northern Boulevard (Route 25A), then east on Northern Boulevard (Route 25A) a short distance to the site.

FOR FURTHER INFORMATION: 212/358-9636.

BOWNE HOUSE, at 37–01 Bowne Street, was built in 1661 by John Bowne, a Quaker who resisted Dutch Governor Peter Stuyvesant's demands to recant his faith and thus became a symbol of the struggle for religious freedom. The house, which contains original Bowne furnishings, was the site of preaching by George Fox, the founder of Quakerism, and the scene of early Friends' meetings.

HOW TO GET THERE: From the Long Island Expressway, take Main Street (Exit 23) north to Northern Boulevard (Route 25A), then east on Northern Boulevard (25A) two blocks to Bowne Street.

FOR FURTHER INFORMATION: 212/359-0528.

GARDEN CITY

CRADLE OF AVIATION MUSEUM is located in hangars at the former Mitchel Air Force Base in the heart of the Hempstead Plains where aviation really took off in the early twentieth century. The museum is a rich repository of planes and memorabilia from the first days of flight to the space age. It also contains a comprehensive aviation reference library.

HOW TO GET THERE: From the Long Island Expressway, take Glen Cove Road (Exit 39S) south to Stewart Avenue, then east on Stewart Avenue to Nassau Community College entrance, then through college to museum.

FOR FURTHER INFORMATION: 516/222-1191

GLEN COVE

GARVIES POINT MUSEUM, at Barry Drive, is part of a 68-acre preserve overlooking Hempstead Harbor. Devoted to geology and prehistoric archaeology, it provides the most sophisticated displays of these subjects on Long Island. There are dioramas, changing exhibits, films, and educational programs dealing with Long Island life before the arrival of European settlers.

HOW TO GET THERE: From the Long Island Expressway, take Route 107 (Exit 41N) or Glen Cove Road (Exit 39N) north to Main Street, Glen Cove, and follow signs to the museum.

FOR FURTHER INFORMATION: 516/671-0300.

HEMPSTEAD

BLACK HISTORY MUSEUM, at 106A North Main Street in the Hempstead Bus Terminal, depicts the black experience on Long Island from slavery to the present. Changing exhibits portray various aspects of Afro-American history, including contributions of blacks to the nation's culture, illustrated with films, photographs, and artifacts.

HOW TO GET THERE: From the Long Island Expressway, take Glen Cove Road (Exit 39S) south and continue as it becomes Clinton Street to Jackson Street in the village of Hempstead, then west on Jackson Street to North Main Street.

FOR FURTHER INFORMATION: 516/538-2274.

ST. GEORGE'S EPISCOPAL CHURCH occupies a site on the corner of Front and Main Streets where people have worshipped since 1648. Anglican services were first held at that location in 1702, an Anglican church was constructed there in 1735, and the present structure was built in 1822. It contains the silver chalice, paten, and prayer book sent by England's Queen Anne in 1706, and the royal charter granted in 1735 by King George II, which still governs the church. A golden rooster weathervane with 16 Revolutionary War bullet scars decorates the steeple.

HOW TO GET THERE: From the Long Island Expressway, take Glen Cove Road (Exit 39S) south and continue as it becomes Clinton Street to Front Street in the village of Hempstead, then west on Front Street two blocks to the Main Street intersection.

FOR FURTHER INFORMATION: 516/483-2771.

HUNTINGTON

HECKSCHER MUSEUM, on Prime Avenue, was built in 1920 in neoclassical style by August Heckscher to house his extensive collection of paintings that spans the fifteenth to twentieth centuries. This art museum contains works by European masters, English portraitists, French landscapists, and Americans of the Hudson River School through the contemporary period. It also features changing exhibits relevant to Long Island.

HOW TO GET THERE: From the Long Island Expressway, take Route 110 (Exit 49N) north to Route 25A (Main Street, Huntington), then east to Prime Avenue, and north on Prime Avenue to the museum.

FOR FURTHER INFORMATION: 516/351-3250.

THE ARSENAL, a red, wooden structure located on the west side of Park Avenue just south of Route 25A, has been restored to its colonial origins. Built in 1740, Long Island's only remaining arsenal was used by the Huntington Militia to store arms and gunpowder until 1776, when it fell to the British.

HOW TO GET THERE: From the Long Island Expressway, take Deer Park Avenue (Exit 51) north, then continue north as Deer Park Avenue (Route 231) becomes Park Avenue (County Road 35).

FOR FURTHER INFORMATION: 516/351-3244.

THE HUNTINGTON HISTORICAL SOCIETY offers central Long Island-oriented collections of furniture, textiles, paintings, prints, costumes, vehicles, pottery, and tools dating from colonial times to the mid-nineteenth century at the Powell-Jarvis House, 434 Park Avenue, built in 1795, and the David Conklin Farmhouse, 2 High Street, built about 1750, as well as changing exhibits and a 4,000-volume research library at The Trade School, 209 Main Street, built in 1905.

HOW TO GET THERE: From the Long Island Expressway, to reach the Powell-Jarvis House, take Deer Park Avenue (Exit 51) north, then continue north as Deer Park Avenue (Route 231) becomes Park Avenue (County Road 35). To reach The Trade School from there, continue north on Park Avenue to Route 25A (Main Street), then west a short distance. To reach the David Conklin Farmhouse from there, continue west on Main Street to Route 110 (New York Avenue), then south a few blocks to High Street.

FOR FURTHER INFORMATION: 516/427-7045.

HUNTINGTON STATION

WALT WHITMAN HOUSE, at 246 Walt Whitman Road, is the birthplace of America's great poet, which has been preserved and furnished with nineteenth-century beds, tables, and chairs, although not the originals. Built about 1810 by Whitman's father, a carpenter, the small, brown-shingled farmhouse was occupied by the family until 1823, when the future journalist and poet was four years old. The second floor contains an exhibit of Whitman material: photographs, excerpts from his writings, and letters.

HOW TO GET THERE: From the Long Island Expressway, take Route 110 (Exit 49N) north to Schwab Road, then west to the old Walt Whitman Road. The house is a short walk from the Walt Whitman Mall.

FOR FURTHER INFORMATION: 516/427-5240.

JAMAICA

KING MANOR HOUSE, or Rufus King House, located in Kings Park on Jamaica Avenue between 150th and 153rd Streets, is a colonial farmhouse built originally in 1730 that has served as an inn and a church rectory. It was purchased in 1805 by King, who remodeled the structure and added a section. An important Revolutionary-era figure and early opponent of slavery, King was a member of the Continental Congress and Constitutional Convention, served in Congress, was an unsuccessful presidential candidate against James Monroe, and ended his career as ambassador to Great Britain. The house is decorated with period furniture.

HOW TO GET THERE: From the Long Island Expressway, take the 164th Street exit, then south on 164th and 163rd Streets to Jamaica Avenue, then west on Jamaica Avenue to the site.

FOR FURTHER INFORMATION: 212/523-1653.

U.S. MERCHANT MARINE ACADEMY, on Steamboat Road, includes the former estate of Walter P. Chrysler and is open to visitors who may wish to attend the impressive regimental reviews.

HOW TO GET THERE: From the Long Island Expressway, take Lakeville Road (Exit 33) north and continue through Great Neck as it becomes Middle Neck Road, then west onto Steamboat Road to the academy's entrance.

FOR FURTHER INFORMATION: 516/482-8200.

AMERICAN MERCHANT MARINE MUSEUM, on the academy grounds, presents a history of the merchant marine from the age of steam propulsion to the present, with ship models, marine paintings, and a maritime hall of fame.

HOW TO GET THERE: See U.S. Merchant Marine Academy.

FOR FURTHER INFORMATION: 516/466-9696.

KINGS POINT

ROCK HALL, at 199 Broadway, was built in 1767 by Josiah Martin, a wealthy West Indian planter, and served as the Hewlett family homestead for 124 years. An impressive example of Georgian architecture, it features hand-planed walls, Chippendale furniture, antique toys, and period furnishings.

HOW TO GET THERE: From the Long Island Expressway, take Cross Island Parkway south onto Southern Parkway and continue west to Springfield Boulevard, then south on Springfield Boulevard to Rockaway Boulevard, then Rockaway Boulevard south to Broadway, then west on Broadway to site.

FOR FURTHER INFORMATION: 516/239-1157.

LAWRENCE

CAUMSETT STATE PARK, on Lloyd Harbor Road, is the 1,500-acre site of the former Marshall Field III estate, with its fifty-room, brick, Georgian manor house, stables, and barn. Although the buildings are closed to the public, the property, overlooking Long Island Sound, not only is beautiful but contains unspoiled examples of Long Island landscape features, such as cliffs, meadows, and woodlands; trails lead to a primeval-looking beach and sand spit.

HOW TO GET THERE: From the Long Island Expressway, take Route 110 [Exit 49N] north to Route 25A, then west on 25A three blocks to West Neck Road, and north on West Neck Road to Lloyd Harbor Road and the park.

FOR FURTHER INFORMATION: 516/423-1770.

JOSEPH LLOYD MANOR HOUSE, on Lloyd Harbor Road, was completed in 1767 in the pre-Revolutionary high style. It has been restored and furnished by the Society for the Preservation of Long Island Antiquities.

FOR FURTHER INFORMATION: 516/941-9444.

HOW TO GET THERE: See above.

LLOYD NECK

MANOR OF ST. GEORGE, on Neighborhood Road, was the site of Fort St. George, a major British military installation on Long Island's South Shore during the Revolutionary War. The fort was attacked and burned by Patriot troops in 1780 under Major Benjamin Tallmadge. The ancestral home of Colonel William (Tangier) Smith, later first chief justice of New York, contains the original 1693 charter from King William III and Queen Mary II, family papers from 1641, and Indian deeds and artifacts. There also is a family cemetery. The manor serves as the headquarters of the Queens Rangers, a reconstituted Revolutionary War military unit.

HOW TO GET THERE: From the Long Island Expressway, take William Floyd Parkway (Exit 68) south to Neighborhood Road.

FOR FURTHER INFORMATION: 516/475-0327.

WILLIAM FLOYD ESTATE, on Washington Avenue, is located on 613 acres and includes a 25-room house which was built in 1724 and has evolved with the Floyd family to include many architectural alterations and additions. It is the birthplace of William Floyd, who was commis-

MASTIC BEACH

sioned a general at the end of the Revolution but is notable principally as one of the two Long Islanders to sign the Declaration of Independence. The furnishings reflect the 250-year history of the Floyds. There are eleven barns and a family cemetery.

HOW TO GET THERE: From the Long Island Expressway, take William Floyd Parkway (Exit 68) south to Neighborhood Road, then east to Mastic Road, north to Washington Avenue, and east on Washington Avenue for about one mile.

FOR FURTHER INFORMATION: 516/399-2030.

OAKDALE

BAYARD CUTTING ARBORETUM, on Montauk Highway, a 643-acre preserve begun by William Bayard Cutting in 1887 and turned over to the Long Island State Park Commission by his family, includes nature walks, flower displays, and the Tudor-style residence which houses a small museum and is representative of the great estates that preceded the Gold Coast mansions. The museum contains a display of stuffed birds and an exhibit of Indian archaeological artifacts.

HOW TO GET THERE: From the Long Island Expressway, take Ocean Avenue (Exit 59) south to Sunrise Highway (Route 27), then Sunrise Highway (Route 27) west to Montauk Highway (Route 27A) to entrance. Motorists coming from the west can use the Heckscher Spur of the Southern State Parkway and get out at Exit 45E.

FOR FURTHER INFORMATION: 516/581-1002.

OLD BETHPAGE

OLD BETHPAGE VILLAGE RESTORATION, on Round Swamp Road, is Long Island's most ambitious historical project. Composed of some two dozen antebellum structures moved to the site from their original locations, it represents a typical Island community of the mid-nineteenth century. There is the Manetto Hills Methodist Church (1853), the John M. Layton general store and home (1865), and the Powell Farm with its barn, carriage house, icehouse, smokehouse, other outbuildings, and barnyard animals. Appropriately costumed citizens, including a blacksmith, are on hand to lend authenticity and demonstrate skills.

HOW TO GET THERE: From the Long Island Expressway, take Round Swamp Road (Exit 48) south.

FOR FURTHER INFORMATION: 516/420-5280.

OLD WESTBURY

OLD WESTBURY GARDENS, on Old Westbury Road, the 70-acre former estate of John S. Phipps, is an outstanding example of Georgian architecture and formal English gardens. The mansion features eighteenth-century furniture by Chippendale, and paintings by Constable, Reynolds, Gainsborough, and Sargent. There are five gardens, each exemplified by a different type of shrubbery. The estate was once maintained by more than 300 people.

HOW TO GET THERE: From the Long Island Expressway, take Glen Cove Road (Exit 39S) south to I. U. Willets Road, then east on I. U. Willets Road to its end at Old Westbury Road, then north on Old Westbury Road a short distance to the entrance.

FOR FURTHER INFORMATION: 516/333-0048.

ORIENT

OYSTERPONDS HISTORICAL SOCIETY, on Village Lane, is housed in a post-Revolutionary period tavern and the former residence of Augustus Griffin, Orient historian. It contains local artifacts and furnishings of the colonial and Victorian periods, a natural history room, and a room of North Fork Indian materials. The grounds include two one-room schoolhouses, the dormitory and cookhouse of the "scientific" Hallock Farm, Civil War memorabilia, maritime and fire-fighting equipment, a carriage and sleigh collection, and a penny-candy store.

WEBB HOUSE, nearby, an eighteenth-century inn that once accommodated George Washington, was moved from Stirling, north of Greenport, and is handsomely furnished with period art and furniture. Behind the house is a nineteenth-century carpentry shop.

HOW TO GET THERE: Take the Long Island Expressway to its eastern end, then Route 58 east to Route 25, continue into the village of Orient and turn south at the monument at Village Lane.

FOR FURTHER INFORMATION: 516/323-2480.

OYSTER BAY

PLANTING FIELDS ARBORETUM, on Planting Fields Road, is located on the 400-acre former estate of William Robertson Coe and includes 150 acres of landscaped plantings that make the property a horticultural showplace. Particularly noteworthy are the rhododendrons and azaleas, greenhouses with exotic plants and flowers, and a five-acre synoptic garden of indigenous plants. Visitors may take self-guided tours along nature trails and go to the Bea Jones Memorial Contemporary Garden.

HOW TO GET THERE: From the Long Island Expressway, take Cedar Swamp Road/Route 107 (Exit 41N) north to Chicken Valley Road, then Chicken Valley Road to Planting Fields Road, then Planting Fields Road to entrance.

FOR FURTHER INFORMATION: 516/922-9200.

RAYNHAM HALL, at 20 West Main Street, was built in 1738 and served as the homestead of Samuel Townsend and his son, Robert, a leading Quaker and a key member of General George Washington's spy ring (Code Name: Culper Junior) during the Revolutionary War, when it served as a British headquarters. Furnished with eighteenth-century and Victorian pieces; a wing was added in the mid-nineteenth century.

HOW TO GET THERE: From the Long Island Expressway, take Jericho-Oyster Bay Road/Route 106 (Exit 41N) north to Oyster Bay village, then west on West Main Street.

FOR FURTHER INFORMATION: 516/922-6808.

SAGAMORE HILL, on Cove Neck Road, is the famous 23-room Victorian home of Theodore Roosevelt that served as a summer White House during his presidency from 1901 to 1909. Furnished in period style, it features the mementos of TR's robust life in the West, his big-game hunting trophies, and gifts from rulers throughout the world. There is a film shown in the Old Orchard Museum on the grounds and a taped tour of the house, narrated by his late daughter, Ethel.

HOW TO GET THERE: From the Long Island Expressway, take Jericho-Oyster Bay Road/Route 106 (Exit 41N) north to Oyster Bay village, then east on East Main Street, then continue on Cove Neck Road to entrance.

FOR FURTHER INFORMATION: 516/922-4447.

SAG HARBOR

CUSTOM HOUSE, on Garden Street facing Main Street, the first in New York State, was authorized in 1789, opened in 1791, and moved in 1948 to its present location. It contains period furnishings and memorabilia relating to Henry Packer Dering, who was named in 1790 the first custom master of Sag Harbor by President George Washington. Dering was given the additional title of postmaster three years later and lived in the structure. The interior has been carefully restored and the furnishings are based on an 1820 inventory by Dering.

HOW TO GET THERE: From the Long Island Expressway, take County Road 111 (Exit 70) south to its end, then Route 27 east to Bridgehampton, then north on Bridgehampton-Sag Harbor Turnpike (County Road 79), which becomes Main Street in Sag Harbor. Garden Street runs west off Main Street.

FOR FURTHER INFORMATION: 516/725-0064.

SAG HARBOR WHALING MUSEUM, on the corner of Main and Garden Streets, is housed in a striking Greek Revival structure with a portico supported by four Corinthian columns. The entrance is through the jawbones of a right whale, which sets the tone for the whaling memorabilia that fill the first floor and include paintings, log entries, scrimshaw, harpoons, lances, and other implements and tools associated with the industry that made Sag Harbor one of the world's foremost whaling ports in the nineteenth century.

HOW TO GET THERE: From the Long Island Expressway, take County Road 111 (Exit 70) south to its end, then Route 27 east to Bridgehampton, then north on Bridgehampton-Sag Harbor Turnpike (County Road 79), which becomes Main Street in Sag Harbor.

FOR FURTHER INFORMATION: 516/725-0770.

WHALER'S CHURCH, on Union Street, is constructed in a style called Egyptian Revival and evokes ancient temples. It was built in 1843 by Minard Lafever during the height of the whaling era, and was topped by an unusual steeple which was blown down by the 1938 hurricane. The interior is a mixture of many styles but contains a whaling motif.

HOW TO GET THERE: From the Long Island Expressway, take County Road 111 (Exit 70) south to its end, then Route 27 east to Bridgehampton, then north on Bridgehampton-Sag Harbor Turnpike (County Road 79), which becomes Main Street in Sag Harbor. Union Street runs east off Main Street.

FOR FURTHER INFORMATION: 516/725-0894.

SANDS POINT

SANDS POINT PRESERVE, off Middleneck Road, includes both the Castlegould estate created by Howard Gould and purchased by Daniel Guggenheim, and Falaise, the estate of Guggenheim's son, Harry, and his wife, Alicia Patterson, the founders of *Newsday*. Each has a different focus: Castlegould houses the Nassau County Museum's artifact collections; Falaise offers a view of life as it was lived on the Gold Coast by a financier, sportsman, art collector, and publisher.

HOW TO GET THERE: From the Long Island Expressway, take Searingtown Road/Route 101 (Exit 36) north, continue as it becomes Port Washington Boulevard and Middleneck Road to the preserve.

FOR FURTHER INFORMATION: Preserve and Castlegould: 516/883-1610; Falaise: 516/883-1612.

SHELTER ISLAND

MASHOMACK PRESERVE, on Route 114, provides a glimpse of a Long Island that civilization has barely touched. Its 2,037 nearly pristine acres contain examples of almost every landscape feature to be found on Long Island: salt marshes, ponds, coastal areas, eroding cliffs, woodlands, and open fields. It abounds in wildlife of all kinds, even rarely seen golden eagles, ospreys, and otters. Comprising one-third of Shelter Island, between Long Island's fishtails, it was purchased in 1980 by The Nature Conservancy.

HOW TO GET THERE: Shelter Island can be reached from either the North Fork (via ferry from Greenport) or the South Fork (via ferry from North Haven). The entrance to the preserve is on the east side of Route 114, one mile north of the dock for the North Haven ferry.

FOR FURTHER INFORMATION: 516/749-1001.

SOUTHAMPTON

SOUTHAMPTON HISTORICAL MUSEUM, at 17 Meetinghouse Lane, a few doors east of Main Street, is an 1843 sea captain's home, complete with widow's walk. It contains rooms furnished as a sea captain's bedroom and living room, a colonial bedroom, and Montauk and Shinnecock Indian artifacts. Other buildings on the grounds include a one-room schoolhouse, barn with whaling and early farm implements, carriage house with wagons and sleighs, country store in a pre-Revolutionary barn, apothecary store, and blacksmith and carpenter shops.

HOW TO GET THERE: From the Long Island Expressway, take County Road 111 (Exit 70) south to its end, then Route 27 east into County Road 39, then south on North Sea Road, which becomes Main Street in the village of Southampton.

FOR FURTHER INFORMATION: 516/283-2494; if no answer: 516/283-0605.

OLD HALSEY HOMESTEAD, a short walk away on South Main Street, was built at its present site in 1648 by Thomas Halsey, an original settler, and is described as the oldest English frame house in New York State. It is furnished with seventeenth- and eighteenth-century furniture and has colonial herb and flower gardens.

HOW TO GET THERE: See Southampton Historical Museum.

FOR FURTHER INFORMATION: 516/283-3527.

PARRISH ART MUSEUM, in the center of the village at 25 Jobs Lane, offers a respite from noise and traffic in its well-tended rear sculpture gardens. The museum features changing exhibits and houses a permanent collection of Renaissance, nineteenth- and twentieth-century American paintings and prints.

HOW TO GET THERE: See Southampton Historical Museum.

FOR FURTHER INFORMATION: 516/283-2118.

SOUTHOLD

SOUTHOLD HISTORICAL SOCIETY MUSEUM, on Main Road, is housed in the Hallock Currie-Bell Victorian home and contains period rooms with antique dolls and toys, as well as collections of costumes. The grounds include the restored pre-1653 Thomas Moore House, containing furnishings from 1640–1840, a mid-nineteenth-century carriage house and blacksmith shop, an eighteenth-century barn, an eighteenth-century boxwood garden, and a buttery.

SOUTHOLD CEMETERY, also on Main Road, contains graves of the earliest settlers, as well as being the site of the first English meeting house in New York State.

HORTON'S POINT LIGHTHOUSE, at the end of Lighthouse Road, was commissioned by President George Washington in 1790 but not built until 1858; it contains a marine museum featuring paintings, logs, and artifacts.

HOW TO GET THERE: Take the Long Island Expressway to its eastern end, then Route 58 east to Route 25, which becomes Main Road in the village of Southold.

FOR FURTHER INFORMATION: 516/765-5500.

STONY BROOK

MUSEUMS AT STONY BROOK, on Route 25A, offer changing exhibitions and programs that involve a wide range of arts and artifacts. Of particular interest is the Carriage Museum with its collection of more than 100 horsedrawn vehicles; the Art Museum, featuring the largest collection of paintings, drawings, and archival materials by the nineteenth-century American genre painter William Sidney Mount; a renowned collection of decoys; a costume collection of period clothing from the late eighteenth century to the present; as well as a blacksmith shop and a restored nineteenth-century schoolhouse.

HOW TO GET THERE: From the Long Island Expressway, take Nicholls Road/County Road 97 (Exit 62) north to Route 25A, then west on 25A to intersection at Main Street, Stony Brook, and entrance to museum complex.

FOR FURTHER INFORMATION: 516/751-0066.

MUSEUM OF LONG ISLAND NATURAL SCIENCES, at the State University of New York at Stony Brook, deals with the relationship of mankind and nature on Long Island. It focuses on geological and ecological processes through the use of changing exhibits, dioramas, slide shows, displays, and educational programs.

HOW TO GET THERE: From the Long Island Expressway, take Route 97 (Exit 62) north to the main entrance of the State University of New York at Stony Brook, and follow signs to the museum in the Earth and Space Sciences Building.

FOR FURTHER INFORMATION: 516/246-8373 or 516/246-6541.

SAGTIKOS MANOR, on Route 27A, built in 1692, became the headquarters of the commander of British forces on Long Island during the Revolutionary War and a stopover for President George Washington on his 1790 tour. It is furnished with period items and there are displays of family memorabilia and Indian artifacts.

HOW TO GET THERE: From the Long Island Expressway, take Sagtikos State Parkway south into Robert Moses Causeway to Montauk Highway (Exit C2), then east on Montauk Highway (Route 27A) to site on north side of Route 27A across from Gardiner Park.

FOR FURTHER INFORMATION: 516/665-1244.

WEST BAY SHORE

SUFFOLK MARINE MUSEUM, on Suffolk County West Sayville golf course, focuses on the importance of the sea to Long Island's development and is devoted to all aspects of Suffolk's maritime history including yachting, shipbuilding, and fishing. Displays include restored oyster vessels, South Bay sailboats, ice scooters, oyster shacks, and exhibits on the U.S. Life Saving Service, forerunner of the Coast Guard.

HOW TO GET THERE: From the Long Island Expressway, take Ocean Avenue (Exit 59) south to Lakeland Avenue (County Road 93), then Lakeland Avenue (County Road 93) into Railroad Avenue to Montauk Highway (Route 27A), then go west on Montauk Highway (Route 27A) to entrance.

FOR FURTHER INFORMATION: 516/567-1733.

WEST SAYVILLE

BROOKHAVEN NATIONAL LABORATORY was built in 1946 on the site of Camp Upton, an Army training base in World Wars I and II. Operated by a consortium of universities and funded primarily by the federal government, the laboratory's broad purpose is to carry out essential research in the physical, biomedical, and environmental sciences and in energy technologies. The Exhibit Center, housed spectacularly in the Old Graphite Reactor building, displays the background of the site and the new frontiers of science and technology. There are multi-media shows about the laboratory and a tour of the complex facility.

HOW TO GET THERE: From the Long Island Expressway, take William Floyd Parkway (Exit 68) north to the Brookhaven National Laboratory entrance.

FOR FURTHER INFORMATION: 516/282-2345.

YAPHANK

Historical Societies

BROOKLYN

Flatbush Historical Society
P.O. Box N
2255 Church Ave.
Flatbush, N.Y. 11226
212/856-3700

Fort Hamilton Historical
Society and Museum
Fort Hamilton
Brooklyn, N.Y. 11252
212/836-4100 x4149

Gravesend Historical Society
and Museum
P.O. Box 1643

Gravesend Station
Gravesend, N.Y. 11223
212/339-9089

Kingsborough Historical
Society and Museum
2001 Oriental Blvd.
Brooklyn, N.Y. 11235

Long Island Historical Society
128 Pierrepont St.
Brooklyn, N.Y. 11201
212/624-0890

National Maritime Historical
Society and Museum
2 Fulton St.

Brooklyn, N.Y. 11201
212/509-9606

QUEENS

Bayside Historical Society
P.O. Box 133
Bayside, N.Y. 11361

Flushing Historical Society
153-10 60th Ave.
Queens, N.Y. 11355
212/961-7236

Greater Astoria
Historical Society

c/o Community Planning
    Bd. #1
34-31 35th St.
Astoria, N.Y. 11102

Kingsland Homestead Museum
143-35 37th Ave. at
    Parsons Blvd.
Flushing, N.Y. 11354
212/939-0647
Hq. of Queens
    Historical Society

NASSAU COUNTY

Baldwin Historical Society
    and Museum
1980 Grand Ave.
Baldwin, N.Y. 11510
516/223-6900

Bayville Historical Society
    and Museum
34 School St.
Bayville, N.Y. 11709
516/628-1720; 628-8975

Cow Neck Peninsula
    Historical Society
336 Port Washington Blvd.
Port Washington, N.Y. 11050
516/365-9074

Farmingdale-Bethpage
    Historical Society
P.O. Box 500
Farmingdale, N.Y. 11735
516/249-4594   516/249-0093

Franklin Square
    Historical Society
P.O. Box 45
Franklin Square, N.Y. 11010

Freeport Historical Society
    and Museum
350 S. Main St.
Freeport, N.Y. 11520
516/FR8-1761

Garden City Historical Society
P.O. Box 179
Garden City, N.Y. 11530

Glen Cove Historical Society
P.O. Box 229
Glen Cove, N.Y. 11542

Historical Society of
    the Merricks
2279 S. Merrick Ave.
Merrick, N.Y. 11566

Historical Society of the
    Town of North Hempstead
    and Museum
220 Plandome Rd.
Manhasset, N.Y. 11030
516/627-0590

Historical Society of
    the Westburys
454 Rockland St.
Westbury, N.Y. 11590
516/333-0176

Long Beach Historical Society
Long Beach Public Library
111 W. Park Ave.
Long Beach, N.Y. 11561
516/432-7201

Lynbrook Historical Society
56 Lenox Ave.
Lynbrook, N.Y. 11563

Nassau County
    Historical Society
P.O. Box 207
Garden City, N.Y. 11530

Roslyn Landmark Society
William M. Valentine House
Paper Mill Rd.
Roslyn, N.Y. 11576

Sea Cliff
    Landmarks Association
P.O. Box 69
Sea Cliff, N.Y. 11579
516/671-8277

Seaford Historical Society
    and Museum
2234 Jackson Ave.
Seaford, N.Y. 11783
516/781-5217

Valley Stream Historical Society
123 Central Ave.
Valley Stream, N.Y. 11580

Wantagh Preservation Society
P.O. Box 132
Wantagh, N.Y. 11793
516/781-4328

SUFFOLK COUNTY

Amagansett Historical
    Association
Montauk Hgwy.,
    P.O. Drawer A-S
Amagansett, N.Y. 11930
516/324-4083

Amityville Historical Society
170 Broadway, P.O. Box 764
Amityville, N.Y. 11701
516/598-1486

Babylon Village Historical and
    Preservation Society
117 W. Main St., P.O. Box 484
Babylon, N.Y. 11702
516/661-3400 (weekdays)

Bayport Heritage Association
P.O. Box 4
Bayport, N.Y. 11705
516/426-4625

Bellport-Brookhaven
    Historical Society
Bellport Lane
Bellport, N.Y. 11713
516/286-8773

Historical Society of Brentwood
1769 Brentwood Rd.
Brentwood, N.Y. 11717

Bridgehampton
    Historical Society
Montauk Hgwy.
Bridgehampton, N.Y. 11932
516/537-1088

Brookhaven Town
    Historical Society
P.O. Box 297
Port Jefferson Station, N.Y.
    11776
516/473-9445

Cultural Resource Center
18 South Street
Greenport, N.Y. 11944
516/477-1121

Cutchogue-New Suffolk
    Historical Council
Main Rd., P.O. Box 575
Cutchogue, N.Y. 11935
516/734-6571 (evenings)

East Hampton
    Historical Society
135A Main St., P.O. Box 819
East Hampton, N.Y. 11937
516/324-6850

Friends for
    Long Island's Heritage
1864 Muttontown Rd.
Syosset, N.Y. 11791
516/364-1050

Greenlawn-Centerport
    Historical Society

Sanders St., P.O. Box 354
Greenlawn, N.Y. 11740
516/261-1198

Hallockville Inc.
P.O. Box 765
Riverhead, N.Y. 11901
516/722-4744, 516/727-2881

Hampton Meadows
    Historical Society
P.O. Box 693
Westhampton Beach, N.Y.
    11972
516/653-4113

Huntington Historical Society
209 Main St.
Huntington, N.Y. 11743
516/427-7045

Lake Ronkonkoma
    Historical Society
328 Hawkins Rd., P.O. Box
    716
Lake Ronkonkoma, N.Y. 11779
516/558-5024

Lindenhurst Historical Society
215 S. Wellwood Ave., P.O.
    Box 296
Lindenhurst, N.Y. 11757
516/957-4385

Lloyd Harbor Historical Society
P.O. Box 582
Huntington, N.Y 11743
516/549-2027

Long Island Antiquities
See Society for the
    Preservation of Long Island
    Antiquities

Mattituck Historical Society
Main Rd., P.O. Box 1133
Mattituck N.Y. 11952
516/298-8830

Miller Place Historical Society
P.O. Box 651
Miller Place, N.Y. 11764
516/473-1505

Montauk Historical Society
Montauk Hgwy., P.O. Box 651
Montauk, N.Y. 11954
516/668-2726 (evenings)

Moriches Bay Historical Society
Montauk Hgwy., P.O. Box 31
Center Moriches, N.Y. 11934
516/878-1776

National Railway
    Historical Society
Long Island-Sunrise
    Trail Chapter
75 Parkwood Rd.
West Islip, N.Y. 11795
516/587-9841

Northport Historical Society
215 Main St., P.O. Box 545
Northport, N.Y. 11768
516/757-9859

Oysterponds Historical Society
Village Lane
Orient, NY. 11957
516/323-2480

Parrish Art Museum
25 Jobs Lane
Southampton, N.Y. 11968
516/283-2118

Historical Society of
    Greater Port Jefferson
115 Prospect St., P.O. Box
    586
Port Jefferson, N.Y. 11777
516/473-2665

Quogue Historical Society
Quogue St.,
    Old Schoolhouse Museum
Quogue, N.Y. 11959
516/643-4224

Riverhead Town Preservation
    and Landmarks
P.O. Box 493
Riverhead, N.Y. 11901
516/727-1255

Sachem Historical Society
1057 Waverly Avenue
Holtsville, N.Y. 11742
516/472-9366

Old Sag Harbor Committee
Madison St.
Sag Harbor, N.Y. 11936
516/725-0064

Sayville Historical Society
P.O. Box 41
Sayville, N.Y. 11782
516/589-2822

Shelter Island Historical Society
16 S. Ferry Rd., P.O. Box 122
Shelter Island, N.Y. 11964
516/749-0025

Smithtown Historical Society
N. Country Rd., P.O. Box 69
Smithtown, N.Y. 11787
516/265-6768

Smithtown Landmarks Society
104 New Mill Rd.
Smithtown, N.Y. 11787
516/360-5516

Society for the Preservation of
    L.I. Antiquities
93 North Country Rd.
Setauket, N.Y. 11733
516/941-9444

Southampton Colonial Society
17 Meeting House Lane
Southampton, N.Y. 11968
516/283-2494

Southold Historical Society
Main Rd. and Maple Lane
Southold, N.Y. 11971
516/765-5500

Springs Historical Society
Fireplace-Springs Rd.
East Hampton, N.Y. 11937
516/324 2805

Suffolk County
    Historical Society
300 W. Main St.
Riverhead, N.Y. 11901
516/727-2881

Suffolk County
    Whaling Museum
Main St., P.O. Box 1327
Sag Harbor, N.Y. 11963
516/725-0770

Suffolk Marine Museum
Montauk Hgwy., P.O. Box 144
West Sayville, N.Y. 11796
516/567-1733

Three Village Historical Society
P.O. Box 1776
East Setauket, N.Y. 11733
516/941-4635; 928-9534

William K. Vanderbilt
    Historical Society
P.O. Box 433
Oakdale, N.Y. 11769
516/567-2277

Yaphank Historical Society
P.O. Box 111
Yaphank, N.Y. 11980

Selected Bibliography

Adams, James Truslow. *History of the Town of Southampton*. Southampton: Hampton Press, 1917.

Adkins, Edwin. *Setauket: The First Three Hundred Years, 1655–1955*. New York: Three Village Historical Society, 1980 reprint.

Bailey, Paul. *A History of Two Great Counties, Nassau and Suffolk*. New York: Lewis Historical Publishing Co., 1949, 3 Vols.

Bailey, Paul. *Colonial Long Island*. Amityville: The Long Island Forum, 1958.

Bayles, Richard M. *History of Suffolk County, New York*. New York: W. W. Munsell & Co., 1882.

Braff, Phyllis. *Thomas Moran, a Search for the Scenic: His Landscape Paintings of the American West, East Hampton, and Venice*. East Hampton: Guild Hall, 1981.

Braunlein, John. *Colonial Long Island Folklife*. Stony Brook: Museums at Stony Brook, 1976.

Bunce, James and Harmond, Richard. *Long Island as America—A Documentary History to 1896*. Port Washington: Kennikat Press, 1977.

Caro, Robert A. *The Power Broker: Robert Moses and the Fall of New York*. New York: Alfred A. Knopf, 1974.

Carse, Robert. *Rum Row*. New York: Rinehart and Co., 1959.

Cavaioli, Frank J. "The Ku Klux Klan on Long Island." Amityville: *Long Island Forum*, May 1979.

Denton, Daniel. *A Brief Description of New York, Formerly Called the New Netherlands, With the Places Thereunto Adjoyning, etc.* London, 1670.

DiScala, Raymond V. *Development of the Aerospace Industry on Long Island, A Chronology: 1833–1965*. Vol. III. Hempstead: Hofstra University Yearbook of Business, 1968.

Doggett, Marguerite. *Long Island Printing, 1791–1830*. Brooklyn: Long Island Historical Society, 1979.

Dyson, Verne. *Anecdotes and Events in Long Island History*. Port Washington: Ira Friedman, 1969.

———. *A Century of Brentwood*. Brentwood: Brentwood Village Press, 1950.

———. *The Human Story of Long Island*. Port Washington: Ira Friedman, 1962 reprint.

———. *Modern Times: the Founding of Brentwood, L.I.* Smithtown: Rambler Publishing Co., 1964.

Epstein, Jason and Elizabeth Barlow. *East Hampton: A History and Guide*. Wainscott, Medway Press, 1975.

Failey, Dean. *Long Island is My Nation: The Decorative Arts & Craftsmen, 1640–1830*. Setauket: Society for the Preservation of Long Island Antiquities, 1976.

Flint, M. B. *Long Island Before the Revolution*. Port Washington: Ira Friedman, 1967 reprint.

Frankenstein, Alfred. *William Sidney Mount*. New York: Harry N. Abrams, 1975.

Furman, Gabriel. *Antiquities of Long Island*. Port Washington, Ira Friedman, 1968 reprint.

Gabriel, Ralph. *The Evolution of Long Island*. New Haven: Yale University Press, 1921.

Gardiner, David. *Chronicles of the Town of East Hampton*. Sag Harbor: private printing, 1973.

Gass, Margaret. *History of Miller's Place*. Port Jefferson Station: St. Gerard Printing, 1971.

Gonzalez, Ellice B. *Storms, Ships and Surfmen: the Life Savers of Fire Island*. New York: Eastern Acorn Research Series, Fire Island National Seashore, 1982.

Hall, Warren. *Pagans, Puritans and Patriots: Yesterday's Southold*. Cutchogue: Cutchogue-New Suffolk Historical Council, 1975.

Hazelton, Henry. *The Boroughs of Brooklyn and Queens Counties of Nassau and Suffolk, N.Y., 1609–1924*. New York: Lewis Historical Publishing, 1925. 7 Vols.

History of Suffolk County. New York: W. W. Munsell, 1882.

Howell, George P. *The Early History of Southampton, Long Island, New York, with Genealogies*. 2nd ed. Southampton: Yankee Peddlar Book Co., 1970 reprint.

Huntington Vignettes. Huntington: The Huntington Historical Society, 1976.

Ireland, Ralph R. "Slavery on Long Island: A Study of Economic Motivation." *The Journal of Long Island History*, 1966.

Jaray, Cornell, ed. *Historic Chronicles of New Amsterdam, Colonial New York and Early Long Island*. Port Washington: Ira J. Friedman, Empire State Historical Publications Series No. 35, 1968.

Kaiser, William K., ed. *Development of the Aerospace Industry on Long Island; 1904–1964*. Vol. I. Hempstead: Hofstra University Yearbook of Business, 1968.

Kammen, Michael. *Colonial New York: a History*. New York: Scribner, 1975.

Klein, Howard and Patricia Windrow. *Three Village Guidebook*. Port Jefferson Station: Three Village Historical Society, 1976.

LaGumina, Salvatore J., ed. *Ethnicity in Suburbia: The Long Island Experience*. Private printing: 1980.

Levine, Gaynell Stone, ed. *Readings in Long Island Archaeology and Ethnohistory*. Stony Brook: Suffolk County Archaeological Association. 1977–83. Vols. I–VII.

Lewis, Cyril A. *Historical Long Island, Paintings and Sketches*. Westhampton Beach: The Long Island Forum, 1964.

Luke, Myron and Robert Venables. *Long Island in the American Revolution*. Albany: N.Y.S. Bicentennial Commission, 1976.

Mabee, Carleton. "Long Island's Black 'School War' and the Decline of Segregation in New York State." *New York History*. October 1978.

Manley, Seon. *Long Island Discovery—An Adventure into the History, Manners, and Mores of America's Front Porch*. New York: Doubleday & Co., 1966.

Martin, Linda and Bette Weidman. *Nassau County, Long Island, in Early Photographs, 1869–1940*. New York, Dover, 1981.

Mather, Frederic. *The Refugees of 1776 from Long Island to Connecticut*. Albany: J. B. Lyon Co., 1913.

McDermott, Charles. *Suffolk County, New York*. New York: James Heineman, Inc., 1965.

Ment, David. *The Shaping of a City: A Brief History of Brooklyn*. Brooklyn: The Brooklyn Educational & Cultural Alliance, 1979.

Monner, Fred and Linda. *Where to Go on Long Island*. Smithtown: SCOPE, 1979.

———. *Museums on Long Island*. Syosset: Long Island Museums Assn., 1983.

———. *Guide to New York City Landmarks*. New York: New York City Landmarks Preservation Commission, 1982.

Onderdonk, Henry. *Revolutionary Incidents of Suffolk and Kings Counties*. New York: Ira Friedman, 1970 reprint.

Overton, Jacqueline. *Long Island's Story*. Garden City: Doubleday & Co., 1929.

———. *The Rest of the Story, 1929–1961*. Bernice Marshall, ed. Port Washington: Ira Friedman, 1961.

Pisano, Ronald. *The Long Island Landscape, 1865–1914: the Halcyon Years*. Southampton: Parrish Art Museum, 1981.

Prime, N. S. *A History of Long Island from Its First Settlement by the Europeans to the Year 1845*. New York and Pittsburgh: R. Carter, 1845.

Prince, Helen Wright, ed. *Civil War Letters & Diary of Henry W. Prince: 1862–1865*. Private printing: 1979.

Randall, Monica. *The Mansions of Long Island's Gold Coast*. New York: Hastings House, 1979.

Rattray, Everett. *The South Fork: The Land and the People of Eastern Long Island*. New York: Random House, 1979.

Rattray, Jeannette. *East Hampton History*. Garden City: Country Life Press, 1953.

Rattray, Jeanette. *Ship Ashore!* New York: Coward McCann, 1955.

Rockwell, Verne. *Colonel Rockwell's Scrapbook*. Smithtown: Smithtown Historical Society, 1968.

Ross, Peter. *A History of Long Island*. Philadelphia: The Lewis Historical Publishing Co., 1902. 3 Vols.

Sclare, Liisa and Donald. *Beaux-Arts Estates: A Guide to the Architecture of Long Island*. New York, Viking Press, 1980.

Scott, Kenneth and Susan E. Klaffky, *A History of the Joseph Lloyd Manor House*. Setauket: Society for the Preservation of Long Island Antiquities, 1976.

Seyfried, V. F. *The Long Island Railroad*. New York: Garden City, 1961.

Smith, M. H. *History of Garden City*. Manhasset: Channel Press, 1963.

Smits, E. V. *Nassau—Suburbia U.S.A.* New York: Doubleday, 1974.

Stevens, William O. *Discovering Long Island*. New York: Dodd, Mead, & Co., 1939.

Strong, Kate. *True Tales from the Early Days of Long Island*. Amityville: The Long Island Forum, 1939.

Thompson, Benjamin. *History of Long Island*. 3rd ed. New York: Dodd & Mead, 1918. 3 Vols.

Tomlinson, R. G. *Witchcraft Trials of Connecticut*. Hartford: The Bond Press, 1978.

Tooker, William Wallace. *The Indian Place-Names on Long Island and Islands Adjacent*. Port Washington: Ira Friedman, 1962 reprint.

Tuckerman, Bayard, ed. *Diary of Philip Hone, 1828–1857*. New York: Dodd, Mead & Co., 1889.

Vagts, Christopher. *Huntington at the Turn of the Century*. Huntington: Huntington Historical Society, 1974.

———. *Huntington in Our Time*. Huntington: Huntington Historical Society, 1975.

Van Liew, Barbara F. *Long Island Domestic Architecture of the Colonial and Federal Periods: An Introductory Study*. Setauket: Society for the Preservation of Long Island Antiquities, 1974.

Waller, Henry D. *History of the Town of Flushing*. Harrison: Harbor Hill Books, 1975 reprint.

Weigold, Marilyn. *The American Mediterranean—An Environmental, Economic and Social History of Long Island Sound*. Port Washington: Kennikat Press, 1974.

Weisburg, Henry and Lisa Donneson. *Guide to Sag Harbor*. Sag Harbor: The John Street Press, 1975.

Williamson, W. M. *Adriaen Block: 1611–14*. New York: Marine Museum of the City of New York, 1959.

Williamson, W. M. *Henry Hudson, Discoverer of the Hudson River, 1609*. New York: Marine Museum of the City of New York, 1959.

Wines, Roger. "Vanderbilt's Motor Parkway: America's First Auto Road." *Journal of Long Island History*, Fall 1962.

Wood, Silas, *A Sketch of the First Settlement of the Several Towns of Long Island*. New York: A. Spooner, 1828.

Wood, Simeon. *A History of Hauppauge*, 2nd ed. revised by Jack Marr. Hauppauge: Exposition Press, 1981.

Ziel, Ron and George Foster. *Steel Rails to the Sunrise*. New York: Hawthorn Books, 1965.

Acknowledgments

The planning, preparation, writing, and editing of this book have constituted a rich learning experience about the subject, about myself, and about others. Among those at *Newsday* to whom I am particularly grateful are Stan Asimov, who involved me in this project, was an enthusiastic and considerate resource throughout, and a keen critic, too; Mary Ann Skinner, who cheerfully and speedily lent expert assistance in obtaining information and authenticating facts; Leo Seligsohn, who was unfailingly responsive to my excessive requests for advice and support; Dave Kahn, who gave confidence based on experience; Andy Ippolito, who was cooperative beyond expectation; and Dave Laventhol and Tony Insolia, who generously provided the opportunity and permitted total independence.

Of those I met through this experience, I am especially appreciative of the extensive help and expertise afforded by Steve Englebright; of the depth of commitment, unremitting energy, broad knowledge, and vital insights offered by my researcher, Gaynell Stone; and of the deep understanding, solid judgment, and thoughtful restraint furnished by my editor, Nora Beeson. In addition, I wish to acknowledge the immeasurable contributions of Marilyn Frucht, of which I alone am aware.

Many colleagues and strangers responded to requests for historical materials, and I would like to thank them for their spirit and their trust, although it was not always possible to utilize what they offered. They include: Audrey Clinton, Dick Zander, Cyril A. Lewis, Rhoda C. Milligan, Dan Russell, Mary Ann Mrozinsky, George Bailey, Frank Cavaioli, Mark Moro, Arthur L. Pollinger, Mrs. Mary Dougherty, D. W. Houghton, Prof. Ronald Lipp, Robert Winowitch, Anthony Marino, Steve Gonsalez, George Lobner, Ralph W. Bastedo, Mary Miller, Sister Frances Maureen Carlin, Fred Monner, William Cahill, Francis McGee, Jean Kadlic, Mary Jane Lippert, Loraine Erickson, Mrs. Thomas P. Duggan, Hank Boerner, Dr. Sidney Canarick, Helen Tylenda, Teresa Roberts, Barbara Randall, Morris Silverman, Charles F. Krauss, Ruth Winkler, Gladys Grimm, Tristram Walker Metcalfe II, R. Surprenant, Patricia Vars Nance, Edward Ferrea, William J. Ferguson, Jr., Carolyn K. Creed, Ward Ackerson, Mrs. George Mack, D. E. Edcris, William Benham, Mrs. Ardell Beckhans, Marilyn Mello, Dorothy Kappenberg, Harry Huson, Sister Anne F. Pulling, Carol Goldstein, Mary Klem, and Cliff Weinberg.

I am also indebted to many historians, librarians, educators, and other professionals who extended cooperation far beyond the requirements of their positions or responsibilities. They include: Rufus Langhans, Richard Winsche, Dan Kaplan, William Kaiser, Gary Hammond, Phyllis Braff, Mrs. Irwin Smith, Louis Harson, Robert Farwell, George A. Finckenor, Sr., Christopher Vagts, Preston R. Bassett, Beverly Tyler, Ron Ziel, Carl Starace, Vincent Seyfried, Frank Turano, Ronald Pisano, Dr. Betsy Kornheiser, Kenneth Newman, James Abbe, Valdemar Peterson, William Golder, Dr. and Mrs. Roger Gerry, Jean Lauer, Frank Braynard, John Drennan, Dr. Ralph Solecki, Donna Ottusch-Kianka, Mrs. Orme Wilson, and Mrs. Louise Hall.

Index

Numbers in *italics* refer to pages on which illustrations appear.

Acadians, 192–93
Adams, Samuel Hopkins, 234
Addams, Charles, 234
Adelphi University, 226, 227, *227*
aerospace industry, 238–40, *238*
Amagansett, 158, 219–21, *220*
Amityville, 158, 231–32
Andros, Thomas, 71
Annesley, Richard, 63, 64
Aqueduct Raceway, 141
Arnold, Benedict, 81
Arnold, Henry H., 165
Arrows, soccer team, 241
Ashcan Group, 234, *234*
Astor, John Jacob, 53
auto racing, 160, *160*, *161*, 162
aviation, 162, 164–65, *164*, *165*, 217–19, 238–40, *238*

Babylon, 98, 100, *132*, 136, 138, 192, 194
Baruch, Bernard, 183
Battle of Long Island, 13, 59, *64*, 65–71, 79
Beecher, Henry Ward, 119, *120*
Bellport, 234
Belmont, August, 138, 151
Belmont, August Jr., 142
Belmont Lake State Park, 138
Belmont Racetrack, 141, 142, *143*, 165
Berlin, Irving, 174, *175*
Bertoldi, Allen, *187*
Bethpage, *107–109*, 218, *218*, 238
Bethpage State Park, *157*, 202–204
bicycling, 156, 158, *158*, 160
blacks, 92, 94, *94*, 191–92, 231–32, *233*; population figures, 119, 120, 191, 232
Block Island, 32
Blue Point, 129
boating, 145, *148*, *149*
Boese, Henry, *99*
bootlegging, 188–91, *189–91*
Bostwick family, 138, 147
Bowne, John, *48*, 49
Braes, Glen Cove mansion, 182
Brentwood, 110, 228, 233
Brewster, Caleb, 80, 81
Brewster, Charles, 232
Bridgehampton, *57*, 98, 110, *128*
Broad Hollow, Old Westbury estate, 186, *187*
Brookhaven, 35, 63, 96, 98
Brookhaven National Laboratory, 174, 223, *239*, 241
Brooklyn, 25, 92, 112, 115, *118*, 126, 142, 151; churches,

32, 119, 193, 194, 197; Civil War, 119–20, *120*; colonial period, 32, 33, 35, 231; growth and industrialization, 117, 119, 123, 124, 193; Revolutionary War, 65, 68–71; transportation, 98, 104, 105, 110
Brooklyn Bridge, 123–24, *125*
Brooklyn Heights, 14, 63, 68, 69, 117
Brookville, 178, 227
Brown, Jim, *243*
Brown Brothers Pottery, *138*
Brush, Jesse, 65
Bryant, William Cullen, *139*
Buell, Samuel, *51*, 52, 228
Burr, Aaron, 216
Bushwick, 117
Byrd, Richard, *198*

Calverton, *116*
Camp Black, 167, 171
Camp Hero, 221
Camp Mills, 172, *173*, 174
Camp Siegfried, 208–209
Camp Upton, *173*, 174, 175, 221, *221*, 223, 241
Camp Wikoff, 110, 167, 168, 170
Canarsie, 27
Capote, Truman, 234
Captree Island, 151
Carmans River, 18, *130–31*, 151
Castlegould, 183, *185*
Catholics, 192–94, *195*
Caumsett State Park, *15*, *41*, 42
Cedarhurst, 147, 196
Cedarmere, Roslyn estate, *139*
Centerport, *4–5*, *26*, *140*, *148*, 178, *181*
Centreville, 144
Chamberlin, Clarence, *198*
Charles I, 25, 35
Charles II, 35–36
Chase, William Merritt, 234, *235*
Christy, Howard Chandler, *174*
churches, 32, *92*, *97*, 119, *136*, *137*, 193–98, *195*, *197*, *198*, 231
Civil War, 95, 119–23, *121*, *123*, 167, 174
Clark, F. Ambrose, 186, *187*, 228
Clemmons, Viola Katherine, 183
Clinton Academy, *51*, 52
Cobb, Irvin S., 234
Cody, William F. (Buffalo Bill), 183
Coe, William Robertson, 186
Cold Spring Harbor, 14, *76*, 78, 92, *140*
Cold Spring Harbor Laboratory,

239, 241
colonial period, 11, 25–57, *61*, 98, 127, 228, 231; farming, 18, 42, 53; religion, 32, 38, 192–93, 196, 197; whaling, 86, *87*, 90
Commack, 194
Coney Island, 14, 142, 156
Connetquot River, 18, 151, *157*
Connetquot River State Park, *152*, 153
Conway, Moncure Daniel, 110, 112
Cooney, Gerry, *243*
Cooper, James Fenimore, 234
Cooper, Mercator, 94
Copiague, 194
Corbin, Austin, 106, 110, 168
CORE, 232, *233*
Cornbury, Lord, 57, 90
corruption, 210, 211, 226, 230, *230*, 231
Cullen, John C., 219–21
Culper Spy Ring, 80
Currier and Ives, *87–89*, 142
Curtiss, Glenn H., 162, *164*, 165
Cutchogue, *45*, 190
Cutting, W. Bayard, 151

D'Amato, Alfonse, 231
Davies, Arthur B., 234
Davis, James, 232
Deepdale Golf Club, *155*
Deer Park, 105, 194, 217
De Kooning, Willem, 234, *236*
De Lancey, Oliver, 72
Democratic Party, 119, 120, 210, 230, 233
Dennison, H. Lee, 230
Denton, Daniel, 28, 30–31, 42, 141
Depression, 201–205, 210, 226
Dering, Henry Packer, *91*
De Vries, David, 31–32
Dewey, Thomas E., 212–14, *212*
Dix Hills, 162, 229
Dongan, Thomas, 192
Doolittle, Jimmy, *164*
Doughty, G. Wilbur, 210–11, 213
Dove, Arthur, *236*
duck farming, 129, *129*, 133
Dunn, Willie, 154
Durant, Will, 178
Dutch East India Company, 25, 38
Dutch settlement, 11, 35–38, 46, 47, 49, 52, 53; religion, 32, 38, 196, 197; slavery, 38–39, 119, 231
Dutch West India Company, 31, 49

Earl, Ralph, *61*, *78*

East Hampton, *8*, *12*, *34*, *56*, 59, 196; artist colony, 234, *237*; colonial period, 35, *45*, *46*, 50, *51*, 52, 90, 228; transportation, 98, 100
East Island, 182–83, *185*
East Mattituck, *128*
East Meadow, 194
East Moriches, *128*
Eastport, 133
East River, 69, 117, *118*, 123
East Setauket, 196, *197*
Eaton's Neck, 97
Edwards, Jonathan, 52
Elmont, 63, 142, *143*, 194, 197
Englebright, Steven, 244
English, John F., 230
English settlement, 11, 27–30, 33–57, 197–98
Erie Canal, 117
Erving, Julius, *243*
estates, 135, 136, 138, *139*, 145, 177–88, *179*, *181*, *184*, *185*, *187*, 194

Falaise, 183, *184*, 186
farming, *10*, 17, 23, *107–109*, *116*, *118*, 122, 127, *127–31*; colonial period, 18, 42, 53; Revolutionary era, 74, 83, *84*, 85, *85*
Farmingdale, 105, 160, 218–19, 226, 227, *238*
Farrett, James, 35
Feke, Robert, *79*
Fickel, Jacob, 165
Fire Island, *2–3*, 17, 40, 63, 190, 202
Fisher, Carl, 205
fishing, 18, 40, 127; commercial, *10*, 85, *91*, 129, *132*, *153*, *154*; sport, *132*, 153, *157*
Fitzgerald, Francis Scott, 177–79, *179*
Fitzgerald, Zelda, 178, 179, *179*
Five Towns, 196, 210
Flagg, James Montgomery, *180*
Flanders, *129*
Flanders Club, 151, 153
Flatbush, 117, 123
Floral Park, 197
Floyd, Anna, *61*
Floyd, William, *58*, *61*, 63
Flushing, 74, 144, 155; colonial period, 33, 35, 47, *48*, 49
Flushing Meadows, 156
Fordham, John, 94–95
Forest Hills, 156
Fort Pond Bay, 106, 110, 168, 221
forts, British, *76*, 77–79, *77*
Fox, George, 49
fox hunting, 150–51, *150*
Franklin, Benjamin, 77
Franklin Square, 194, 197, *209*
Freeport, 190–92, 196, 197, 205, 232, 234
French and Indian War, 59, 63
Fresh Meadow Country Club, 155

Frick estate, *187*
Frothingham, David, 216
Fulton, Robert, 117
Furman, Gabriel, 98, 100

Garden City, 165, 198, 204, 219, 226, 227, 231; building of, 135–36, *136*, *137*; World War I, 172, *173*, 174
Gardiner, Lion, 33, *34*, 35, 50
Gardiner, Robert David Lion, 24
Gardiner's Island, *24*, 33, *37*, 80, 92
Garlick, Elizabeth and Joshua, 50
geology, *12*, 13–18, *15*, *16*, *19*
George III, 60, 65
German-American Bund, 208–10, *209*
German immigrants, 194, 196–97
Gibson, Charles Dana, *144*
Gillies, Clark, *242*
Glackens, William J., 234
Glen Cove, 126, *126*, 145, *146*, 178, 182; ethnic groups, 194, 232, 234; Garvies Point, *12*, *21*, *22*, *26*, *55*
Goddard, Robert, 183
Gold Coast, 177, 183, 186, *187*, 194, 227
golf, 153–56, *155*, *157*
Gordon Heights, 232
Gould, Howard, 183, *185*
Gowanus Creek, *64*, 68
Grace Estate, 138, *150*
Gravesend, 49, 68, 117, 123, 142
Great Cow Harbor, 79
Great Neck, 14, *150*, 177–79, *179*, 196
Great South Bay, 18, 129, *132*, 151, 234
Greenlawn, *128*
Greenport, 104, 105, 158, 190, 192, 193
Greentree Estate, 182
Greenwood, Ernest, 214
Grumman Aircraft Engineering Corp., 218, *218*, 219, 238–40, *240*
Guanill, Elizabeth, 233
Guest, Winston, 147
Guest family, 138, 147
Guggenheim, Daniel, 183, *185*, 186
Guggenheim, Harry, 183, *184*, 186, *200*, 214, *214*, 231
Guy, Francis, *118*

Hale, Nathan, 80
Hall, Mary and Ralph, 50
Hamilton, Alexander, 216
Hammerstein, Oscar II, 178
Hanley, Joe R., 213, 214
Harbor Hill estate, 138, 186
Harbor Hill Moraine, 14
Hardy, T. M., 92
Harmon, Clifford B., 165

Harrison House, 182
Hassam, Childe, 234
Hathway, Alan, 231
Hazlehurst, 165
Hazlehurst, Leighton W., 172
Hazlehurst Field, 171–72
Hazleton, Edgar, *213*
Heard, Nathaniel, 62
Heckscher, August, 202
Heckscher, John G., 151
Heckscher State Park, 202, *204*
Hedges, Mary, 196
Held, John Jr., *180*
Hempstead, 98, 126, 144, 172, 210, 211, 214, 217, 224–26; colonial period, 35, 42, 47, *53*; ethnic groups, 232, 234; Revolutionary era, 39, 60, 63; *see also* North Hempstead
Hempstead House, 183, *185*, 186
Hempstead Plains, 14, 17, 42, 70, 135, 141, 196; air flights, 162, 164, *164*, 165; military bases, 167, 171
Henri, Robert, 234
Hewlett, 196
Hicksville, 127, 162, 194, 196, 234
Hispanics, 233–34
Hitchcock family, 138, 147
Hobart, Josiah, *45*
Hofstra University, 226, 227, *227*
Homer, Winslow, *120*, *123*, 234
Home Sweet Home, *8*
horse racing, 141–44, *142–45*, 182, 183
Houldsworth, Jonas, 52
housing, 44–47, *44*, *45*, 194, 223–26, *224*
Howard, Leslie, 178
Howe, Richard, 68, 69, 72
Howe, William, 68, 72
Howell, Elizabeth, 50
Hoxsey, Arch, 165
Hudson, Henry, 25, 32
Hughes, R. Ford, 214
hunting, 150–51, *150*, *153*
Huntington, *138*, *140*, *150*, *159*, 186, 217; colonial period, 35, 52, 228; historic buildings, *6–7*, *67*, 97, 112, *114*; Revolutionary era, 62, 64–65, *66*, *67*, 77, 78

immigrants, 119, 124, 191–97, 233–34
Indians, 11, 17–23, 53, 86, 92, 95, 98, 127; colonists' relationships with, 25–33, 35, 38, 53
industry and industrialization, 74, 90–98, 117, 238–40; colonial period, 53, 57, 85–90, *138*; post-Civil War, 123–24, 126; World War II, 217–19
Inwood, 155, 194, 196, 210, 232

Isaacs, Aaron, 196
Islanders, hockey team, 241, *242*
Islip, 138, 162, 213, 233; Central Islip, 192; East Islip, 202
Italians, 194, 213

Jamaica, 83, 98, 141, *142*, 144; colonial period, 28, 33, 35; Revolutionary War, 68, 70, 81
Jamesport, *128*
Jazz Age, 177–99
Jefferson, Thomas, 92, 142
Jericho, 98, 160
Jersey, *70*, 71, 81
Jews, *195*, 196
Johnston, Ralph, 165
Jones, Bobby, 155
Jones, Thomas, 64
Jones Beach, 17, 202, *206–207*

Kahn, Otto, 186
Kaufman, George S., 178
Kellum, John, 135
Kerouac, Jack, 234
Kidd, Captain William, 80
Kieft, William, 31, 32
Killenworth, 182
Kings County, 38, 117, 119, 124, 158, 191, 193
Kings Point, 221
Korean War, 172, 238, *238*, 239
Krasner, Lee, *237*
Kuhn, Fritz, 208–10, *209*
Ku Klux Klan, 191, 192, *193*, 198, 232

Lake Ronkonkoma, 162, 231
Lake Success, *155*, 160, 178, 219, 223
Lange, Edward, *96*, *138*
Lardner, Ring, 178
Lattingtown, 182, *185*
Laventhol, David, 231
Lawrence, 196, 211
Lawson, Ernest, 234
League of American Wheelmen (L.A.W.), 156
Lefferts, John, 39
Lefferts Mill, *73*
Levittown, 194, 223–26, *224*
Levy, Asser Van Swellem, 196
Levy, George Morton, 144
Lewis, Francis, *61*, 63
L'Hommedieu, Ezra, *61*, 85
Liberty Aircraft Products Company, 219
Lichtenstein, Roy, 234
Lido Beach, 221
Liebling, A. J., 234
Lincoln, Abraham, 119, 120
Lindbergh, Charles, 183, *198*, 199, *199*
Lindenhurst, 196
Livingston, Philip, 63
Lloyd Harbor, 72, *73*
Lloyd Neck, *15*, *41*, *42*, *75*, *76*, 77, 171
Locust Valley, 178

Long Beach, *1*, 17, 196
Long Island City, 196
Long Island Railroad, 100–106, *101–104*, 110, 126–27, 129, 133, 158, 160, 174, 226; growth, 168, 196, 201
Long Island Sound, 13, *15*, 79, 95–97, 145, *148*, *149*, 165
Long Island University, 227
Lorillard, Pierre, 151
Loyalists, 60, 62, 63, 71, 72, 77, 79, 81
Luks, George, 234, *234*
Lunar Module, 238, *240*
Lynbrook, 196
Lynch, Lincoln, 232, *233*

MacArthur, Douglas, 172
Mackay, Clarence, 138, 186
Macy, W. Kingsland, 213, *213*, 214
Mailer, Norman, 234
Manhasset, 14, 182, 231, *243*
Manhasset House, *134*, *135*
Manorville, 105
Marchant, Edward Dalton, *136*
Margiotta, Joseph M., 230
Martin, Josiah, *79*
Marx, Groucho, 178
Mashomack Preserve, *15*, *19*
Massapequa, 27
Mastic Beach, *58*, 63, 77, *77*
Matinecock, 27, *48*
Matinecock Indians, *26*, 27, *29*, 167, 231
Mead, Edward S., 154
Meadow Brook Club, 147, *147*, 151
Megapolensis, Domine Johannes, 32
Melville, *84*, 231
Melville, Herman, 94
Middle Island, *16*
Miller Place Academy, *226*
Milling, Thomas D., 165
Mill Neck, *33*, 197
Mills, Albert L., 172
Mineola, 144, 167, 171, 204, 210, 234; aviation, 162, 164, 165, 172
Mitchel, John Purroy, 172
Mitchel Field, 165, 172, 221, 228
Modern Times, utopian community, 110, 112
Montauk, 95, 106, 110, *111*, 115, *132*, 190, 221; camps, 110, 167, 168, 170, 221; Manor Hotel, 205, *205*, 221
Montauk Indians, 25, 27, *29*, 33
Montauk Steamboat Company, *134*
Moran, Thomas, 234
Morgan, J. P., 182–83, *185*
Morgan, J. Pierpont, 145
Morgan, Junius Spencer, 183
Morgan family, 138, 182–83
Moriches Bay, 18, 133
Moses, Robert, 162, *200*,

201–202, *203*, 213
Mount, William Sidney, 112, *112*, *113*
Mt. Sinai, 65, 79, *245*
Murphy, Charles M. "Mile-A-Minute," 141, 160
Muttontown, 178

Napeague, *132*
Narragansett Indians, 35
Nassau Collegiate Center, 204
Nassau Community College, 228
Nassau County, 17, 126, 182, 186, 203, 210, 226, 234; Depression era, 201, 204, 205; politics, 171, 194, 210–13, 230–31
Nassau County Museum, *187*
Nazi demonstrations, 208–10
Nazi saboteurs, 219–21, *220*
New Amsterdam, 33, 36
New Cassel, 232
Newhouse, S. I., 217
New Hyde Park, 197
New Netherland, 32, 36, 38, 47, 196
Newsday, 186, 214–17, *215*, 224, 225, 228–29, *230*, 231
newspapers, 214–17
New Utrecht, 83, 117
New York City, 117; English/Dutch seizures, 36, 38; formation of Greater New York, 126, 210; Revolutionary War, 68, 72, 80
New York Institute of Technology, 182, *187*, 227–28
Nickerson, Eugene H., 230
Nicolls, Richard, 36, 38, 141
Nissequogue River, 18, 151
Nissequogue River State Park, *152*, 153
North Hempstead, 60, 126, 160, 203, 210
Northport, *4–5*, *19*, *23*, 79, 95, *148*, *149*, 178
Norton, Ken, *243*

Oaks Hunt Club, *150*
Occom, Samson, 27–28
Old Field, *20*
Old Westbury, 178, 182, 186, *187*, 188, 202, 227–28
Old Westbury Gardens, *176*, *184*, 186
Old Westbury Golf and Country Club, 182
Orient (Oysterponds), 14, *85*, *96*, *121*, *154*
Ossorio, Alfonso, 234, *237*
Outerbridge, Mary, 156
Ovington, Earl, 165
Owen, Robert Dale, 112
Owen, Russell, 199
Oyster Bay, 18, 98, 126, 145, 186, 194, 210, 228; colonial period, *29*, 35, 49, 50; historic buildings, *76*, *84*, *166*, 167, *168*, 171; Revolutionary War, 76, 77, 80

parks, *15*, *41*, 42, 138, *152*, 153, *157*, 202, 203, *203*, *204*
parkways, *see* roads
Parrish, Samuel, 153, 154
Pastorius, Franz, 221
Patchogue, 83, *99*, 100, 129, *153*
Patriots (Whigs), 60, 62, 63, 71, 72, 81
Patterson, Alicia, *184*, 186, 214–16, *214*, 231
Patterson, Joseph Medill, 215
Payne, John Howard, 196
Payson, Joan Whitney, 182
Peale, Charles Willson, *82*
Peconic Bay, *20*, 23, 151, 154
Peconic River, 18, 105
Pelletreau, Elias, Sr., *53*
Phipps, John S., *184*, 186
Pierpont, Hezekiah B., 117
Planting Fields, 186
Plowden, Edmund, 25
Polhemus, Johannes Theodorus, 197
Polish immigrants, 194
politics, 119, 120, 171, 194, 210–14, 230–31, 233
Pollock, Jackson, 234, *237*
polo, 145, 147, *147*, 186
Pope, John Russell, 162
population figures, 117, 124, 142, 191, 201, 225–26, 234; blacks, 119, 120, 191, 232
Port Jefferson, 95, 126, 158
Port Washington, 204
Post, Marjorie Merriweather, 227
Potter, Gilbert, 65, 70
Potvin, Dennis, *242*
Pratt family, 138, 182
Prendergast, Maurice, 234
Prime, Ebenezer, 78, 228
Prime, Ezra, *139*
Prince, Henry W., 121–23, *121*
prohibition, 188–91, *189–91*
Promised Land, *10*
Puerto Ricans, 233–34
Puritanism, 33, 47, 50, 138, 197, 198

Quakers, *29*, 39, 47–50, 198
Quantuck Bay, 208
Queens, 14, 63, 117, 126, 158, 160, 162, 193, 210; colonial period, 38, 231; Revolutionary War, 60, 62, 70, 74
Quimby, Harriet, *165*

Raiche, Bessica Faith, 165
Rauschenberg, Robert, 234
Rego Park, 144, *144*
Reifschneider, Felix, 172
religion, 32, 38, 192–98; *see also* churches
Remsenburg, *163*
Republican Party, 210–14, 230–31
Republic Aviation Corporation, 218–19, *219*, *238*, 239
resort industry, 133, *134*, 135, *135*, 138

Revolutionary War, 13, *54*, 59–81, 92, 98, 167
Rinehart, Mary Roberts, 234
Riverhead, *10*, 158, 194, 228
Rivers, Larry, 234
roads and parkways, 63, 98–100, 158, 160, 162, 191, 201–203, 228; pictured, *84*, *98*, *99*, *133*, *203*, *222*
Rockaways, 27, 86, 151, *159*
Rockville Centre, *158*, 194, *195*, 204, 205, 217, 223, 234
Roe, Austin, 80, 81
Roebling, John A. and Washington, 123
Roosevelt, 192, 232
Roosevelt, Edith Carow, 167, *170*
Roosevelt, Franklin D., *203*, 204, 211, 213, 215, 221
Roosevelt, Quentin, *170*, 172
Roosevelt, Theodore, *166*, 167–71, *168–70*, 210
Roosevelt family, 138, *170*
Roosevelt Field, 165, 172, 199, *225*, 226
Roosevelt Raceway, 141, 144, *145*
Roslyn, 14, *121*, 138, *139*, 186, *187*, 232
Rumford, Count, 77
Rum Row, 177, 188, *189*, 190
Russell, Lillian, 178
Ryan, Patrick, 191

Sagamore Hill, Oyster Bay, *166*, 167, *168*, 170, 171
Sag Harbor, 79, 92, 98, 100, 192, 196, 216, 234; churches, 193, *195*; historic buildings, *91–93*, whaling industry, 92–95
Saint-Gaudens, Augustus, 234
salt marshes, 18, *19*, *41*, 42
Salutations, 183
Sands Point, 183, *185*, 186
Sandy Hook, 32
Sarazen, Gene, 155
schools, *51*, 52–53, 226–28, *226*, 231–32
Schulberg, Budd, 234
Scudder, Henry, 79
Scudder, James Long, *139*
Sea Cliff, *26*
Seawanaka Club, *158*
Seawanhaka Corinthian Yacht Club, 145
Seldon, 228
Setauket, 27, 50, 83, 95, 112, *113*; East Setauket, 196, *197*; historic buildings, *54*, *195*; Revolutionary War, 69, 80–81
Seversky Aircraft Corporation, 218
Sheepshead Bay, 142
shellfish, 18, *20*, *21*, 40, 127, 129, *132*
Shelter Island, *15*, 115, *134*, *135*, 190, 231; colonial period, *19*, 35, 49, *51*
Shinn, Everett, 234

Shinnecock, 18, 27, 95, *104*, 208, *235*
Shinnecock Canal, *149*
Shinnecock Hills Golf Club, 154, *155*
Shinnecock Indians, 27, *31*, 154, 231
shipbuilding, 95, *96*, 97–98, 126
Shoreham, 226, *244*
slavery, 38–40, *39*, 119, 231
Sloan, John, 234
Slongo, George, 78
Smith, Alfred E., 202, 213
Smith, Richard "Bull," 35
Smith, Valentine W., 162
Smith's Point, 79
Smithtown, 35, *36*, 72, 98, 151, *152*, 158
Snead, Sam, *155*
Southampton, 100, 191, 227; colonial period, 35, 38, 86, 90, 197
South Haven, 151
Southaven County Park, 153
Southold, 85, 121, 122; colonial period, 35, 38, *45*, 197
Southside Sportsmen's Club, 151, *152*, 153
Spanish-American War, 110, 167–70
Speonk, 133
Sperry Gyroscope Company, 219, 223
Spooner, Alden, 216, *216*, 217
Sprague, J. Russel, 211–13, *212*
Staten Island, 36, 68, 156
steamships, 117, *118*, *134*
Steinbeck, John, 234
Steinberg, Saul, 234
Stevenson, Adlai, 183
Stewart, Alexander Turney, 135, 136
Stewart, Mrs. Alexander T., 136, *136*
Stiles, James E., 217
Stimson, Henry L., *150*
Stirling, Earl of, 35
Stirling, William, *64*, 70
Stony Brook, 14, *73*, 95, *113*; State University, 227, 228, 244; The Museums, *34*, 112, *133*, 153
Stuyvesant, Peter, 36, 47, 49, 196, 197
suburban growth, 117, 123, 138, 193, 194, 201, 215; post-World War II, 223–30
Suffolk Club, 151, 153
Suffolk County, 96, 112, 121, 191, 192, 193, 209–10, 216, 217, 226, 228, 234; colonial period, 27, 35, 36, 38; Depression years, 201, 204, 205; farming, 126, *127*, 128, 133, 244; politics, 120, 194, 213–14, 230; recreation, 158, 160; Revolutionary War, 60, 63

Sullivan, John, 70
Swope, Herbert Bayard, 178
Syosset, 127

Tallmadge, Benjamin, 69, 78–81, 78
Taylor, George C., 138, 202, 213
Thompson, Benjamin, 77, 78
Thompson, C.G., 139
Tiffany, Charles, 151
Tiffany, Louis Comfort, 160, 160
Townsend, Robert, 80, 81
Townsend, Samuel, 76, 77
transportation, 95–106, 99, 123–24, 133; see also Long Island Railroad; roads; water transportation
Trevelyan, George O., 69
Truex, Ernest, 178
Tryon, William, 72
Turner, William Bradford, 174
Twenties, Roaring, 177–99

Underhill, John, 33
Union Course, racetrack, 141–42, 142, 144

Valley Stream, 203
Van Anden, Frank, 162
Vanderbilt, Cornelius, 97
Vanderbilt, Gertrude, 182
Vanderbilt, William K., 151
Vanderbilt, William K. Jr., 154, 160, 162, 178
Vanderbilt Cup Race, 160, 160, 161, 162
Vanderbilt family, 138, 178, 181, 191

Vanderbilt Museum, 26, 181
Verrazzano, Giovanni da, 24, 25

Wading River, 63, 65
Waldon, Henry W., 164
Wales, Prince of, 147, 186
Walker, James J., 213
Wallabout Bay, 70, 71
wampum, 53, 54
War of 1812, 92, 167
Warren, Josiah, 110, 112
Washington, George, 64, 78, 80, 81, 82, 83, 85, 92; Battle of Long Island, 65, 68–72
water transportation, 95–98, 96, 104, 117, 118, 127, 134
Watson, James D., 239, 241
Wa-Wa-Yanda Club, 151
Webb Institute of Naval Architecture, 182
Welwyn, 182
West Bay Shore, 54
Westbury, 127, 145, 147, 147, 162, 194
Westhampton, 17, 221
Westhampton Beach, 205, 208, 208
West Hills, 112, 114, 150
West Island, 182, 183
Weston, Andrew, 211
West Sayville, 151, 152
whaling, 86, 87, 90–95
White, Stanford, 154, 234
Whitman, Walt, 112, 114, 115, 216–17, 234
Whitney, C.V., 228
Whitney, Cornelius Vanderbilt (Sonny), 182
Whitney, Harry Payne, 178, 182

Whitney, William C., 142, 178
Whitney, William Payne, 178, 182
Whitney family, 134, 147, 182
Wilde, Oscar, 150, 151
wildlife, 8, 17, 18, 20, 21, 104, 152, 153
Willard, Charles F., 162
Wills, Helen, 156, 156
Wilson, Woodrow, 171, 210, 211
windmills, 8, 37, 56, 57
Winfield, 178
Wisconsinan Glacier, 13, 14, 17
witchcraft trials, 50
Wodehouse, P. G., 178, 234
Wood, George, 50
Wood, Mrs. Willis Delano, 78
Woodhull, Abraham, 80
Woodhull, Nathaniel, 65, 70–71
Woodmere, 196
Wooley, Charles, 86, 90
Woolworth, F. W., 178
World War I, 165, 167, 171–75, 173, 174
World War II, 186, 194, 215, 217–21, 232, 238
Wright, Frank Lloyd, 183
Wright, Mary, 50
Wright Brothers, 162, 165
Wyandanch, 232
Wyandanch, Indian chief, 33, 35
Wyandanch Club, 151, 152, 153

yachting, 145, 148, 149
Yaphank, 105, 208, 209, 229, 232
York, Duke of, 36, 192

Photo Credits